AFTER
POSTSTRUCTURALISM

Rethinking Theory

AFTER
POSTSTRUCTURALISM

*Interdisciplinarity and
Literary Theory*

Edited by
Nancy Easterlin and
Barbara Riebling

Northwestern University Press
Evanston, Ilinois

Northwestern University Press
Evanston, Illinois 60208-4210

ISBN: cloth 0-8101-1096-2
    paper 0-8101-1097-0

    Library of Congress Cataloging-in-Publication Data

After poststructuralism : interdisciplinarity and literary theory /
edited by Nancy Easterlin and Barbara Riebling.
    p.   cm. — (Rethinking theory)
    Includes bibliographical references.
    ISBN 0-8101-1096-2 (cloth). — ISBN 0-8101-1097-0 (pbk.)
    1. Criticism—History—20 century. 2. Structuralism (Literary
analysis) I. Easterlin, Nancy. II. Riebling, Barbara.
III. Series.
PN94.A34 1993
801'.95'09045—dc20   93-2256
                                                     CIP

The paper used in this publication meets the minimum requirements of the American National
Standard for Information Sciences—Permanence of Paper for Printed Library Materials, ANSI Z39.48-
1984.

Contents

Foreword

Frederick Crews

For about two decades now, the Anglo-American profession of literary study has found itself challenged—or, depending on one's quotient of cynicism, simply provoked—by a militant critical avant-garde. Let us call it, for want of an already consensual term, the Poststructuralist Vanguard. When it first emerged in the mid-sixties, that movement was pleased to be regarded as a guerrilla insurgency against the old-boy humanism that in one guise or another had ruled the academy for well over a century. By today, however, the movement has been all but officially recognized as the new academic establishment. Although literature departments still harbor representatives of other tendencies and methods, many, perhaps even most, of those professors now feel themselves regarded as throwbacks whose best contribution to the emergent order would be simply to disappear.

In the 1990s, scarcely anyone finds it necessary to argue directly for poststructuralism as a distinct body of thought. Rather, poststructuralist assumptions are often (though by no means always) treated as self-evidently valid within those cutting-edge schools of practice—feminist, Marxist, gay and lesbian, ethnic, psychoanalytic, new historicist—that seek to highlight and favor previously suppressed interests within both literature and society. As a result, most literary academics now assume, however ingenuously, that there must be a necessary connection between poststructuralism and radical virtue. And that assumption in turn has ensured that, until now, few critics who are not themselves politically conservative have cared to challenge the methodological dubieties of poststructuralism.

Supremely powerful, then, within its small domain, the Poststructuralist Vanguard nevertheless meets with nothing but hostility from baffled outsiders, who feel, ignorantly yet not without cause, that something must have gone terribly wrong with reality testing in the academy. Tellingly, however, this faction scarcely seems to mind its luxurious house arrest within the English and modern language departments. And after all, it is perhaps just as well that actual political power, beyond the power to affect academic appointments and curricula, lies beyond this faction's reach. In the long run, traditionally mistreated groups would surely be ill served by having their fortunes entrusted to "discourse radicals," who have contracted such an allergy to "positivism" that they have tended to insulate themselves against unwelcome but important facts, and whose arcane lingo is in any case preposterously unsuited to the leadership of masses.

In the eyes of some nostalgic academics and still more right-wing journalists, the Poststructuralist Vanguard has brought about nothing less than the abandonment of the Western literary tradition and the wholesale indoctrination of students in revolutionary dogma. But this is a lurid misrepresentation not only of the state of the academy but even of the Vanguard's own politics, which tend to be "anticapitalist" only in a distant theoretical manner that means no one any practical harm. For the most part, these academics are simply egalitarian, lending their tortuously rationalized blessing to expanded rights for women, minorities, and the poor. What bothers many of us who rub shoulders daily with the Poststructuralist Vanguard is not its announced value system but its use of moral intimidation to discourage critiques of its own flagrant apriorism. Real harm is being done not to the indifferent body politic but to the cause of empirical rationality, which has been tacitly devalued by many poststructuralists and explicitly condemned as oppressive by some others.

Harboring these views, I felt both encouraged and wary when, in 1989, I received a letter from a graduate student in English at Temple University, Nancy Easterlin, asking if I would be interested in helping her and another graduate student, Barbara Riebling of Penn, in their launching of this present book. The project struck me as timely and, given the powerless status of the would-be editors, heroic; they could only hope that their lack of either prestige, financial resources, or a committed publisher would be outweighed in potential contributors' minds by the opportunity to begin assessing the intellectual costs of poststructuralism and posing alternatives to it. But I also hoped that the book would not turn out to be simply a defense of the liberal-humanist status quo ante, a brief for "literature" against "theory." Could Riebling and Easterlin show that the academic Left itself would be better off without acquiescing in the clichés of poststructuralism? And could they assemble a collection that would go beyond the exposure of current fads and offer us new methodological directions to explore?

I needn't have worried on either count. The editors have done a remarkable job not just of securing fresh essays by knowledgeable academics but also of placing rival theories in juxtaposition so that their consequences can be fairly weighed. Despite some spirited chapters that do tweak our latest intelligentsia for its tunnel vision and its insensitivity to literary texture, this book is not an exercise in satire or polemics. Rather, it points optimistically toward fresh theoretical possibilities that could allow literary study to interact more fruitfully with other academic fields.

Nor, I trust, could anyone accuse *After Poststructuralism* of political backwardness. Several chapters assess the damage done to the Left itself by what

Paisley Livingston identifies as a key poststructuralist fallacy, the confusion of semiotic with political freedom. The point acquires extra force when it is made by someone like William Cain, whose radical credentials are impeccable but whose exasperation with the extra-academic impotence of poststructuralism has become acute. Or again, one could point to Carol Siegel's chapter on film criticism, which assesses the damage done to women's interests when the post-structuralist denigration of "the subject" conjoins with psychoanalytic dogma to muffle the brutal reality of rape. Neither intellectually nor politically, this chapter among others suggests, can we afford to discount individual consciousness, will, and moral responsibility in the theory-laden way that has by now become academically routine.

In emphasizing interdisciplinary inquiry of various kinds, this book strikes me as taking a promising tack. "Interdisciplinarity," as Richard Levin's contribution incisively shows, is at once the chief pride of poststructuralism and its point of maximum vulnerability. More particularly, the essays by Barbara Riebling and David Bell reveal that the poststructuralists' reliance on speculative Gallic versions of the "sciences of man" has led them into a grave misconstruction of modern science and an inadvertent reassertion of the Newtonian-Laplacean determinism that they flatter themselves on having left behind. Meanwhile, the actual sciences of our time beckon invitingly—evolutionary biology (Robert Storey), nonequilibrium dynamics (Barbara Riebling), cognitive psychology (David Anderson), theories of time (Saul Morson), and game and play theory (Paisley Livingston, Nancy Easterlin), to name a few.

In most of these chapters about scientific parallels, the proposed improvement over poststructuralist fatalism should be immediately apparent. Contemporary science, like the recent history of Europe, teaches us to withhold judgment about the inevitability of certain likely looking outcomes. Decisive factors, we are learning, can sometimes be found in the least likely quarters, and when conditions are propitious, awesome power can be toppled with previously unimaginable ease. This rehabilitation of the individual actor on the historical stage ought to be welcome news for social activists as well as for relatively disinterested students of the past who have wearied of specious determinisms, from Marx's through Foucault's.

Of course, not all contemporary science offers such immediately heartening implications. Some readers will surely wonder, for example, whether anything of value can be gleaned from the new biology of gender dimorphism, which appears to provide an evolutionary rationale for patriarchal structures. Careful attention, however, to the chapter in question will disclose that its author, Robert Storey, has an emancipating purpose in mind. He wants to free us from utopian assumptions about the benevolence and rectitude of nature—assumptions that will be found to underlie most poststructuralist arguments about the "social construction" of this or that conventional trait. If we want to make a nonsexist social world for ourselves, Storey argues, let us do so without sentimental appeals to a precapitalist natural paradise that probably never existed. Moreover—and this could be seen as the central lesson of *After Poststructuralism* as a whole—let us face up to the best available knowledge of our world, whether or not it reinforces our preconceptions.

Throughout this book, one senses an admirable yearning to honor the empirical spirit that has been neglected and disdained in the heyday of poststructuralism. That these writers disagree with specific poststructuralist readings is of only incidental importance. What they chiefly seek to restore, I believe, is a set of impartial ground rules for critical inquiry, so that students and teachers of literature can once again know the excitement of genuine investigation. This, I think, is the real reason why science looms so large here. The point is not that critics should indiscriminately apply recent scientific discoveries to literary interpretation but that they should cultivate the scientist's alertness against doctored evidence, circular reasoning, and willful indifference to counterexamples. It is a modest goal, but given the current state of our field, I cannot think of a more urgent one.

Acknowledgments

This collection would not have been possible without the unstinting support of many people. We are grateful to our friends and advisers among the graduate students and on the faculties of Temple University and the University of Pennsylvania, including Robert Storey, Timothy Corrigan, Deirdre David, Mary Tiryak, Michael Carroll, David DeLaura, Rebecca Bushnell, David McWhirter, Phyllis Rackin, Gary Dyer, Chris Fassler, and David Columbia, for their advice and support; we are particularly indebted to Elisabeth Magnus for her editorial and critical insights. To those mentors who believed that we could undertake and complete this project even while working on our doctorates, we are especially grateful. Nancy acknowledges the University of New Orleans for a course reduction in the spring of 1992, which provided time to bring the manuscript to completion. Thanks also to both our families for their ongoing encouragement, especially to Peter McNamara. Above all, we extend our profound gratitude to the contributors to this collection—for their ready trust in us and our abilities, for their ongoing and invaluable advice throughout this project, and for their generous contribution of the fine pieces we are so honored to include in this book.

Robert Storey's "'I Am I Because My Little Dog Knows Me': Prolegomenon to a Theory of Mimesis" was first published in slightly different form in *Criticism* Fall 1990 and is reprinted here by permission.

Introduction

Nancy Easterlin and Barbara Riebling

Poststructuralism dominates contemporary literary studies. The influence of its leading theorists—from Derrida and Barthes to Foucault, Lacan, and Althusser—has profoundly altered historical, textual, psychoanalytic, feminist, and Marxist criticism and given these once-divergent approaches a new similarity. Indeed, practitioners of poststructuralism have become "the Establishment" in most English and comparative literature departments. In *After Poststructuralism: Interdisciplinarity and Literary Theory*, the editors and contributors try to go beyond the work of that establishment. Our purpose is positive: using a wide variety of approaches, we hope to chart future directions for literary theory and criticism.

The contributors' political views, positions in the profession, and theoretical perspectives vary widely, and their essays reflect this diversity. The authors range from graduate students to senior members of the profession. In its scope and variety this collection is anything but programmatic; it does not represent any single school or system of thought. What the essays share is a sense of openness—particularly openness to ideas from other disciplines and a conviction that the current orthodoxies derived from poststructuralism inhibit originality and growth in literary theory, criticism, and pedagogy.

Poststructuralism initially generated excitement because it seemed to tear the field of literary studies wide open, subjecting texts to radically subversive readings. Specific texts could be made to embarrass their own logical structures by collapsing the binary oppositions upon which those structures rested. Through an endless play of signifiers, the tyrannical world of finite textual meaning was replaced by a free realm of infinite ambiguity. By declaring the death of the author, Roland Barthes and other theorists transferred creative power in that realm to the critic. Liberated from fixed systems of meaning, s/he ruled a vast empire of play and pleasure.

In other words, poststructuralism was heady stuff, promising unprecedented freedom and power to the literary critic who embraced it. However, inherent within its promise was a catch: a strict adherence to deconstructive "antilogo-centrism" meant that the play of signifiers had to be infinite—that meaning was perforce and in every case to be exposed as an arbitrary construct. Critics were, therefore, all "free" to come to the same conclusion. The point of every text became its own unraveling, the endless exposure of its empty core. And because truth claims were considered to be wholly relative to the discourse that produced them, critics also found themselves "always already" confined within one or another "prison house of language." Given these developments, it should not come as a surprise that for many in the profession, poststructuralism came to represent neither freedom nor power but a profound loss of agency on the part of critic and author alike.

Poststructuralists have also taken a radically constructivist approach to reality and truth. They have attacked, and rightfully so, scientistic notions of transcendent and transparent "truths" that exist eternally, waiting to be discovered by a process entirely free from cultural context or conditioning. But although such naive positivism may represent the popular view of science, it does not really characterize twentieth-century scientific theories. Therefore, the poststructuralist attack upon it can be seen as a dated and specious argument. More important, radical constructivism is not the only alternative to scientism: even though we must admit we cannot know *everything*, that is not the same as asserting that we cannot know *anything*. As the essays in this collection demonstrate, despite some poststructuralists' attempts to "narrativize" them, various sciences are now fruitfully engaged in expanding our knowledge, a knowledge that is still possible even when partial or subject to revision.

Furthermore, the radical constructivist approach that grew out of poststructuralism is itself highly problematic. After nearly three decades, the assertion that the world is a mere linguistic or social construct has begun to wear thin, and poststructuralism is facing some of its most challenging critiques from scholars influenced by current scientific theories: for example, Paisley Livingston's *Literary Knowledge: Humanistic Inquiry and the Philosophy of Science* and Alexander Argyros's *A Blessed Rage for Order: Deconstruction, Evolution, and Chaos*. New scientific theories, while more provisional in their knowledge claims than their nineteenth-century predecessors, are nevertheless tightly bound to the natural world through rigorous observation and experiment. Thus science can provide both theoretical inspiration and models of methodological rigor.

The collection's contributors are not, however, calling for the wholesale application of unmodified scientific theories and methods to literary studies; they are acutely aware of the ineluctable differences between literature and the natural world. But models drawn from both the hard and the social sciences can guide literary studies in a promising direction, offering alternatives to constructivist theorizing and critical practices constrained by "free play." As Richard Levin points out in his essay, scientific methods at the minimum insist that to be meaningful claims must be "falsifiable": each claim must be presented in a way that both asserts a position (its hypothesis) and at the same time leaves it open to refutation by contrary evidence (its null hypothesis). By contrast, poststructuralism has placed its doctrines beyond refutation, because its central tenet is the blanket negation of all claims to truth, fact, or discernible meaning. Its defense against criticism is like Sir Philip Sidney's response to the classic accusation that the poet lies: the poststructuralist, like the poet, "nothing affirmeth, and therefore never lieth." This volume's contributors, however, make assertions whose force and clarity leave them open to a hostile critique, here viewed as a necessary part of open-ended dialogue.

In order to assess honestly the state of theory in the profession and to call for a more open atmosphere in which to practice, one must engage the question of politics. The politics of poststructuralism are a welter of contradictions, probably because they are as much institutional and hegemonic as they are ideological and activist. Some scholars—for example, most Althusserians and feminists influenced by Lacan and Kristeva—believe that the poststructuralist assault on meaning is so inherently disruptive of the status quo as to be ipso facto subversive of the reigning political order. To this group, the acceptance of poststructualist orthodoxies can act as a political as well as a theoretical litmus test. A dissenting group of scholars—most notably Terry Eagleton, Edward Said, and Frank Lentricchia—find that poststructuralism's assault on meaning coupled with the hopelessness that characterizes Foucauldian models of power makes significant political action impossible. The situation is made even more confusing by the presence of a third group that shifts as rhetorical conditions demand between foundationalist and relativist political claims.

The authors in this collection hold a wide variety of political convictions. Moreover, they vary considerably in how they view the relation between politics and literary studies. Some call for a retreat from politicized discourse. Others see politics as integral to theory, criticism, and pedagogy but want it to operate in an open arena. They prefer critics and teachers to be independent from demands to conform while responsive to lived experience. All, however, want to free the profession from pressures to work exclusively within received orthodoxies. And all are concerned with making sure that theory is always held accountable to a "real" world, whether social, political, or natural.

Whether responding to the changed political scene that follows the fall of communist regimes around the world, recognizing the rapidly eroding credibility and prestige of the Freudian psychoanalytic establishment, or facing the need to create a workable pedagogy in a politically charged classroom climate, the authors point up the inability of accepted theoretical systems in literary studies to describe the complexities of current political events or to engage with pressing political and social problems as they are lived. They consequently draw on philosophy, history, and new paradigms within the sciences in order to show how theorists might better conceptualize both the processes of political or social change and the role of literature in those processes. They use recent biological, psychological, cybernetic, and other kinds of interdisciplinary research to subject poststructuralist assumptions about agency, intertextuality, literary realism, and the psychology of reading to more rigorous examination, and they suggest models that are more attuned to developments in these fields. All these strategies demonstrate the authors' commitment to interdisciplinary work that represents, not a selective appropriation of ideas to confirm already existing theoretical tenets, but a genuine dialogue with other disciplines that opens up our own field to new developments in a variety of previously neglected directions.

Because our ultimate purpose is positive, we have arranged the essays in three categories that move progressively away from criticisms of poststructuralism and toward elaborations of new theoretical possibilities. The essays do not, however, fall rigidly into these categories: all contain criticisms of current theory as well as implications and suggestions for future research. None is simply a narrow attack on poststructuralism.

The first section, "Poststructuralism and Interdisciplinarity: Questions of Models, Assumptions, and Definitions," contains three essays that challenge specific poststructuralist assumptions. Implicitly or explicitly, each of the essays also recommends a more rigorous methodological course for interdisciplinary literary studies.

Richard Levin's essay, "The New Interdisciplinarity in Literary Criticism," initiates the collection with a critique of current interdisciplinary practices in the profession. Levin argues that many interdisciplinary critics "do not even try to acquire an overall sense of the other discipline" but merely "raid" it for a convenient theory. And they choose this theory, as he shows by quoting their own rationales, not on the basis of its cogency or of its standing in the discipline, but according to their "comfort" with it, that is, its utility for their political or critical projects. Typically, after borrowing a theory, they wantonly modify it to suit their aims. Finally, they "aprioritize" it, giving it the status of truth rather than treating it as a testable hypothesis. Often the theories that they borrow, such as Freudianism, are themselves aprioritizing in the sense that they act as closed, self-confirming systems. Levin offers numerous suggestions for advancing a genuine interdisciplinarity in the profession; among them are proposals for graduate training and journal review that would encourage literary scholars to become more knowledgeable and responsible in their engagements with other fields.

In "'I Am I Because My Little Dog Knows Me': Prolegomenon to a Theory of Mimesis," Robert Storey counterbalances the current theoretical emphasis on the cultural and linguistic construction of the subject with an appeal to recognize as well a prelinguistic, cross-cultural, biologically based "human nature" of emotions and feelings shared with much of the animal world. Drawing on abundant research from neurophysiology, anthropology, ethology, and psychology, Storey disputes the constructivist notion that human nature is infinitely malleable. He claims that language, culture, and moral responsibility all developed out of social instincts present in human beings from their earliest beginnings, and that the emotions associated with these social instincts remain powerful sources of motivation and agency. Such assertions need not lead to a simplistic biological determinism. For Storey, the evolutionary heritage of the human race presents the individual with a variety of often conflicting "inducements"; reason permits us to choose among them, and "culture is the record of our complex and shifting allegiances" to them.

The last essay in this section, David Bell's "Simulacra, or, Vicissitudes of the Imprecise," shows how the concept of the simulacrum, developed in science as a tool for constructing meaning, has in literary theory become a weapon for destroying meaning. In science, the simulacrum is a model used to study complex, nonlinear phenomena that cannot be assessed by precision-measurement strategies. Although not set up to explain phenomena causally, it permits the researcher to grasp certain repetitive structures and thereby to gain some predictive power. In literary theory, by contrast, the simulacrum has become an image that, unlike the faithful and subordinate "copy," distorts or perverts the original on which it is based and threatens to replace it.

French poststructuralists of the 1960s and 1970s (Deleuze, Baudrillard) envisioned the simulacrum as a destructive force that could empty the ideal Platonic hierarchy of all operational validity. In Bell's words, once simulacra were unleashed upon the world, there would be "no going back, no return to safe haven, only a[n] . . . endless circulation of images, each a pretender but none capable of ending the strife of ideas by establishing an origin and founding point." From here it was a small step for poststructuralist theorists to misrepresent scientific simulation as this kind of destructive activity. For Baudrillard, contemporary science constructs a variety of competing simulacra that produce facts and events in as many ways as the theorist cares to imagine, much like contemporary literary criticism. Bell suggests that literary theorists, instead of projecting their own methods and aims onto science, might find it more productive to adapt the actual scientific processes of simulation to uses in the humanities.

The essays in the second section of this book, "Poststructuralism and the Pragmatic Test: Theory in the World of Art and Criticism," explore how literary practices, including writing, reading, teaching, and criticism, inform our notions of what literature is. They also explore how theory can be held accountable to our experience of these practices.

Paisley Livingston opens the section with "From Text to Work," an essay that inquires into the potential losses involved in replacing a notion of literary "works"—classifiable, closed, belonging to their authors—with a notion of "texts" that can be endlessly remade by their readers, fragmented and recombined with one another. He argues that although this strategy appears at first glance to offer a maximum degree of critical freedom and of interaction between texts, the actual "dissolution of all classificatory notions in the sea of textuality" would strip readings of all intellectual value and aesthetic pleasure. This conclusion is made vividly credible by a thought experiment that details what the experience of reading and writing would be like if all the world's written documents were stored in a central textual data bank with all their author-identifying information removed. Yet Livingston does not advocate a return to the kind of scholarship Barthes and other wished to replace. At the end of his essay he draws on game theory to suggest a new, more useful model for textual interaction.

Whereas Livingston's essay addressed epistemological considerations involved in literary criticism, Nancy Easterlin's explores the psychological nature of literary experience itself. Contending against the cultural materialist position that equates literary realism with indoctrination into bourgeois ideology, she suggests that the fundamental distinctions we make between literary and other forms of experience render the materialist claim highly questionable. Additionally, as research from anthropology and cognitive and developmental psychology focusing on play suggests, literary experience may serve an adaptive function similar to that performed for our human ancestors by ritual and physical contest. Given that we live in a world of increasing complexity in which our need for psychological and intellectual adaptation increasingly supersedes our need for physical adaptation, it follows logically that we would benefit most from a wide variety of literary works and genres. Returning to the materialist denigration of realism, Easterlin suggests in closing that such universalizing claims about genres fail to account for the specific value literary works yield in experience.

In "The Crisis of the Literary Left: Notes toward a Renewal of Humanism," William E. Cain points out that the literary Left, far from awakening students to troublesome social realities, has been sociopolitically ineffective thus far. He maintains that at the same time that the Left prospered in the academy and became increasingly rigid politically, the public sphere became more conservative and the situation of minorities deteriorated alarmingly. He suggests that the Left's cause would be better served by a skeptical and open-minded approach toward politically charged issues of literary practice within the academy. Taking the canon debates as a case in point, he argues that academics on the Left need to balance their emphases. Instead of focusing exclusively on the differences between minority and mainstream traditions and the particularity of minority themes, they should also explore the connections between canonical and non-canonical texts. Cain uses passages from Emerson and Douglass to suggest a dialectical method of criticism and teaching that, while highlighting differences, also fosters a moral inquiry that does not depend on race, gender, or ethnicity to make itself meaningful.

Carol Siegel's essay, like the others in this section, concerns the ways in which the universalization of interpretive claims poses problems for specific interpretive situations. "When No Means No and Yes Means Power: Locating Masochistic Pleasure in Film Narratives" illustrates the ethical problems raised for feminists by the use of psychoanalytic paradigms and concepts. Focusing on discussions of masochism in film gender studies, Siegel points out that the psychoanalytic equation of suffering with masochism ignores the issue of choice and thus perpetuates the tendency to "blame the victim." The Freudian model by its nature undervalues conscious choice. Whereas feminism as a political movement has been largely concerned with issues of consent in sexual matters, the adoption by academic feminists of a psychoanalytic paradigm that confuses voluntary with involuntary suffering undermines feminist aims. Through interpretations of male masochism in the films *if . . .* and *Lord Jim*, Siegel demonstrates the necessity of considering how masochism functions differently in the overall narrative of any given work.

The third and final section, "Revisionary Interdisciplinarity: A Selection of New Approaches," offers a sampling of interdisciplinary literary research not based on poststructuralist assumptions. While the subjects and approaches of these essays are varied, all three employ models that respond to the complexity and dynamism of specific texts in their social, historical, and political contexts.

David Anderson's essay, "Razing the Framework: Reader-Response Criticism after Fish," argues that problems of interpretive limits, interpretive change, and the social negotiation of meaning cannot be adequately explained by existing cultural framework theories of reader response such as Stanley Fish's idea of interpretive communities. For a reader does not simply reflect the shared assumptions of a large community but continually constructs and transforms meanings with other readers. Meaning is not assimilated but negotiated. Mechanistic framework models that conceptualize readers as "just so many electrons within a magnetic field" obliterate "the tremendous agency that all readers (and minority readers in particular) exercise daily to construct viable selves and meaning in indifferent or hostile social environments."

Anderson's own model of reader response draws on cognitive psychology, catastrophe theory, and the psychology of reading to describe how readers combine impressions, according to probability and convention, to form interpretive structures and then modify those structures in response to new information. Catastrophe theory, which explores how major changes in a system can result from minor changes in external variables, helps to describe a reading process in which small and gradual disappointments to one's initial expectations may lead to abrupt shifts in reading strategy. Anderson's readings of poems by Williams, Whitman, and Frost illustrate his model by indicating that interpretive stability is based upon a dynamic process of continuous self-organization and self-correction.

In "Remodeling Truth, Power, and Society: Implications of Chaos Theory, Nonequilibrium Dynamics, and Systems Science for the Study of Politics and Literature," Barbara Riebling takes issue with the Foucauldian/new historicist analysis of power in society and its relation to literary texts. A theory that defines truth entirely as an effect of power cannot explain historical instances in which dissident acts of truth telling have brought down regimes. Furthermore, the assumptions that both political and textual systems exist in a continuous equilibrium process of subversion and containment rest on obsolete models of mechanistic determinism, which cannot account for political conflict or social transformation.

Riebling's alternative approach employs models drawn from the new paradigm sciences. Scientists developed catastrophe theory in mathematics, and theories of order through fluctuation in various physical and life sciences, to describe nongradualist patterns of change in complex systems. Riebling asserts that these theories can also be used to explain explosive discontinuities in the history of nations, such as the sudden downfall of totalitarian regimes in Eastern Europe. Chaos theory's discovery of "sensitive dependence on initial conditions"— the so-called butterfly effect—calls into question the classical determinist idea that minor individual actions are necessarily overwhelmed by the giant systems containing them, whether those systems are physical or social. Finally, Riebling looks at the role political literature has played in history. She applies new paradigm theories, particularly systems theories of feedback, to medieval and Renaissance "counsel literature"—works that advocate confronting rulers with painful truths in order to ensure the survival of the state.

The final essay in the collection, Gary Saul Morson's "For the Time Being: Sideshadowing, Criticism, and the Russian Countertradition," examines two contrasting ideas of time—one held by the Russian intelligentsia of the prerevolutionary period and the other held by a "countertradition" of theorists and artists, most notably Bakhtin and Tolstoy. As he phrases the point, members of the intelligentsia were not only utopians but "uchronians": apocalyptic thinkers who held in contempt the prosaic events of daily life while impatiently anticipating the abolition of time and the end of history. For them, the unfolding of history was governed by one or another teleology. By contrast, the countertradition emphasized the openness of every moment, whether past, present, or future, and stressed the multiplicity of possible outcomes that can spring from each moment. Such a view of time invests even small choices or undramatic daily actions with profound ethical implications and expands the domain of individual responsibility and choice. According to Morson, the realistic novel, particularly as Tolstoy developed it, exemplifies this view of time. It heightens the reader's awareness of time's multiple possibilities and the responsibilities of people who are temporal to the core.

For several reasons, Morson's essay serves as a fitting conclusion to this volume. It argues that today's prevailing critical habits repeat key assumptions of the Russian intelligentsia that reflect a mistaken notion of temporality. One such habit is to act as if one's insights and one's moment in time lay at the end point of history, from which one could judge a benighted past and close off divergent futures. Another naive practice proceeds as if human actions were entirely "transcribable" by a set of abstractions that a given theory provides. Our hope is that the profession will begin to move in the opposite direction, toward the values of the countertradition that Bakhtin's and Tolstoy's work epitomizes: "epistemic modesty," respect for the mundane, emphasis on agency and responsibility, and the recognition that what gets left out of a grand system—what Bakhtin called "the surplus"—is the matrix from which new understanding can emerge.

Poststructuralism and Interdisciplinarity: Questions of Models, Assumptions, and Definitions

The New Interdisciplinarity in Literary Criticism

Richard Levin

It seems clear that one of the best things a literary critic can do today is to become interdisciplinary. Anyone who doubts this has only to look at the publishers' advertisements, which regularly urge us to buy some critical book or anthology because it "succeeds in crossing traditional disciplinary boundaries" or words to that effect. The impression they are designed to create is that this is a courageous, difficult, and cutting-edge undertaking that is valuable in itself, implying that critics who remain within their own discipline are timid (or at least lazy), narrow-minded, and hopelessly out-of-date. And in recent debates in the field the failure to be interdisciplinary is usually viewed as a serious fault, almost as serious as the failure to theorize. Indeed the two failings are often linked as the products of formalism, and we will see that there is an obvious connection between interdisciplinarity and theorizing, as the terms are now used.

Despite the current excitement about it, interdisciplinarity is not new in criticism; it appears in the oldest critical texts we possess. For Plato all true knowledge must be interdisciplinary, since any inquiry within the confines of a single science has not reached the highest level of the divided line where the separate sciences are integrated dialectically. Thus in his dialogues art is never treated as independent but is always subsumed under more general considerations. Aristotle's system is based on a separation of the sciences, one of which is poetics; but his book on that science begins with the concept of "imitation" derived from metaphysics, its analysis of "character" in chapter 2 depends on ethics, and the discussion of "thought" in chapter 19 refers us to the *Rhetoric*. These two inter-disciplinary traditions continued into the Renaissance, where most critics adapted some Aristotelian concepts to a Platonic scheme. Sidney's *Apology*, for instance, judges poetry in terms of ethics and in competition with history and philosophy.

The early study of English literature in the university also drew on other disciplines such as philology, and the dominant mode of interpretation in the period preceding the New Criticism was historical, which often involved other fields as well. Lily Bess Campbell's *Shakespeare's Tragic Heroes*, to take a notable example, is based on a survey of Elizabethan moral philosophy and humor psychology, but she did not think she was crossing traditional disciplinary boundaries; she was being traditional. Even formalists could go to science: I. A. Richards, often seen as an ancestor of the New Critics, introduces us to the physiology of sensation, complete with diagram (116), and Norman Rabkin, one of the last of the breed, to the physicists' principle of complementarity (22, no diagram).[1] And frequently in the New Criticism we find borrowings from other disciplines that are unacknowledged and perhaps unrecognized; in *The Well Wrought Urn* Cleanth Brooks reports that "a river is the most 'natural' thing that one can imagine" (6), a fact presumably learned from geology, and he later relies on knowledge of obstetrics (44), the Irish school system (166), and so on. It would be impossible to interpret a literary text without recourse to some inter-disciplinary knowledge in this sense.

Virtually all English departments of the forties, when I had my training, professed a number of different disciplines: literary history, criticism, linguistics, the history of the language, textual bibliography, rhetoric, and composition. Yet no one thought it was interdisciplinary, since the departmental organization defined all these as "English." There was, however, some activity in this period that was regarded as interdisciplinary (though the word was not used),[2] such as the committees formed at the University of Chicago to bring together members of several departments. One was the Committee on Social Thought, to which we owe Allan Bloom's closing of the American mind, and I can remember that even in my student days it was known as a hotbed of conservatism. I mention it because crossing traditional disciplinary boundaries is now usually seen as a radical project; but in order to understand this it will be necessary to investigate the nature of the new interdisciplinarity. My investigation, of course, makes no claim to cover all contemporary interdisciplinary criticism, which would be impossible. I have instead focused on what seem to be the basic problems of some of the dominant trends in this body of criticism, produced by some of the more prominent critical approaches. And while most of my examples come from recent studies of Shakespeare, I believe these trends dominate other fields as well.

Selecting a Theory

I am using Joseph Zinker's views [on Gestalt psychology] because, first, they meet these conditions. Second, I am comfortable with the language in which he talks about therapy because it is frequently the language of literary criticism.
—Jean Kennard

A good way to start would be to ask how most critics today go about becoming interdisciplinary. They usually do not proceed by first selecting another *discipline* and then trying to master it, which would take a lot of time and would be unnecessary, as we will see. My impression is that most of them do not even try to acquire an overall sense of the other discipline, of the sort that could be derived from a few good introductory courses. Instead they typically begin by selecting from the discipline a particular *theory* that they want to use. This is the obvious connection between the new interdisciplinarity and theorizing noted earlier, for in the current critical scene to theorize usually means to adopt a theory from another discipline.[3] But since this procedure in effect bypasses the other discipline itself as an organized body of knowledge and mode of investigation, critics do not select a theory on the basis of its standing in its own discipline, and so we must ask on what basis they do select it. Here it will help to look at some examples, which I have limited to the selection of theories taken from psychology.

A revealing example is provided by Coppélia Kahn's 1982 essay in which she introduces and recommends the neo-Freudian theory of Nancy Chodorow, Dorothy Dinnerstein, and Adrienne Rich to American feminist critics.[4] Early in the essay she admits that Freud's concept of penis envy "has justifiably angered many feminists and regrettably alienated them from psychoanalysis" (34). One can see why this concept alienated feminists (and nonfeminists) and led them to question the assumptions and methodology of a system that features it, but for Kahn their reaction is regrettable since she wants to detach and change this concept (and others that seem masculinist) without giving up Freudianism. And the theory she is recommending does this: it retains the Freudian assumption that a single basic cause in the child's "family drama" accounts for all our problems, but simply relocates it in the "pre-Oedipal" instead of the "Oedipal" stage and so foregrounds the mother rather than the father. It also retains the methodology required to support this assumption—the reliance on a fixed and universal scheme of developmental stages, the hypostatizing of mental entities like "the unconscious," and the multiplication of mechanisms (displacement, condensation, splitting, etc.) that can force all possible data to fit the prescribed thesis, which now turns out to be that young boys' experience with mothering is responsible for misogyny and all the gender conflicts in society.

Our concern, however, is not with the theory itself but with the basis of Kahn's recommendation. It cannot be the evidence, for she makes only one passing reference to "clinical evidence" in favor of the theory (34), without noting that it was the clinical evidence of orthodox Freudians that confirmed penis envy (a point we will return to); nor can it be the standing of the theory in its own discipline, which she never mentions. Instead she gives another kind of reason for adopting it, or rather two related reasons: that it can serve the feminist cause in opposing the "oppression of women" in "patriarchal society" (33), and that it can serve feminist criticism in uncovering a "maternal subtext" in "patriarchal texts" (36). She selects the theory, in other words, on the basis of its utility rather than its truth. Now most scientists, who are skeptical about absolute truths, could agree with this. They would also judge a theory by its utility, that is, by whether it proves more useful than competing theories in accounting for all the relevant data, in making predictions, and in generating productive research to test, refine, and expand it. That would determine its standing in the discipline and would be what they mean by its "truth"; it will also be what I mean by the term here. But that is not how Kahn views the utility of this theory, which for her is its usefulness, not to its own discipline, but to her political agenda. The question of whether it is true, in this sense, seems to be irrelevant.

A similar project underlies Toril Moi's essay that introduces and recommends some French "feminist theoreticians," primarily Julia Kristeva, to a group of British critics, most of whom are Marxists. She begins by attacking Anglo-American feminist criticism because its "empiricist and humanist" concept of the subject and the text is in "fundamental complicity" with "bourgeois ideology" and is "inherently reactionary" (4, 10), and contrasts it to Kristeva's theory of human development. Again we can pass over the details of the theory (which takes the child from the "semiotic *chora*" of the mother to the "symbolic order" of the father, roughly analogous to Chodorow's "pre-Oedipal" and "Oedipal" stages), since we are only interested in the reasons Moi gives for recommending it. And again we find they are not based on any evidence for it (that apparently would be "empiricist" and hence "reactionary") or on the evaluation of it in its own discipline. It is recommended because it provides a theoretical ground for "disrupt[ing] the strict symbolic order" and the "identity" of the subject, and so can "be a valuable dimension of any Marxist analysis of the conditions for revolutionary activity" and can also give us "a revolutionary form of criticism" (9–10).

The choice between these two ways of judging a theory is even more explicit in Catherine Belsey's essay on Freudianism, also aimed at a Marxist audience, which starts out by asking what the present status of this theory is: "The question is not, to my mind, as it once was, an epistemological one ('is it true?', 'how do we know?'). Post-Saussurean linguistic theory . . . closes off questions about how accurately language represents the world. . . . In asking 'what is the status of psychoanalysis?', I want to pose a political question: 'what challenge to the existing order is inscribed in [it]?'; 'what is its radical potential?'" ("Romantic" 57). Thus she goes further than Kahn or Moi by deliberately rejecting the criterion of truth and arguing that the theory should be judged only by the criterion of utility, which is defined again by a political agenda—challenging "the existing order." And she finds it is useful in this sense for much the same reason that Moi found Kristeva's theory useful: because it "radically undermines" the "unitary subject of bourgeois ideology" that is "the central justification of liberal humanism" and of "bourgeois criticism" (58, 75). Presumably, if it could be shown that the humor psychology surveyed by Campbell had even more "radical potential," Belsey would prefer it to psychoanalysis.

Although all three critics choose a theory primarily for its political utility, they all claim that it is also useful for criticism; but this is not an independent factor, since the kind of criticism they favor is determined by their politics. There are others, however, who focus on critical utility. David Leverenz explains that he is selecting Sullivan's "interpersonal theory" rather than other psychiatric theories because "it is more useful for literary criticism" (126); but its usefulness in criticism, like its usefulness in politics, cannot tell us if it is true, or even if it is more true than other theories that are less useful here. Moreover, many other critics claim that Freudian theory is the most useful for criticism, so this too depends on the kind of criticism each critic prefers. That preference need not be based on the critic's politics, but it functions in the same way as the political agendas of Kahn, Moi, or Belsey in determining the choice of a theory.

My last example is the passage by Jean Kennard used as the epigraph to this section, where she states that she is adopting Zinker's psychological theory because she is "comfortable" with it (67). (The other "conditions" it meets, we will not be surprised to learn, have nothing to do with the evidence for it or the evaluation of it by psychologists.) She does not realize that the test of a scientific theory is not whether it makes people comfortable, or that some of the most important theories of modern times made many people very uncomfortable.[5] But then all these critics could be said to choose a theory because it makes them comfortable, which means that it serves their needs, although different things serve those needs and so give them comfort.

While this section has focused on the way interdisciplinary critics select a psychological theory, the same procedure seems to apply in many of their borrowings from history, sociology, and the other "soft" sciences. It seems fair to conclude, then, that the world of the new interdisciplinarity is seen by these critics as a kind of cafeteria presenting a tempting array of theories that have been produced by other disciplines but are now detached from them, where they are free to choose whatever suits their taste, which turns out to be whatever is useful for their political or critical projects. And there is a clear connection between these two aspects of the scene, for if the theories are detached from their discipline, then a critic cannot select one in terms of the criteria of that discipline and so the only criterion that remains is the critic's own "comfort."

Improving the Theory

My use of Freudian terms does not mean that I endorse its ahistorical, Europocentric and sexist models of psychical development. However, a materialist criticism deprived of such concepts as displacement and condensation would be seriously impoverished.

—Paul Brown

Although it is not a necessary step in the process of becoming interdisciplinary, it is not uncommon for critics, after selecting a theory, to set about changing it. One might have thought they would hesitate to do this, since they usually know so little about the discipline that generated the theory and provides its context, but the opposite is true. It is because they do not know the other discipline, and because the theory has been validated, as it were, by their own choice rather than by the discipline, that they feel free to improve it. And since its validity depends entirely on its usefulness to them, they can improve it by making it more useful. The neo-Freudian theory sponsored by Kahn can be seen in this way as an improvement of Freud, though we do not owe it primarily to literary critics.[6] Kahn herself derives from it another account of penis envy to replace Freud's (which, we saw, she wished to separate from his system): the little girl now wants a penis because "she wants to detach herself from her mother and become an autonomous person, not because she feels castrated without one" ("Excavating" 34). No evidence is given for this change, but it clearly makes the theory more useful for her agenda.[7] Belsey, from a Marxist position, objects to the "universal, transhistorical and transcultural" nature of Freudian theory ("Romantic" 57), yet thinks she can amputate that and still keep enough of the theory alive to retain its "challenge to the existing order." And the epigraph to this section shows that Brown, another Marxist, also believes he can improve Freudian theory by dropping the parts he dislikes and keeping those he finds politically useful (71). Nor is he troubled by the fact that in Freud displacement and condensation occur within the human psyche, while he wants to relocate them in the text or "colonialist ideology" where there is no psychic mechanism to explain them. And Moi, after endorsing Kristeva's theory on political grounds, adds that its conclusions are "politically unsatisfactory" but reassures the audience that this "should not prevent us from drawing others" (9)—that is, from improving the politics of those conclusions.

Critics can also enhance the utility of the theory they select by making it a universal law. Freud's theories were supposed to be universal since they derived from a single basic cause of all human behavior, as we saw, and critics employing the new improvement of Freud often make similar claims. Edward Snow says that Othello's gynophobic reaction to the consummation of his marriage is felt in "every civilized white man," which he later extends to "every sexual relationship" (400, 402). He does not explain how this law (in either version) was derived, but it is obviously useful for establishing Othello's gynophobic reaction, which escaped the notice of virtually all viewers and readers of the play and all the characters in it. And Kahn's revised theory of penis envy is presented as a universal law, as was Freud's original account. One might think it would first be helpful to find out whether all girls in all family configurations in all societies actually want a penis before arguing about why they want one, but neither the orthodox Freudians nor the neo-Freudians have shown any interest in such an investigation.

Unlike the Freudians, Marxist critics profess to reject universal laws (we saw Belsey attacking the "universal" claims of Freudian theory), but they have many of their own, since their theory too posits a single basic cause of human behavior. When Frank Lentricchia refers to "the ultimate problem of linking repressed and master voices as the agon of history, their abiding relation of class conflict" (131), the terms "ultimate" and "abiding" tell us this is supposed to be a universal law determining all historical events and thus all literary texts. But probably the most useful universal law for these critics (derived from this law of class conflict) is found in Jean Howard's assertion that "a dominant ideology . . . always bears traces of the contestatory or subversive elements it has attempted to recuperate" (355), for this guarantees that every text will contain "traces" of ideological conflicts or contradictions. (And they will always be unresolvable, which is another universal law derived from the "abiding" nature of class conflict.) There is, however, a difference between the universal laws of the Marxists and neo-Freudians and those of orthodox Freudians, since the first two groups insist that their laws depend on social arrangements and will be repealed in the future when we have a society without classes or without a gender division of labor that assigns mothering to women. This is very important to them, since both groups, unlike the Freudians, believe the situation their laws describe can be ended by political action;[8] but it seems clear that until this day arrives their laws are supposed to be just as universal as the Freudians'. It also seems clear that the critics in all three groups have no notion of the evidence that would be required to establish this kind of universal law in the discipline involved.

Seeing if (Proving that) the Theory Works

The imprint of mothering on the male psyche, the psychological presence of the mother in men whether or not mothers are represented in the texts they write or in which they appear as characters, can be found throughout the literary canon.

—Coppélia Kahn

After selecting (and perhaps improving) a theory from another discipline, the critic must then apply it to the interpretation of a literary text. This is the last step in the process of becoming interdisciplinary and it is regarded as the payoff, a kind of test to see if the theory really works in criticism. The trouble is that all theories always pass this test; no failure has ever been recorded. We can get an idea of why this happens by looking at the neo-Freudians' application of their theory to Shakespeare, which requires that all his male heroes must have problems with mothering, which in turn requires that all his works must have a mother. There are many mothers in Shakespeare, but except for Volumnia they have usually been ignored by these critics because their relationship to the hero does not fit the theory, and because the theory is based on unconscious motivation and therefore seems to call for a surrogate mother figure concealed in a "maternal subtext" that is repressed by the hero or the text or Shakespeare (the critics are often uncertain about this), so that, as Kahn explains, "the absence of a mother in the play serves to highlight her psychological presence," though she later adds that in *Coriolanus* "the mother's psychological presence within the hero is no less strong for being represented" ("Excavating" 37, 39). Heads I win, tails you lose.

As a result of the application of this theory, Shakespearean mother figures have been proliferating at a remarkable rate and are now as plentiful as his Christ figures were under the older dispensation. In her essay introducing the theory, Kahn applied it to Lear and argued that he unconsciously views his daughters as mothers, which was a good choice since there really is evidence of this in the play. But much less likely mother figures have been found for many other heroes in the canon: Portia is supposed to be a mother figure for Bassanio (Wheeler), Desdemona for Othello (Erickson; Novy, *Love's*; Snow), Lady Macbeth for Macbeth (Adelman, "Born"; Kahn, *Man's*; Wheeler), Cleopatra for Antony (Erickson, Stockholder), Rosalind for Orlando (Wheeler), Cressida for Troilus (Adelman, "This"), Helena for Bertram (Adelman, "Bed"; Stockholder), Hermione for Leontes (Adelman, "Male"; Erickson; Kahn, *Man's*; Nevo; Wheeler; Stockholder), Imogen for Posthumus (Nevo), Miranda for Prospero (Novy, "Shakespeare"), and Venus for Adonis (Kahn, *Man's*).[9] But they do not have to be female, since mother figurehood has been conferred on Shylock (Sundelson) and Falstaff (Traub). They do not even have to be human; the hero's mother figure has turned up in the witches in *Macbeth* (Stockholder, Wheeler), the lioness in *As You Like It* (Erickson, Montrose), mother England in *Richard II* (Kahn, *Man's*) and *Henry IV* (Wheeler), and the sea in *The Comedy of Errors* (Adelman, "Male"; MacCary; Nevo), *Twelfth Night* (MacCary, Wheeler), *Pericles* (Nevo), *Timon of Athens* (Kahn, "Magic"), and *The Tempest* (Nevo).

The sheer variety here helps to explain why we now have as many mother figures in Shakespeare as we had Christ figures, since the searches for both have been conducted under the same golden rule: seek and ye shall find. I once showed how easy it was to find a Christ figure because of the many aspects of Jesus that could be drawn on to make connections to a character (*New* 212–24); and it is even easier to find a mother figure, since the theory splits her into a benign and a malevolent persona, either of which can be used by the critics, and also mandates that she must appear in every play, no matter how concealed she may be. Indeed the concealment is part of the theory, which enabled Kahn ("Absent") to argue that the mother's absence is evidence of her presence, something the Christ figure seekers could not claim. (Alert readers will have noticed that some plays already have two mother figures, and if the trend continues we can anticipate more competition, with readings that begin by asserting that "My Mother Figure Can Lick Your Mother Figure.") Therefore, the fact that the theory can be shown to work in Shakespeare tells us nothing about its validity. This is just what we would expect, and we must remember that orthodox Freudians and Jungians were able to show that their theories worked in the same way in the same plays, as did Campbell with Elizabethan humor psychology, and Leverenz with interpersonal psychiatry, and Kennard with Zinker's Gestalt theory.

The Marxists also have no trouble proving that their theory works in every Shakespeare play, for it tells them that whatever the play seems to be about, it must really be about Lentricchia's "ultimate problem" of "abiding" class conflict. It also tells them, like the neo-Freudians' theory, that this real subject is usually concealed by the play and thus must be "deconcealed" (Jameson's term) by the critic.

The operation is now so widespread that a listing would be pointless, so I will limit myself to one example, Peter Stallybrass's reading of *Othello*, which is a kind of test case (though I do not know if he intended this), since the play does not seem to have anything to do with class conflict: the conflicts in it, insofar as they can be treated abstractly, all involve the first two terms of the race-gender-class triad. But he saves the play for Marxism by using the Freudian concept of displacement to subsume gender and race under class.[10] "Class aspiration," he says, is "displaced onto the enchanted ground of romance, where considerations of status are transformed into considerations of sexual success"; and Othello's race is "the displaced condition" of his status as "class aspirant" (134–35). Even Iago's villainy is a displacement, because the ruling class's fear of "subversion is localized" in him, so he becomes "the projection of a social hierarchy's unease in the hypostatized form of envy" (140).[11] Thus *Othello* passes the test and proves that the theory works. The problem is that this reading is a test case in another sense that certainly was not intended by Stallybrass, for if the theory works in this play then it will work in any play, which means it has not been and cannot be proved. In order for a theory to be provable it must be disprovable—that is, we must be able to conceive of a situation where it would *not* work. And this also applies to the neo-Freudian theory. The readings produced by either theory would be convincing only if there could be a play that did not involve a maternal subtext or a class conflict. But the claimed universality of the two theories and the methodology used in applying them preclude such a possibility. They have no negative test.

Aprioritizing Theory

A rigorous knowledge must beware of all forms of empiricism, for the objects of any rational investigation have no prior existence but are thought into being.
                                                                          —Pierre Machery

Having examined the current procedure for becoming interdisciplinary, we can now try to explain why it developed in this way. One of the main causes is what I call "aprioritizing theory," which includes two related phenomena implied in the two meanings of the phrase: the tendency of interdisciplinary critics to aprioritize theory, that is, to treat "theorizing" as an a priori mode of thought, and their tendency to borrow theories that are themselves aprioritizing in the sense that they depend on a priori thinking.

It is no accident that most of these borrowings (and hence most of my examples) come from Marxism or Freudianism, since they are already interdisciplinary. Although each has a home discipline, as it were, in economics or psychology, we saw that both claim to have found the basic cause of all human behavior studied in other disciplines as well, which makes it so easy to apply them to literature. Of course both Marx and Freud intended to construct an empirical science, but they proceeded in isolation from and in opposition to the other sciences, including those they were supposed to be representing (or supplanting). The result was that Marxism and Freudianism developed along different lines than those sciences, which were viewed as enemies, and became closed, self-confirming systems that never confronted the criticisms levied against them on empirical grounds—in fact both systems were able to explain away these criticisms.[12] They are named for their founders, like a religion, and even have canonical texts and excommunications for heresy.[13] They also have separate associations and journals preaching to the converted. And this isolation has affected interdisciplinary criticism: many Marxist and Freudian critics know a great deal about the theories of the founding fathers and their descendants but virtually nothing about the relevant discipline. They do not have to, and if they are even aware of the low standing of these theories in that discipline, this is just further proof that it is the enemy.

Any charge that Freudianism is not empirical must confront the claims of Freud himself and the schools derived from him, including the revisionists, that their theories are generated and confirmed by "clinical evidence." Chodorow, for instance, invokes "the clinical situation that ultimately provides psychoanalysis its truths" (*Feminism* 12). The clinical situation can provide analysts with promising hypotheses (which can come from anywhere, even an overflowing bathtub or falling apple), but it can never prove they are true because it is always contaminated by the analysts' a priori theory, as several commentators have shown.[14] Analysts are not trying to deceive us (or themselves), but out of all the evidence coming from the patient they only hear things that fit their theory, which is why each school of psychoanalysis is able to validate its own theories from the clinical evidence of its own practitioners. It is similar to the situation described earlier in which critics showed that very different psychological theories "worked" in the same play, since they were in effect treating the play (or playwright) as a patient providing data that they read in the light of their favorite theory. But the clinical situation is even more contaminated than these readings, for the play itself is not affected by the critic, while patients clearly are affected by their analyst's expectations, as acknowledged by Judd Marmor (himself an analyst): "Patients of each school seem to bring up precisely the kind of . . . data which confirm the theories . . . of their analysts!" (289).[15] Feminist neo-Freudians should be especially sensitive to this, since the clinical evidence of orthodox Freudians was supposed to prove theories like penis envy. Yet they have shown no more interest than the Freudians in submitting their evidence to empirical verification, which would require objective tests that could be administered by nonbelievers and could yield negative results. When the theory of two female orgasms, another Freudian truth proved by clinical evidence, was put to such a test it flunked badly. It seems clear that clinical evidence is not empirical but deduced from a priori theories.

Marxists have nothing equivalent to clinical evidence, although their analyses of society, both diachronic and synchronic, seem just as aprioritized as the interpretations of Freudian therapists and critics. Their theory in its latest versions, however, is even more obviously a priori than the Freudians', since it is not merely nonempirical but antiempirical, as shown in the epigraph to this section and in the earlier quotation from Moi asserting that empiricism is "inherently reactionary" (10). This would have surprised Marx, who spent many hours collecting data for those tables in *Das Kapital*; but there are several reasons for this antiempiricist swerve of the new Marxism. Surely the most important is that the empirical facts have not been kind to Marx's theory or the predictions based on it.[16] That in turn has contributed to the tendency of the new Marxists to distance their theorizing from the real world of political action, despite their claim to be "activists." And this is related to their wholesale condemnation of all modes of thought they associate with the bourgeoisie and the Enlightenment, including empiricism, idealism, objectivism, positivism, and realism, which have all become bad words in their vocabulary.[17] They have also been influenced by the general thrust of poststructuralism, which questions the possibility of access to an external reality and hence of empirical knowledge. As a result, the new Marxists not only deduce their facts from their theory (as did the old Marxists) but now insist this is the proper way for state-of-the-art revolutionaries to proceed. Nor has this poststructuralist influence been limited to them, for many interdisciplinary critics of other schools have joined the attack on empirical evidence and so contributed to the aprioritizing of theory.[18]

Politicizing Theory

[Our] claim is not that such a history . . . is more accurate, but only that it is more radical.

—Catherine Belsey

The interdisciplinary critics' lack of concern for the empirical verification of the theories they borrow is closely connected to their lack of concern for the evaluation of these theories by the disciplines involved (which is based on empirical verification), and therefore to their belief that they are free to borrow any theory and make any improvement in it that suits their purposes. And since these purposes are often political, as we saw, aprioritizing theory is also closely connected to politicizing theory, which I use again in two related senses: the tendency of these critics to treat all "theorizing" as a political activity and their tendency to borrow theories that are themselves politicizing in that they are directed to the transformation of society. That is one reason why interdisciplinarity is now seen as a radical project.

Many of these critics justify this politicization with the argument that all critical approaches are political, and specifically that the formalist approach, though it may seem politically neutral, really supports "liberal humanism," which is supposed to be the ideology of the bourgeoisie that legitimates the oppression of workers or women. Therefore they link formalism and liberal humanism to the other bad isms on the hit list compiled above (empiricism, idealism, etc.), which are opposed to the good isms that are linked to class or gender liberation. Politicization thus leads these critics to polarization, with all truth and virtue on "our" side and all error and vice on "theirs." And not far beneath the surface of this polarized view of the world are glimpses of a vast conspiracy that is imposing the bad isms on us, including pluralism, which is seen as a devious strategy to maintain the status quo (like the "repressive tolerance" we heard about in the sixties).[19] Even the boundaries separating the disciplines become part of this conspiracy, since they prevent us from learning about our oppression, which is another reason why interdisciplinarity is now held to be radical and liberating.

Like other conspiracy theories, this sounds neat and simple, but it simply is not true. There is no necessary connection between critical approaches and political beliefs. Many of the early New Critics were conservatives, yet during its heyday this formalist approach attracted people of all political persuasions, including Marxists and feminists. There was also a thriving group of Marxist formalists in the USSR before they were liquidated by Marxist realists, who are now opposed by the new Marxists because realism is bourgeois. Historical criticism is practiced by conservatives, liberals, and radicals, and so is psychological criticism. The alleged connection between critical approaches and political actions (rather than beliefs) is even more dubious, as Stanley Fish and Gerald Graff assert in one of their rare moments of agreement ("Forum" 220, "Pseudo" 150–52). Formalists can work for radical causes, and many new Marxists, we saw, distance themselves from political activity. This disjunction is noted in the essay by Moi cited earlier, where she attacks Anglo-American feminist critics for adopting a "humanist" approach that is "inherently reactionary" and praises French "feminist theoreticians" for their "revolutionary form of criticism," but then praises the Anglo-Americans for being "politically committed" to "challenging the social and political strategies of the literary institution," while the French have shown "a scandalous lack of interest in the social and political aspects of women's oppression" (6,11). Yet she insists that the French approach is politically superior.

It also seems clear that there is no necessary connection between political beliefs or actions and the theories these critics choose to borrow from other disciplines, even though we found that their choices are often based on political grounds. Moi and Belsey urged the (partial) adoption of the theories of Kristeva and Freud since they disrupt the unitary subject of liberal humanism and so pave the way for communism. But disrupting the subject need not promote Marxist goals; it was also on the fascist agenda, which was just as hostile to liberal humanism as Marxism is. This lack of connection is also demonstrated in the endless debates among these critics on whether some theory is really on "our" side or can serve "their" side by appropriation, co-option, and so on.[20] The debates are endless because the theories they argue about are not linked to specific political positions. This also applies to the passage from Belsey used as the epigraph here: she endorses one version of history since it is "more radical" than others, but we have no way of determining which history is more radical. The same historical interpretations are used by different political factions, and so are the larger historical theories—there are leftist and rightist Hegelians, for instance, and the idea of history as a fall from a lost Eden figures in reactionary and radical rhetoric.[21]

There is a more basic objection to these politicizers, however, for even if we could establish a necessary connection between some theories taken from another discipline and specific political positions, it would still be wrong to judge *any* theory by political criteria instead of the criterion of truth. That is easy to see when we disagree with the political criteria; I do not think many of my readers support the assault on the theory of evolution by the religious right, yet this is the most prominent recent example of the politicization of theory advocated by these critics when their own political beliefs are the criteria. The theory of evolution seems to be true (and is used by political conservatives and radicals), but the criteria are just as objectionable when the theory is false. Freudian theory has been attacked by Marxists and some feminists because it legitimates class or gender oppression; but that cannot make it false.[22] It is false, not because it may have bad political consequences, but because it does not meet the criteria of empirical verification established in the discipline of psychology. And the revision of Freud recommended by Kahn is false for the same reason, even though it might have good political consequences in promoting the feminist cause.

The judging of theories on the basis of their alleged political consequences has itself dire political consequences, for it leads to the politicizing of the disciplines and hence to their destruction as independent modes of inquiry. This is the lesson of Lysenkoism—not of the genetic theory itself (which no one believes anymore), but of the way it was adopted on political grounds as "revolutionary," while opposing theories were outlawed as "reactionary." This was atypical, since Marxist regimes usually kept their hands off the "hard" sciences, which yield useful results when left alone;[23] but they resolutely politicized the rest of the curriculum. Thus a major demand of students after the liberation of Eastern Europe was for the *depoliticization* of the university, by which they meant the elimination, not only of compulsory indoctrination courses in Marxist ideology, but also of ideological criteria in the study of other disciplines, which they wanted to be governed by the criteria of truth defined in those disciplines. Our politicizing critics should listen to these students, who have already been where the critics want to take us.

Welcoming Theory

"At sociology meetings I've wandered from session to session where people were giving papers on how absurd my work is," she recalled. "I find I'm taken more seriously by literary critics."
—Interview with Nancy Chodorow by Daniel Goleman

We should not place all the blame for the present state of interdisciplinarity upon these critics, since a share belongs to the rest of us, or rather to the discipline of literary criticism. It can hardly be a coincidence that our discipline is so hospitable to discredited theories from other disciplines and is able to prove that they "work" in interpreting literature. This must be related to our interpretive procedures, which seem to operate without any rules. Martin Mueller observes that "from the perspective of other disciplines, literary scholars engage in exegetical activities that are peculiarly unconstrained" and that the "hermeneutical license that has long been claimed by literary critics . . . has always been suspect" in those disciplines (27).

This can be partly explained by the nature of the phenomena we deal with. Literary texts and the responses they evoke are highly complex and multiform and hence not amenable to precise demonstrations. As a result, our discipline will always be less rigorous than even the "soft" sciences. But another important explanation lies in the approach that dominated the New Criticism and is still influential, which I call *thematism*. Thematic critics usually begin with the assumption that the real subject of the text they are interpreting cannot be what it seems to be—the particular actions of particular characters—but must be an abstract idea or "central theme" reflected in them, and then look for evidence to prove it, which they always find. And they never find any evidence that might disprove it, because they are not looking for this evidence (that is, they only "see" the data they have already thematized) and because the approach does not define what such evidence would be—there is nothing the text could contain that cannot be accommodated to the theme. They have no negative test, which is why we have no unsuccessful thematic readings.

This should recall our earlier account of how interdisciplinary critics see if the theory they took from another discipline works in interpreting a text, since this operation is also always successful for the same reasons: they only look for evidence in the text that will prove the theory works, and there is no evidence that could disprove it. This also applies to the two favorite theories of these critics. Freudian and neo-Freudian analysts perform a kind of thematic reading of clinical evidence, for their theory tells them in advance that what the patient seems to be talking about is only a reflection of the real problem, and it also tells them in advance what that real problem must be. And Marxists produce thematic readings of history and of society; thanks to their theory, they know in advance that what seems to be happening is only a reflection of what is really happening, and that what is really happening is an aspect of class conflict. We also saw that neither Freudian nor Marxist theory is subject to a negative test, since they cannot be refuted by any conceivable evidence, which is why we concluded that they are both aprioritized.

I suggest that it is partly because of the legacy of thematism that so few critics today appreciate the importance of negative tests, which in turn would explain the fact, noted by Mueller, that our mode of interpretation seems so unconstrained to people in other disciplines. Scientists have long realized that if a theory cannot be disproved, then it cannot be proved. Ideally any scientist proposing a new theory should try all possible means to disprove it,[24] which may be asking too much; but we do not have to rely on this because the theory must be formulated in such a way that others can do the job—that is, it must "invite falsification" by objective tests that can produce negative results. A theory that is not "falsifiable" in this sense would not be taken seriously; it would be what Frank Cioffi calls pseudoscientific. The failure of interdisciplinary critics to grasp this principle is seen in the assumption of Marxists and neo-Freudians, noted earlier, that they can prove their theory works by finding a class conflict or maternal subtext in every play, without defining a possible situation in which it would not work. And because these critics operate in this a priori mode with no negative tests, they see nothing wrong in adopting theories that operate in the same way, which helps to account for the strange situation described by Chodorow in the epigraph to this section.

This may explain why these critics do not reject a priori theories, but there are also positive reasons why they accept Marxism and Freudianism (especially the revised version). The most important is the politicization of theory discussed above: those who see criticism as the continuation of political struggle by other means are drawn to a theory that seems useful for this purpose and do not care that it is discredited in its own discipline (which they view as itself politically motivated by the "enemy"). We also saw that both theories distinguish between the apparent and real meaning of the phenomena they deal with, just as many critics do, and that they both locate this real meaning in one basic cause of all human behavior that can be easily grasped by critics and applied to any text. And it is a very dramatic cause featuring conflicts between hypostatized entities (parts of society or of the psyche), which appeals to critics who like to find conflict in literary works.[25] These seem to be the main reasons why Marxism and Freudianism are thriving in literature departments when they are in full retreat everywhere else in the world.

The fact remains, however, that these theories could not become popular in interdisciplinary criticism if critics recognized the importance of negative tests, both for the theories they borrow and for the application of those theories in interpreting literature, so I now want to turn to such tests. Their role in interpretation is too complicated to discuss here,[26] but there are two simple and obvious tests for the theories themselves—tests that are easy to use and require no special expertise. I am under no illusion that they will be used by critics who already inhabit (or are inhabited by) Marxism or Freudianism or similar closed, a priori systems, which we saw are impervious to adverse arguments. But they might be helpful to aspiring interdisciplinarians who are not yet committed to a system of this kind and are still willing and able to judge its theories before borrowing them.

Looking at a Real Horse

In the midst of the Middle Ages three learned doctors held a public debate at the Sorbonne on the nature of the horse's hoof. One based his case on a passage from Aristotle. The second disagreed, citing another account from Galen. The third said they were both wrong since Pliny had a different view. They argued for hours until someone in the audience asked, "Why don't we step outside and look at a real horse?"

This is an apocryphal story that probably comes from some anti-Scholastic satire, like that debate over how many angels could dance on the point of a needle; but it tells us something about the nature of a priori thinking, where the facts are deduced from the theory and so are always already "theorized" (just as the textual evidence of the New Critics was always already "thematized"). One obvious negative test of such a theory, then, is to step outside it and look at the facts—the real horse—to see if they are what the theory claims they should be. I will present just a few examples in which these theories fail this test, beginning with Snow's law, stated above, that every man or at least "every civilized white man" has an intense gynophobic reaction to the consummation of his marriage (400, 402), which is presumably derived from the neo-Freudian theory of male pathology and is supposed to explain Othello's murder of Desdemona. If the theory were true, most of our marriages would end like Othello's; but the facts are otherwise. In fact many husbands, even civilized white ones, seem to feel more loving after the wedding night (when the couple abstained until then), which is also true of Othello.

Some feminist critics use Kristeva's theory of the child's progress from the "semiotic order" of the mother to the "symbolic order" of the father (or Lacan's similar scheme) to maintain that language is a masculine construct from which women are "alienated" (Gohlke 166, 170). But in fact women handle the mother tongue at least as well as men and score higher than men in the verbal sections of many aptitude tests; some of them are even able to describe their alienation from language with real eloquence. Similar to this theory of "masculine language" is the theory of "masculine narrative," which also fails the test of fact, since however this narrative is defined, we find that it is employed by some women. And if this is explained away on the ground that they were conditioned to write like men,[27] it would show that the theory cannot be disproved by any conceivable facts, and so cannot be proved. It is simply deduced from some a priori assumption about gender difference.

Many of the Marxist theories also fail this test. It is obvious that every prediction based upon them has been contradicted by the facts. We found that this led Jameson to deny that Marxism is predictive, which would exempt it from this test and make it, too, undisprovable and thus unprovable; but others still prophesy the collapse of "late capitalism,"[28] when in fact we are seeing the collapse of late socialism. More examples are provided by the new Marxists' campaign against the bourgeoisie, which includes the theory of Barker (110–12) and Belsey (*Subject* 124–25) that bourgeois subjects possess a "death drive" impelling them to suicide. But the facts again contradict this idea, since very few bourgeois subjects commit suicide; in fact the suicide rate varies widely in different bourgeois societies, as it does in different nonbourgeois societies, so it is not correlated to the economic system. Another Marxist theory that clearly fails this test, even though it has been endorsed by some feminists,[29] is that gender oppression is caused by class oppression and will end when capitalism is replaced by socialism. But the facts are that the subjection of women long preceded class society and survives under socialism. There are in fact striking differences in the status of women in different capitalist societies, as there are in different socialist societies, showing that this status, like suicide, is not determined by the economic system.

Many more examples of this sort could be cited, but these should be enough to make my point about the nature of a priori thinking. For I cannot believe that I possess some special ability or knowledge that enables me to find the facts that contradict these theories, since they are obvious and available to anyone who looks for them. And this forces me to conclude that the interdisciplinary critics cannot have looked, because they do not want to subject the theory they are borrowing to this negative test.

Do I Contradict Myself? Very Well Then, I Contradict Myself

Human nature is not "natural," but is, rather, shaped by social forces and values. . . . In de Beauvoir's terms, "woman sees herself and makes her choices not in accordance with her nature in itself, but as man defines her."
—Gayle Greene

The second obvious negative test of theories borrowed from other disciplines is to see if they are contradicted, not by the facts, but by a practice or another belief of the critic who borrows them. Again I present only a few of the examples where theories clearly fail this test, most of which are related to the politicizing of theory (just as most failures of the test of fact were related to the aprioritizing of theory). In many of these cases critics adopt a theory about texts or discourse but exempt their own texts or discourse from it, so that they inconsistently "privilege" their practice. Several commentators have noted that this is standard procedure in Freudian criticism (which here includes the neo-Freudians): the critics regularly assume that every text they interpret is shaped by unconscious motives but that their interpretation of it is immune from such motives. Thus a male critic who finds that a play is permeated by castration anxiety never has to ask himself whether that anxiety could be in him rather than in the play or playwright. If he or we did ask this, Freudian criticism would grind to a halt.[30]

Other examples of this self-privileging appear in critics employing the post-Saussurian linguistic theory invoked by Belsey, since they usually treat signifiers as freely floating in the texts they read but as firmly grounded in the texts they write; they will even complain when they are misunderstood, although this theory insists that there can be no correct understanding of a text and that its author has no control over its meaning.[31] They also contradict themselves on the referentiality of language: in the passage referred to, Belsey says this theory "closes off questions about how accurately language represents the world" but then discusses "the existing order" of the world in language that she must believe represents it accurately. More examples come from critics who adopt the theory that interpretation is never objective since it is always affected by the interpreter's ideology (rather than by the intrinsic volatility of language itself). Unlike many post-Saussurians, these critics often admit that the theory applies to their own discourse (as in the epigraph to the section "Politicizing Theory"), yet they can forget this very quickly when it serves their purpose. Barker says all historical interpretation is "reshaped to present needs . . . and to believe otherwise would be to advance a hubristic objectivism,"[32] and two sentences later attacks critics who misinterpret the real historical basis of Shakespeare's texts (15). And a letter signed by twenty-four feminists states that "we forthrightly acknowledge the partiality of our own interpretations," but in the next paragraph presents interpretations of Shakespeare that are meant to be independent of this partiality since they derive from "detailed analyses of the specific actions of particular heroes" (Adelman et al. 77). The explanation of these contradictions is political: the critics believe that the idea of interpretive objectivity belongs to the bourgeois or male enemy and so must be rejected, yet they also believe—and want readers to believe—that their own interpretations are objectively true.

There is another form of this self-contradiction in which critics espouse a theory but exempt certain texts from it, so that they are privileging, not their own practice, but the texts themselves. Most of these examples involve the *"herméneutique du soupçon"*—the theory that a text is never what it seems to be since it must contain concealed or repressed material (ideological contradictions or maternal subtexts)—which these critics adopt from the Marxist or Freudian traditions and apply selectively. Moi notes that many Anglo-American feminist critics use this "suspicious approach" on men-authored texts but not on women-authored texts, which they take straight (2–4). (Characters can also be privileged in this way: neo-Freudians typically probe the unconscious and always pathological motivation of male characters, while female characters seem free of such probing; and Snow, after giving Othello the full "suspicious" treatment, gets indignant when an orthodox Freudian does the same to Desdemona [405].) The new Marxists are just as guilty. Evans applies the *soupçon* theory (with a dash of post-Saussurianism thrown in) to Shakespeare's texts but assumes that radical texts of the Civil War period are just what they seem to be (259–62). And many Marxists who employ this theory in reading bourgeois plays abandon it when they read Brecht.[33] The explanation of these contradictions again lies in the political polarization of criticism, since the critics want the enemy's ox gored but not their own.

The last kind of self-contradiction results not from the inconsistent application of one theory adopted by these critics but from their adoption of two theories that are incompatible. Most of the examples turn on the nature-nurture problematic, which poses problems for critics who are committed to the theory that "human nature" is created entirely by nurture—that, as Rorty puts it, "there is nothing to people except what has been socialized into them" (177)[34]—but find it politically expedient to adopt an opposed position. Marxists get into this contradiction because if "the subject" is simply the product of the dominant bourgeois ideology, they have no way to explain how opposition to it arises or why we should support this opposition,[35] and so must introduce values like "social justice," "equality," "liberation," or "human potential" that cannot have been inscribed in us by that ideology and seem to derive from (and assume) a concept of a basic, indestructible human nature. Thus Jameson begins *The Political Unconscious* with the command "Always historicize!" (9) and later tells us that all history is "the collective struggle to wrest a realm of Freedom from a realm of Necessity" (19), a struggle that could not be the result of historically specific conditioning but is apparently an inherent and unhistoricizable aspiration of humanity itself.

For some feminists the problem of nature vs. nurture centers on the question whether gender differences are innate or acquired, which can involve them in the same kind of self-contradiction, as seen in Greene's two sentences used as the epigraph to this section. Greene begins her essay by insisting that human nature (which for her includes woman's nature) is not natural but is "shaped by social forces" that are patriarchal, and later endorses de Beauvoir's statement that a woman acts "not in accordance with her nature in itself, but as man defines her" ("Shakespeare's" 133, 136). Yet there can be no opposition between woman's "nature in itself" and man's definition of her if man's definition shapes her nature, for then she would have no "nature in itself." Presumably both theories are asserted because each has political advantages: the theory that women's nature is wholly the product of conditioning (that it is all "socialized into them") is useful for arguing that it can be changed by social action, while the theory that they have an inherent nature that this conditioning violates is useful to validate and valorize such action.[36]

Although more examples could be presented, these should be enough to make my point, which is the same one I reached at the end of the preceding section. For again I must say that I did not require any special knowledge or ability to find these contradictions, since they would all be obvious to anyone who looked for them. And so we must conclude once more that these critics could not have looked, because they did not want to apply this negative test either to the theories they borrowed or to their use of them in literary criticism.

For Interdisciplinarity

Interdisciplinary work is most difficult but also most productive when it involves the collision of strongly articulated disciplinary ethnicities. Work of this kind is quite rare, because it requires a hands-on experience of, and deep respect for, the otherness of the other.

—Martin Mueller

I want to end this investigation on a positive note, because I have been arguing not against interdisciplinarity itself but only against its abuses. I am really arguing for a genuine interdisciplinarity, or at least for something much closer to it than the studies we examined. Mueller recognizes that the kind of work he is describing, where the critic has actually practiced the other discipline, is an ideal that can rarely be achieved; but we surely can ask that critics who want to be interdisciplinary know enough about the other discipline to use it in ways that will not seem absurd to its own practitioners. I hope it is clear that I am not calling for a rigid turfism that would discourage critics from using another discipline. Nor am I suggesting that the various disciplines as now constituted are natural, inevitable, autonomous, seamless, God-given, or any of the other inanities that we liberal humanists are supposed to believe in. The disciplines have been constructed by human beings and have evolved through time. But as a result of this evolution they have developed organized bodies of knowledge and methodologies for producing and testing new knowledge that deserve our respect, for even though they are fallible, they are still the best means we have for learning about the world. It follows then that a critic wishing to use a theory from another discipline should first understand what it means in that discipline and how it is judged there. To promote this goal I am presenting four proposals, in an ascending order of their importance and the difficulty in implementing them.

The most obvious step and the easiest would be to ensure that whenever a critical article or book claiming to be interdisciplinary is submitted for publication, its referees include a representative of the other discipline.[37] This is sometimes done today, but the practice should be universal. It would not only help to screen out bad interdisciplinary work but would also have a positive effect on the research of interdisciplinary critics. If they were planning an essay that relied on Lawrence Stone's theory of the "reinforcement of patriarchy," for instance, and knew in advance that it would be refereed by a social historian, they would have a powerful incentive for finding out, before writing the essay, just how this theory is regarded in Stone's own field.[38]

Second, I would recommend changes in our requirements for literature students, both undergraduate and graduate, that would enable them to carry a double major or a strong minor in a second discipline. This, too, is sometimes done today, but it should be made much easier if we hope to encourage responsible interdisciplinary work.[39] We might also offer, as part of our general education component, an introductory course in the methodologies of the disciplines that would explain, among other things, the significance of falsifiability and negative tests and the pitfalls of enumerative inductivism. These are not very recondite concepts, yet most of the critics dealt with here have apparently never heard of them, and we saw this was also true of the older thematic critics. If our students learned about them, therefore, we would reap future benefits not only in interdisciplinary criticism but also in the kinds of criticism practiced within the confines of our own discipline.

The third proposal is to take some of the pressure off our colleagues, especially the younger ones, to engage in interdisciplinarity with its attendant theorizing. I realize this is much more easily said than done since it involves the pressure to publish and hence to adopt the mode of criticism that is now most publishable. One has to sympathize with the plight of those who feel obliged to join this enterprise even though they are not suited for it by training, ability, or inclination, and so find themselves trafficking in undigested scraps of theory, picked up from other disciplines, that they cannot evaluate or apply properly—a practice that has led to many of the errors we examined. Some of them would have trouble theorizing their way out of a wet paper bag. Clearly they would benefit, as would the rest of us, if we could convince them that they are not being timid or narrow or outdated if they stick to their own discipline and do what they know how to do. Perhaps we could even convince them that it takes more courage to buck the current fashion than to follow it.

The final proposal is the most important since it extends well beyond the specific problems of interdisciplinarity to the general state of our discipline. I would like to see an end to the political polarization noted earlier, which locates all truth and virtue on one side and all error and evil on the other. This polarization bears most of the responsibility (much more than the lack of ability) for the problems of the new interdisciplinarity that we surveyed: for the selection and improvement of theories from other disciplines on political grounds, with the resulting arguments over whether some theory is really on "our" side or "theirs"; for the self-contradiction and the disregard of empirical evidence; for the inconsistent privileging of "our" discourse and "our" texts; and the rest. It has also created an atmosphere that is harmful to all other areas of our discipline, since it prevents us from talking to and learning from each other. Depolarization would therefore benefit not only the targets of the polarizers but also the polarizers themselves. The reason has already been suggested in the discussion of negative tests, for we tend to be lax in applying such tests to our own work or the work of critics like us. That is why we need critics with different orientations to apply the tests for us, so we will be able to refine or correct our views. I have learned more from those who disagree with me than from those who agree; but we cannot learn in this way if we dismiss adverse criticism as the machinations of the enemy.[40]

The blame for this polarizing belongs to both extremes of the political spectrum. All my examples were on the Left, since that is where the new interdisciplinarity is coming from, but the Right is equally guilty, as can be seen in Allan Bloom's book (a product of the old interdisciplinarity), with its nostalgic idealizing of a lost Eden and wholesale condemnation of all new developments, which is just as absurd and pernicious as the opposite stance.[41] We would all benefit if we could abandon this warfare between the two sides, and even abandon the idea of two sides. There are many different political positions and many different critical positions and no necessary connection between them, as I have tried to show. And in most of them we find well-meaning, intelligent people who have useful things to tell us about our discipline and interdisciplinarity and the world we all share.

Notes

1. Graff discusses some other attempts at interdisciplinarity during the period dominated by the New Criticism in *Professing*, chap. 13.

2. The earliest citation of *interdisciplinary* in the *OED* is dated 1937, but Frank's study, which I highly recommend, records its appearance in 1926.

3. For Stewart, "Doing theory and doing interdisciplinary work are inseparable projects" (11); and for Dollimore, "One of the most important achievements of 'theory' in English studies has been the making possible a truly interdisciplinary approach" ("Introduction" 2).

4. Kahn presents the same argument in "Hand" and "Absent," but in "Hand" 79 she also cites some clinical evidence from Horney as support (see n. 15 below). For convenience I refer to these theories collectively as a single feminist revisionist or neo-Freudian theory, though I do not deny (nor does Kahn) their differences; I am less interested in the theories themselves than in how these critics view and use them. And although I call this revision "feminist," I realize that a great many feminist critics never employ it.

5. Kennard adds that "in borrowing Zinker's ideas, I do not imply that other theories might not work as well" (67); but a scientific theory is supposed to preclude some competing theories (see the discussion of falsifiability below).

6. Chodorow is a sociologist and psychoanalyst, and Dinnerstein a psychologist; Rich of course is primarily a poet and critic.

7. Some feminists also improve Lacan (e.g., Belsey, "Romantic" 60–61; Moi 6), which is understandable since his theory is even more phallocentric than Freud's; what is hard to understand is why any feminist would want to use it.

8. Thus Dollimore, after explaining the nature of class oppression, concludes that "it did not, and still does not, have to be so" ("Introduction" 15); and Chodorow says her theory "asks how we might change things" (*Reproduction* 4). She now disavows her search in that book for a single cause and cure of gender oppression (*Feminism* 5–6, 15), but critics have not yet caught up with her.

9. Of course Cleopatra and Hermione really are mothers and Bertram really has one in the cast, but these relationships, as I said, do not fit the theory.

10. Stallybrass increases his interdisciplinarity by also using Bakhtin's theory of the "grotesque body," after improving it to include all women's bodies (126), which makes the theory more useful for inserting "woman" into class conflict.

11. Snow, using the neo-Freudian mode of this same logic, says Iago "is really only the name and local habitation" of society's misogyny (386), which is the real subject of the play.

12. Marxists could argue that people objecting to their doctrines were the bourgeois enemy threatened by the coming revolution, and Freudians that such people were "resisting" the threatened exposure of their own repressions.

13. Bristol defends his view of ideology by claiming he "followed Brecht's injunction to return to the classics, i.e., the Marxist classics, and the early ones at that" ("Where" 43). One cannot imagine a biologist today returning to the classic texts of Darwin to defend her view of evolution. Marxism has an extensive catalog of heresies, including economism, spontaneism, voluntarism, and opportunism (a catchall); Freudian heresies are named for the archheretics, giving us Adlerians, Horneyites, Jungians, Rankians, etc.

14. See, e.g., Crews 81–86, Grünbaum 127–28, 209–14, and Weisstein 209–12, where the problem is viewed from a feminist perspective.

15. This could also explain Horney's report that her men patients reveal an intense envy of pregnancy (60), which Kahn cites to confirm the neo-Freudian theory she endorses ("Hand" 79) (though she ignores the clinical evidence supplied by Horney's women patients, since it does not fit this theory).

16. Jameson now denies that Marxism is predictive ("Science" 290), which would surprise Marx and all his followers who believed the laws of economic determinism gave them the key to the future; but this disclaimer is understandable since none of Marx's predictions has come true. It is like a football coach at the end of a disastrous season denying that he was trying to win games.

17. There are some strange bedfellows here. Empiricism and idealism are supposed to be opposites, but the new Marxists combine them, as in Belsey's reference to "a *humanism* based on an *empiricist-idealist* interpretation of the world" (*Critical* 7, her italics; see also Evans 34, 246; and Kavanagh 163).

18. In one amusing twist, Chodorow now reports that she is "criticized by Lacanian psychoanalytic feminists . . . for being empiricist" (*Feminism* 18).

19. See Barker 48; Bristol, "Where" 40; Eagleton 50, 198–99; and Evans 98, 198, 245, 263.

20. See Dollimore, "Introduction" 11–13, *Radical* 271; Evans 167, 253–54, 264; Gohlke 170; Goldberg 118; Greene, "Feminist" 41; Howard 323; and Sinfield 131–32. A feminist version of the debate turns on the question whether a theory that seems to promote their cause really "reinscribes" gender categories, and a Marxist version on the question whether an apparently "subversive" theory is really implicated in the hegemonic "containment" strategy as part of that vast conspiracy (which includes the pluralism that tolerates the theory).

21. I discuss this Edenic rhetoric in "Bashing" 81–83. Howard also politicizes historical inquiry by insisting that it is always a "history-for" some interest and that we must ask "what interests get advanced" by it (323). Nor would she accept the answer that it advanced the interests of the discipline, which seeks to learn about the past; she wants to know what *political* interests are advanced (see also 363; and Barker 15, 68; Evans 83, 253).

22. See Belsey, "Romantic" 57–58, and the quotation above from Brown (71).

23. One result is that more of the best students there went into science because, as an emigrant physicist explains, it was "not ideological. . . . This was one of the few fields where they could be more or less free" (Kolata C14). Cai reports the same tendency among the best students in communist China (12).

24. Bacon discusses the importance of "the negative instance" in "the establishment of any true axiom" in *Novum Organum* 1.46 and 1.105.

25. Hence most of the "central themes" once in vogue also feature a hypostatized conflict of mighty opposites like appearance vs. reality, emotion vs. reason, wit vs. witchcraft, eros vs. agape, etc.

26. I suggest some tests of this sort in *New* 199–207, but they are limited to the formalist-intentionalist approach.

27. In one version Winnett distinguishes masculine from feminine narrative on the basis of biological differences between the sexes. She explains that some women enjoy masculine narratives because they were "taught to read in drag" (516), but that could not explain why some men enjoy feminine narratives.

28. Bristol, *Shakespeare's* 209–11, says that my work, Stanley Cavell's, and Stephen Greenblatt's reflect "very deep rifts" in our society portending its demise. For many years Marxists have seized on any conflicts to predict the impending collapse of "late capitalism" from its "irreconcilable contradictions," while the absence of conflict in communist lands was supposed to prove their stability.

29. See Moi 10; and Greene, "Feminist" 41–42, "Shakespeare's" 137.

30. Freudian critics who have undergone analysis sometimes claim that this guarantees they will not project their own problems onto the text, but this is a circular argument that assumes the validity of Freudian theory and therapy.

31. Belsey says I misunderstood a sentence of hers in her book *Critical Practice* ("Richard" 455). I did; but in the same paragraph she endorsed the post-Saussurian assault on the "author-as-origin" of meaning, which precludes her from objecting that she was misunderstood since it makes my interpretation of the sentence just as valid as hers. For critiques of post-Saussurianism see Tallis and Jackson.

32. Compare this to Howard's concept of "history-for" (n. 21). In "Leaking" I collect more contradictions of this kind from the new Marxists.

33. See Barker 18, 21; Belsey, *Critical* 89, 94, 125; Dollimore, *Radical* 35, 63–68, 153, 226, 246; Eagleton 136, 170, 187, 191; and Evans 140, 210.

34. There is even a self-contradiction in his formulation, since the "them" that this socialization is put into cannot be an empty space, so there must be something to people beyond "what has been socialized into them."

35. This point is also made in Butler 231–33.

36. Similar contradictions are generated by the question of whether it is politically more advantageous for homosexuals to claim that their condition is innate or acquired (see Kennard 64–65). Many of the disputes cited in n. 20 also involve the nature-nurture problem.

37. This of course will only work when articles are refereed, but a glance at my bibliography will show that many are now written on invitation for special anthologies and so presumably escape any peer review. I do not regard this as a healthy trend, even though my own article is part of it.

38. They might begin with Macfarlane's review of Stone's book on the family. For examples of critics' uncritical acceptance of this book see Callaghan 114; Dollimore, "Introduction" 5; Erickson x; Freedman 255; Gossett 113; Greenblatt 42; Hays 83; Jardine 80–81, 89; Kahn, *Man's* 14–16; and Stimpson 62.

39. I cannot here do justice to the new interdisciplinary programs in women's studies, cultural studies, etc., because they are so varied. In general, I welcome programs that give students a good grounding in two or three disciplines but question the value of those that simply assemble (or cross-list) a collection of unrelated courses from various disciplines.

40. On this important point see Ellis 8 and Mueller 29–30.

41. The most intelligent review of this book that I have seen is by Nussbaum.

Works Cited

Adelman, Janet. "Bed Tricks: On Marriage as the End of Comedy in *All's Well That Ends Well* and *Measure for Measure*." Holland, Homan, and Paris 151–74.

———. "'Born of Woman': Fantasies of Maternal Power in *Macbeth*." *Cannibals, Witches, and Divorce: Estranging the Renaissance: Selected Papers from the English Institute, 1985.* Ed. Marjorie Garber. Baltimore: Johns Hopkins UP, 1986. 90–121.

———. "Male Bonding in Shakespeare's Comedies." *Shakespeare's "Rough Magic": Renaissance Essays in Honor of C. L. Barber.* Ed. Peter Erickson and Coppélia Kahn. Newark: U of Delaware P, 1985. 73–103.

———. "'This Is and Is Not Cressid': The Characterization of Cressida." Garner, Kahane, and Sprengnether 119–41.

Adelman, Janet, et al. "Feminist Criticism." Forum. *PMLA* 104 (1989): 77–78.

Bacon, Francis. *Selected Writings*. Ed. Hugh Dick. New York: Random, 1955.

Barker, Francis. *The Tremulous Private Body: Essays on Subjection*. London: Methuen, 1984.

Belsey, Catherine. *Critical Practice*. London: Methuen, 1980.

———. "Literature, History, Politics." *Literature and History* 9 (1983): 17–27.

———. "Richard Levin and In-different Reading." *New Literary History* 21 (1990): 449–56.

———. "The Romantic Construction of the Unconscious." 1981. *Literature, Politics and Theory: Papers from the Essex Conference, 1976–84*. Ed. Francis Barker et al. London: Methuen, 1986. 57–76.

———. *The Subject of Tragedy: Identity and Difference in Renaissance Drama*. London: Methuen, 1985.

Bloom, Allan. *The Closing of the American Mind: How Higher Education Has Failed Democracy and Improverished the Souls of Today's Students*. New York: Simon, 1987.

Bristol, Michael. *Shakespeare's America, America's Shakespeare*. New York: Routledge, 1990.

———. "Where Does Ideology Hang Out?" *Shakespeare Left and Right*. Ed. Ivo Kamps. New York: Routledge, 1991. 31–43.

Brooks, Cleanth. *The Well Wrought Urn: Studies in the Structure of Poetry*. New York: Reynal, 1947.

Brown, Paul. "'This Thing of Darkness I Acknowledge Mine': *The Tempest* and the Discourses of Colonialism." Dollimore and Sinfield 48–71.

Butler, Christopher. "The Future of Theory: Saving the Reader." *The Future of Literary Theory*. Ed. Ralph Cohen. New York: Routledge, 1989. 229–49.

Cai, Xiao. "China: Outward Conformity, Inner Despair." *Academe* 76 (1990): 8–12.

Callaghan, Dympna. *Woman and Gender in Renaissance Tragedy: A Study of "King Lear," "Othello," "The Duchess of Malfi," and "The White Devil."* Atlantic Highlands, N.J.: Humanities, 1989.

Campbell, Lily B. *Shakespeare's Tragic Heroes: Slaves of Passion*. Cambridge: Cambridge UP, 1930.

Chodorow, Nancy. *Feminism and Psychoanalytic Theory*. New Haven: Yale UP, 1989.

———. *The Reproduction of Mothering: Psychoanalysis and the Sociology of Gender*. Berkeley: U of California P, 1978.

Cioffi, Frank. "Freud and the Idea of a Pseudo-Science." *Explanation in the Behavioural Sciences*. Ed. Robert Borger and Frank Cioffi. Cambridge: Cambridge UP, 1970. 471–99, 508–15.

Crews, Frederick. *Skeptical Engagements*. Oxford: Oxford UP, 1986.

Dinnerstein, Dorothy. *The Mermaid and the Minotaur: Sexual Arrangements and Human Malaise*. New York: Harper, 1976.

Dollimore, Jonathan. "Introduction: Shakespeare, Cultural Materialism and the New Historicism." Dollimore and Sinfield 2–17.

———. *Radical Tragedy: Religion, Ideology and Power in the Drama of Shakespeare and His Contemporaries.* Chicago: U of Chicago P, 1984.

Dollimore, Jonathan, and Alan Sinfield, eds. *Political Shakespeare: New Essays in Cultural Materialism.* Ithaca: Cornell UP, 1985.

Eagleton, Terry. *Literary Theory: An Introduction.* Minneapolis: U of Minnesota P, 1983.

Ellis, John. "Radical Literary Theory." *London Review of Books* 8 Feb. 1990: 7–8.

Erickson, Peter. *Patriarchal Structures in Shakespeare's Drama.* Berkeley: U of California P, 1985.

Evans, Malcolm. *Signifying Nothing: Truth's True Contents in Shakespeare's Text.* Athens: U of Georgia P, 1986.

Ferguson, Margaret, Maureen Quilligan, and Nancy Vickers, eds. *Rewriting the Renaissance: The Discourses of Sexual Difference in Early Modern Europe.* Chicago: U of Chicago P, 1986.

Fish, Stanley. "Forum Reply." *PMLA* 104 (1989): 219–21.

Frank, Roberta. "'Interdisciplinary': The First Half-Century." *Words: For Robert Burchfield's Sixty-Fifth Birthday.* Ed. E. G. Stanley and T. F. Hoad. Wolfeboro, N. H.: Brewer, 1988. 91–101.

Freedman, Barbara. "Misrecognizing Shakespeare." Holland, Homan, and Paris 244–60.

Garner, Shirley Nelson, Claire Kahane, and Madelon Sprengnether, eds. *The (M)other Tongue: Essays in Feminist Psychoanalytic Interpretation.* Ithaca: Cornell UP, 1985.

Gohlke (Sprengnether), Madelon. "'I Wooed Thee with My Sword': Shakespeare's Tragic Paradigms." Lenz, Greene, and Neely 150–70.

Goldberg, Jonathan. "Shakespearean Inscriptions: The Voicing of Power." *Shakespeare and the Question of Theory.* Ed. Patricia Parker and Geoffrey Hartman. New York: Methuen, 1985. 116–37.

Goleman, Daniel. "Fluid Identities." *New York Times Book Review* 21 Jan. 1990: 12.

Gossett, Suzanne. "'Man-Maid, Begone!': Women in Masques." *English Literary Renaissance* 18 (1988): 96–113.

Graff, Gerald. *Professing Literature: An Institutional History.* Chicago: U of Chicago P, 1987.

———. "The Pseudo-Politics of Interpretation." *The Politics of Interpretation.* Ed. W. J. T. Mitchell. Chicago: U of Chicago P, 1983. 145–58.

Greenblatt, Stephen. *Renaissance Self-Fashioning: From More to Shakespeare.* Chicago: U of Chicago P, 1980.

Greene, Gayle. "Feminist and Marxist Criticism: An Argument for Alliances." *Women's Studies* 9 (1981): 29–45. Special issue on "Feminist Criticism of Shakespeare," ed. Gayle Greene and Carolyn Swift.

————. "Shakespeare's Cressida: 'A Kind of Self.'" Lenz, Greene, and Neely 133–49.

Grünbaum, Adolf. *The Foundations of Psychoanalysis: A Philosophical Critique.* Berkeley: U of California P, 1984.

Hays, Janice. "Those 'Soft and Delicate Desires': *Much Ado* and the Distrust of Women." Lenz, Greene, and Neely 79–99.

Holland, Norman, Sidney Homan, and Bernard Paris, eds. *Shakespeare's Personality.* Berkeley: U of California P, 1989.

Horney, Karen. *Feminine Psychology.* Ed. Harold Kelman. New York: Norton, 1967.

Howard, Jean. "Recent Studies in Elizabethan and Jacobean Drama." *Studies in English Literature* 27 (1987): 321–79.

Jackson, Leonard. *The Poverty of Structuralism: Literature and Structuralist Theory.* London: Longman, 1991.

Jameson, Fredric. *The Political Unconscious: Narrative as a Socially Symbolic Act.* Ithaca: Cornell UP, 1981.

————. "Science versus Ideology." *Humanities in Society* 6 (1983): 283–302.

Jardine, Lisa. *Still Harping on Daughters: Women and Drama in the Age of Shakespeare.* New York: Barnes, 1983.

Kahn, Coppélia. "The Absent Mother in *King Lear.*" Ferguson, Quilligan, and Vickers 33–49.

————. "Excavating 'Those Dim Minoan Regions': Maternal Subtexts in Patriarchal Literature." *Diacritics* 12 (1982): 32–41.

————. "The Hand that Rocks the Cradle: Recent Gender Theories and Their Implications." Garner, Kahane, and Sprengnether 72–88.

————. "'Magic of Bounty': *Timon of Athens,* Jacobean Patronage, and Maternal Power." *Shakespeare Quarterly* 38 (1987): 34–57.

————. *Man's Estate: Masculine Identity in Shakespeare.* Berkeley: U of California P, 1981.

Kavanagh, James. "Shakespeare in Ideology." *Alternative Shakespeares.* Ed. John Drakakis. London: Methuen, 1985. 144–65.

Kennard, Jean. "Ourself behind Ourself: A Theory for Lesbian Readers." *Gender and Reading: Essays on Readers, Texts, and Contexts.* Ed. Elizabeth Flynn and Patrocinio Schweickart. Baltimore: Johns Hopkins UP, 1986. 63–80.

Kolata, Gina. "Soviet Scientists Flock to U.S., Acting as Tonic for Colleges." *New York Times* 8 May 1990: A1, C14.

Lentricchia, Frank. *Criticism and Social Change.* Chicago: U of Chicago P, 1983.

Lenz, Carolyn Ruth Swift, Gayle Greene, and Carol Thomas Neely, eds. *The Woman's Part: Feminist Criticism of Shakespeare.* Urbana: U of Illinois P, 1980.

Leverenz, David. "The Woman in Hamlet: An Interpersonal View." 1978. *Representing Shakespeare: New Psychoanalytic Essays.* Ed. Murray Schwartz and Coppélia Kahn. Baltimore: Johns Hopkins UP, 1980. 110–28.

Levin, Richard. "Bashing the Bourgeois Subject." *Textual Practice* 3 (1989): 76–86.

———. "Leaking Relativism." *Essays in Criticism* 38 (1988): 267–77.

———. *New Readings vs. Old Plays: Recent Trends in the Reinterpretation of English Renaissance Drama.* Chicago: U of Chicago P, 1979.

MacCary, W. Thomas. *Friends and Lovers: The Phenomenology of Desire in Shakespearean Comedy.* New York: Columbia UP, 1985.

Macfarlane, Alan. Rev. of *The Family, Sex and Marriage in England, 1500–1800,* by Lawrence Stone. *History and Theory* 18 (1979): 103–26.

Macherey, Pierre. *A Theory of Literary Production.* 1966. Trans. Geoffrey Wall. London: Routledge, 1978.

Marmor, Judd. "Psychoanalytic Therapy as an Educational Process: Common Denominators in the Therapeutic Approaches of Different Psychoanalytic 'Schools.'" *Psychoanalytic Education.* Ed. Jules Masserman. *Science and Psychoanalysis* 5. New York: Grune, 1962. 286–99.

Moi, Toril. "Sexual/Textual Politics." *The Politics of Theory: Proceedings of the Essex Conference on the Sociology of Literature, July 1982.* Ed. Francis Barker et al. Colchester: U of Essex, 1983. 1–14.

Montrose, Louis. "'The Place of a Brother' in *As You Like It:* Social Process and Comic Form." *Shakespeare Quarterly* 32 (1981): 28–54.

Mueller, Martin. "Yellow Stripes and Dead Armadillos." *Profession* 89: 23–31.

Nevo, Ruth. *Shakespeare's Other Language.* London: Methuen, 1988.

Novy, Marianne. *Love's Argument: Gender Relations in Shakespeare.* Chapel Hill: U of North Carolina P, 1984.

———. "Shakespeare and the Bonds of Brotherhood." Holland, Homan, and Paris 103–15.

Nussbaum, Martha. "Undemocratic Vistas." Rev. of *The Closing of the American Mind,* by Allan Bloom. *New York Review of Books* 5 Nov. 1987: 20–26.

Rabkin, Norman. *Shakespeare and the Common Understanding.* New York: Free, 1967.

Rich, Adrienne. *Of Woman Born: Motherhood as Experience and Institution.* New York: Norton, 1976.

Richards, I. A. *Principles of Literary Criticism.* London: Kegan, 1926.

Rorty, Richard. *Contingency, Irony, and Solidarity.* Cambridge: Cambridge UP, 1989.

Sinfield, Alan. "Introduction: Reproductions, Interventions." Dollimore and Sinfield 130–33.

Snow, Edward. "Sexual Anxiety and the Male Order of Things in *Othello.*" *English Literary Renaissance* 10 (1980): 384–412.

Stallybrass, Peter. "Patriarchal Territories: The Body Enclosed." Ferguson, Quilligan, and Vickers 123–43.

Stewart, Susan. "The Interdiction." *Profession* 89: 10–14.

Stimpson, Catharine. "Shakespeare and the Soil of Rape." Lenz, Greene, and Neely 56–64.

Stockholder, Kay. *Dream Works: Lovers and Families in Shakespeare's Plays.* Toronto: U of Toronto P, 1987.

Stone, Lawrence. *The Family, Sex and Marriage in England, 1500–1800.* New York: Harper, 1977.

Sundelson, David. *Shakespeare's Restorations of the Father.* New Brunswick: Rutgers UP, 1983.

Tallis, Raymond. *Not Saussure: A Critique of Post-Saussurean Literary Theory.* Basingstoke: Macmillan, 1988.

Traub, Valerie. "Prince Hal's Falstaff: Positioning Psychoanalysis and the Female Reproductive Body." *Shakespeare Quarterly* 40 (1989): 456–74.

Weisstein, Naomi. "'Kinder, Kuche, Kirche' as Scientific Law: Psychology Constructs the Female." *Sisterhood Is Powerful: An Anthology of Writings from the Women's Liberation Movement.* Ed. Robin Morgan. New York: Random, 1970. 205–20.

Wheeler, Richard. *Shakespeare's Development and the Problem Comedies: Turn and Counter-Turn.* Berkeley: U of California P, 1981.

Winnett, Susan. "Coming Unstrung: Women, Men, Narrative, and Principles of Pleasure." *PMLA* 105 (1990): 505–18.

"I Am I Because My Little Dog Knows Me": Prolegomenon to a Theory of Mimesis

Robert Storey

But what do we know about nature?
　　　　　　　　　　　　　　　　　—Geoffrey Galt Harpham

The hypocrisy of past ages was usually classical and dogmatic, the hypocrisy of this age is romantic and skeptical. We pretend not to know. Instead of trying to see, we shut the curtains and revel in tragic darkness, concentrating carefully on impossible cases and taking the boring possible for granted.
　　　　　　　　　　　　　　　　　—Mary Midgley, *Beast and Man*

1

He was right where we thought he'd be.

He jumped up off the driveway, where we'd left him that morning, and stood staring into the headlights, his tail wagging furiously, his ears drooping in an attitude of abject humility, his whole body trembling with barely contained excitement. My wife and I were back in Philadelphia from a day in Washington, D.C., and Blackie had hardly budged from his usual station in front of the garage. His doggie door had been unlocked, he had fresh water in the kitchen, but not even his thirst (which proved prodigious) had been strong enough to lure him from the spot.

I kept thinking of this scene as I reflected, the next morning, on a remark I had read recently of S. P. Mohanty's: "It is this capacity for a second-order understanding and evaluation [i.e., for a rationality "that distinguishes us from animals" (21)], which enables us to be critically and cumulatively self-aware in relation to our actions, that defines human agency and makes possible the sociality and the historicality of human existence" (22). There was little fit, of course, between the oracular academese of the passage and my physically immediate reunion with my dog, but that was a small discrepancy I could put down to (among other things) the self-important penchant for grand pronouncements

45

that now disfigures Mohanty's profession. (Mohanty is a professor of English.) There was a more serious lack of fit, though, that tended to nag at me, and that was between the "sociality" of Blackie and Mohanty's ascribing that same sociality to "human agency" alone. It was obvious that Blackie had missed our company over that long afternoon: he was as hungry as he was thirsty, but he could hardly settle down to his doggie bowls for his joy at having us home. He kept running from one of us to the other, his tail thrashing wildly, poking at us with his muzzle for a caress, a pat, a fond look.

Of course the skeptical observer would have cautioned against our "anthropomorphizing" the scene (though he wouldn't have given a second thought to anthropomorphizing any signs of internal distress if Blackie had needed a vet). Isn't Blackie's "sociality" a rather opaque kind of dependency, his "excitement" a response that his human caretakers interpret in an all too human way? We are obligated these days to indulge this sort of skepticism, since current advanced opinion holds that biology and "human existence" have parted company, so that whatever an observer reads into an animal's behavior is likely to be a cultural—not to say a verbal—artifact. But it takes a very skeptical observer indeed to deny sociality to various undomesticated animals: ants, bees, the gregarious primates—have these been anthropomorphized, too? I am ready to grant Mohanty that "historicality" (and therefore art) is "made possible" by human rationality, but sociality is by no means its child. The social nature of human life, a nature shared with much of the insect and mammalian world, is the fact from which "agency" springs.

Before arguing and elaborating this point, I should give Mohanty's sentence a context. In many ways his is an interesting and important essay. He is intent on establishing a common ground for understanding human interrelations as they are distributed across cultures, races, and genders, and he is rightly impatient of the relativism that has long held sway in the "progressive" humanities and, to an influential extent, anthropology. The more radical versions (which is to say, the more fashionable versions) of the prevailing orthodoxy are quite impossible as workable propositions: "If the relativist says that everything is entirely context-specific," Mohanty observes, "claiming that we cannot adjudicate among contexts or texts on the basis of larger—that is, more general—evaluative or interpretive criteria, then why should I bother to take seriously *that very relativist claim?*" (14). Mohanty is politically savvy enough to know that he mustn't seem to be subscribing to "the ambiguous imperial-humanist myth of our shared human attributes" (13): what he calls "the Enlightenment's emphasis on a singular rationality underlying and comprehending all human activities" (2) was misplaced to begin with, he predictably declares, a relic of the Dark Ages of critical thought.

But what can we put in its place? Alluding to Talal Asad's call for a "'genuine dialogue' between anthropologist and native, the ex-colonizer and the ex-colonized," Mohanty writes: "A . . . dialogue of the kind Asad envisions would become possible only when we admit that crucial aspects of [a] non-Western culture may have a great degree of coherence as part of a larger web of ideas, beliefs and practices, and moreover that *some* of these aspects may be untranslatable to the language of the Western anthropologist's culture in terms of its historically sedimented and institutionally determined practices of knowing" (15). And he concludes by asserting that "the reason this would constitute the beginning of a *dialogue* is that 'we' are forced to extend our understanding by interrogating its limits in terms of [alien] categories of self-understanding" (16).

We seem to be back at the familiar poststructuralist impasse here. It's hard to understand how an "interrogation" of anything or anyone can be carried out in "categories of self-understanding" that are alien to the inquiring mind. (Notice how quickly the phrase "in terms of" plunges the sentence into referential obscurity.) If those categories are not to some extent the interrogator's own, then communication is completely impossible. It's apparently because Mohanty recognizes this difficulty that he makes his last argumentative move, the declaration that certain "basic claims" must be formulated about *all* human "subjects": "If (as I argued against the relativist position earlier) we are to deal seriously with other cultures and not reduce them to insignificance or irrelevance, we need to begin by positing the following minimal commonality between us and them: the capacity to act purposefully, to be capable of agency and the basic rationality that the human agent must in principle possess" (21).

A disappointingly ironic conclusion. We've dismissed the Enlightenment error of history as "guided by Reason, obeying the logic of Progress and Modernization" (13), only to resurrect it in a stylishly more palatable form. Although Mohanty concedes that the conditions of the world are "not all within [human] control" (19) and that humans as "agents" are only "potentially" self-aware (20), his final emphasis is upon the purposiveness and "rationality" of the human actor, deliberately "making" his or her world. And it's obvious why the emphasis should fall there: "theoretically understanding this 'making,'" he writes, "involves redefining social structures and cultural institutions as not simply given but *constituted*, and hence containing the possibility of being changed" (19). Progress and Modernization are on the horizon, as they are in all sentimental political visions.

It should be clear now why it's important for Mohanty to attribute sociality to agency and hence rationality. The human world is made by and through human relationships, and if the making is to be purposive, those relationships must be rational. For, lacking the self-awareness consequent upon rational control, the agent is not "free" and the world cannot be "changed." The logic is simple, not to say simple-minded, and Mohanty is wise not to spell it out too explicitly. But for those readers with dogs like my obstreperously social Blackie, the shakiness of the edifice is more than apparent.

In opposition to Mohanty, I want to argue that a sustained reflection upon human sociality leads us inevitably to a theory of human nature in which rationality has little part. I'll use "human nature" without apology, not only because (as I'll try to show) important behavioral facts clearly warrant it but because there can be no coherently intelligible criticism of human life and production, including art, without it. The time is long overdue for an abandonment of the cant that both structuralism and poststructuralism have foisted on the academy. That the human "subject" is "indeterminate," the artifact of history and culture and language alone, erecting structures upon their ghostly frames that must be constantly "deconstructed"—this is a piece of stupefyingly romantic fiction that can't bear much serious thought. Of course this charge has been thoughtfully (or splenetically) lodged by a number of previous critics, with most memorable vigor, for example, by Frederick Crews in "The Grand Academy of Theory." But rather than rehearse their arguments or defend the indictment myself, at least just yet, I'll let a poststructuralist take the scythe to his own premises and so clear the ground for our work.

2

Many people, it has been argued, "drift" into identity, battered by contingency rather than guided by will. Four characteristic stages have been identified by [Kenneth] Plummer [in *Sexual Stigma: An Interactionist Account* (1975)]: "sensitization," when the individual becomes aware of the possibility of being different; "signification," when he or she attributes a developing meaning to these differences; "subculturalization," the stage of recognizing oneself through involvement with others; and "stabilization," the stage of full acceptance of one's feelings and way of life. . . . There is no automatic progression through these stages; each transition is dependent as much on chance as on decision; and there is no necessary acceptance of the final destiny, of an open identity. Some choices are forced on individuals, whether through stigmatization and public obloquy or through political necessity. But the point that needs underlining is that *identity* is a choice. It is not *dictated* by internal imperatives.

Thus Jeffrey Weeks in a section entitled "Identity as Choice" in "Questions of Identity" (43–44), his contribution to *The Cultural Construction of Sexuality* (1987), an anthology rather widely adopted in the cultural anthropology classroom. It is a passage, to mangle a familiar phrase, that almost successfully eludes the intelligence. The first sentence immediately introduces an unresolved ambiguity: the "it has been argued" vaguely suggests that Weeks will take an opposing position on the idea that "many people . . . 'drift' into identity," or, at the very least, that he will argue that they should be "guided by will" rather than "battered by contingency." But as he summarizes Plummer's four "stages," he seems to imply that those stages are authoritative, even capping the summary with re-finements of his own ("There is no automatic progression through these stages"). But his final paraphrase of Plummer's position is a bizarre deformation of it: whereas Plummer seems to argue that the rather haphazard route to identity leads to a kind of fated closure, to "full acceptance of one's feelings and way of life," Weeks asserts that "there is no necessary acceptance of the final destiny, of an open identity." And his last two sentences of the paragraph are in flat contradiction to Plummer's whole thesis, at least as Weeks has presented it. Identity *is* "dictated" by "internal imperatives," according to Plummer himself: his "individual" is inducted into "identity" by strong forces within and without; there is hardly any suggestion at all, in fact, that identity for him is a "choice."

Given the discontinuities in the exposition, I am not really sure what Weeks thinks he has done, but a charitable reading would conclude, I suppose, that Plummer's implicit determinism need not always obtain. Identity *can* be "guided by will," according to this reading of the passage, for, in an "open" subject, identities are merely (as Weeks declares at the beginning of his essay) "historically and culturally specific, . . . selected from a host of possible social identities, . . . not necessary attributes of particular sexual drives or desires, . . . not, in fact, *essential*—that is naturally pre-given—aspects of our personality" (31).

But Plummer may prove as seductive for the attentive reader as he seems to have been for Weeks: What are we to do with those autonomously intractable agents of persuasion, the "feelings"? Are they, too, historically and culturally specific and so "inessential"? Not surprisingly, attempts have been made by poststructuralist anthropologists to argue that they are, that "the passions are as cultural as the devices [of political exploitation]"—an attempt dismissed by Edmund Leach as "complete rubbish." Leach's response (he is replying specifi-cally to Clifford Geertz) is worth reproducing in full:

> I can make no sense of a line of thought which claims that "passions" are culturally defined. From my prejudiced position as a social anthropologist this passage reveals with startling clarity the ultimately radical weakness of the basic assumption of cultural anthropology, namely, that not only are cultural systems infinitely variable, but that human individuals are products of their culture rather than of their genetic predisposition. (qtd. in Levy 217)

Subsequent attempts to defend Geertz's position—in extreme terms by Michelle Z. Rosaldo, for example; in more moderate ones by Robert I. Levy—founder, it seems to me, upon a failure to meet the challenge implied by Leach's final remark.

Psychologists of emotion now seem to be converging upon a functional account of "affect," one that assumes, as "a truism at this point in scientific history," that "mental structure" and therefore the operation of the emotions are "influenced by the evolutionary history of the species" (Mandler 54). There is disagreement among them about many things, most significantly about the hypothetical existence of "primary emotions" that some theorists claim are innate, but what most seem to agree on is that emotion is a psychological system that once served—and still serves, though to a disputed extent—biologically adaptive ends.

George Mandler, one of the most respected and persuasive of the theorists (see Ortony, Clore, and Collins 6, for example), argues that "organisms have evolved in such a way that whenever well-organized actions or plans cannot be completed (i.e., fail), two major adaptive mechanisms come into play—one physiological, the other cognitive" (Mandler 172). The first, which generally results in "arousal," disposes the organism to behavior that has (or, I would add, had) "survival value" or to the "protective organization of the group" (172). The second mechanism "is cognitive in that it is concerned with knowledge"—i.e., an assessment of the failure at hand—"and it is interpretive in that it transforms information into functional units" (50). Of course, what may signal failure for one organism may not do so for a conspecific, and Mandler stresses that it is a sense of individual "mastery," variable in intensity across the members of a population, that determines to what extent a disruption seems to endanger actions or plans or seems to offer a momentary, perhaps pleasurable, suspension of them. For the timid (or unprepared) a roller coaster ride may seem a harrowing nightmare; for the bold (or experienced) it may be an exhilarating interruption of a tedious affective routine. As for the "feelings," those thermostats of our daily living that have been called the "little emotions" (Mandler calls them "incomplete" ones [132]), they are as various in their sensitivity and responsiveness as individuals vary in temperament and need. The most important point for our purposes, however, is that *phylogenetically*, so to speak, the evolution of all emotional systems occurred in the service of behavioral adaptation: in the service of survival, reproduction, and nurturance of what the organism was persuaded were its own genetic progeny.

Such a conclusion would hardly surprise the neuroanatomist. As early as 1949, the pioneering Paul D. MacLean began elaborating a model of brain functioning that, extending the research of P. P. Broca in the last century and of J. W. Papez in this, led to the identification of the "limbic system," which has now, as Melvin Konner explains, "won almost universal acceptance as the central neural network of the emotions" (146). In a still-influential theory among non-neuroscientists, MacLean assigned that network to the "paleomammalian" brain, the second of what he calls the "triune" brain's structures, which also include the "reptilian" and "neomammalian" brains. His compartmentalizations have proved much too neat, and most neurobiologists are now skeptical of the triune-brain theory (Reiner 304)—but their skepticism in fact rests on evidence that strengthens my own argument here. For the limbic system has since been identified, not only as a "paleomammalian" phenomenon, but as a possession of even more primitive vertebrates as well. The septum, the amygdala, and the hippocampal complex—all links in the limbic "network"—are found in reptiles, birds, amphibians, and mammals. The cingulate cortex, which seems essential, among other things, for parental behavior, can be assumed not only for avian brains but perhaps for those of the birds' remote extinct ancestors: recent paleontological evidence suggests that some dinosaurs nurtured their young (Reiner 305). The "emotions" (if we may thereby identify the psychological artifact of apparently homologous brain structures) were of early evolutionary origin; their usefulness—in exciting parenting, mating, aggression, play—helps explain their robustness and their antiquity.

In summary, emotions and feelings, which are aroused, in Mandler's words, "at the choice points of actions, of lives, and of intentions" (130), and which are powerful sources (perhaps the *only* sources, if we are to credit thinkers like David Hume) of human motivation, are mechanisms that we share, at least in large part, with the "lower" mammalian world. An unremarkable conclusion, I assume, at least to most lovers of dogs and cats (not to mention most zoologists). To live with a social animal in intimacy is to learn (as I have) how clear a continuity there is across species that are often said to be severed by the gulf of language. ("If a lion could talk," wrote Wittgenstein, "we could not understand him" [223ᵉ]. Another of his philosophical blunders.) Not only do I recognize my own hunger and thirst, my lust and fear and boredom in my dog, but I see in him my love of play and my need for physical affection and comfort from what might most accurately be called "my likes."

Darwin early recognized the continuity, and in his *Expression of the Emotions in Man and Animals* (1872) he gave the motive for the fascinating work of Lorenz and his students—of, most notably, the eminent ethologist Irenäus Eibl-Eibesfeldt. The latter's *Love and Hate* offers compelling arguments for the "ritualization" of functional nonhuman primate behaviors into expressive human signals: so the hiding movements of apes and monkeys became the human's covering of the face in shame or embarrassment that is common to all cultures; so their submissive gestures became the bows, the prostrations—the "making of oneself small"—that stamp most human encounters with rank. These (and the many others that Eibl-Eibesfeldt proposes) are conjectural derivations, of course, but they rest on an evolutionary logic that is very hard to resist. Especially when we realize that the "ritualizations" are involuntary *emotional* signals that emanate from an ancient neural circuitry still deep in the animal brain.

I think it is largely in that shared circuitry, beneath the destabilizations—

negligible, to my mind—of language and "rationality," that human nature resides. This will probably strike most readers as both paradoxical and pointless— paradoxical because it promises to elucidate *human* attributes by confusing them with those of nonhuman species; pointless because it offers to deal with none of the *uniqueness* of human life as opposed to life in the animal order. To take the last first: it is becoming increasingly clear that human uniqueness is an illusion, at least in the strict (and common) usage of the word. Self-consciousness, foresight, tool and language use, culture, none of these is the sole province of the human animal: "It now seems likely," write the sociobiologists Richard D. Alexander and Katharine M. Noonan, "that all occur in other primate species, and chimpanzees alone may possess all five, though not in the form or to the degree that they are expressed in humans" (437). The myth of man as alienated from "nature," a victim of his uniqueness, of his culture and language, rests upon a widespread ignorance of nature in general and, particularly, of man's primate kin. As for the first objection, that comparative reference to that kin reveals little about human realities, it ignores the profound implications of man's indisputable evolutionary origin. To say that human beings evolved is to concede that there is much in their primitive emotional relations that is useless, if not inimical, to modern life; as Jerome H. Barkow reminds us, "Evolution always involves adaptation to past and not present environments" (178). This fact has led Harvard sociobiologist Edward O. Wilson to declare (with the assent of many of his disciplinary colleagues) that human nature is a "hodgepodge of special genetic adaptations to an environment largely vanished, the world of the Ice-Age hunter-gatherer" (196).

The world, in short, of a still unsophisticated primate who's to be understood by reference to an ancient past. In the pages that follow I'll draw from that past and offer evidence, long familiar to the behavioral biologist, for the persistence of its influence on the present. My object is to suggest an enduring "essentiality" of the "subject," though I must caution immediately against the confusion of that essentiality with psychological normality or moral authenticity. The natural, the normal, and the good are by no means synonymous categories: what nature contrives for the survival of the fittest may—and often does—have little to do with the rights (or desired norms) of man. On the other hand, we should guard against the cliché of the human beast, harboring a savage heart of darkness in its civilized breast. Such romance shares with Freud's romance of the id the notion of unstructured instincts propelling life forward in an egomaniacally grasping bloodlust. Like all melodrama, it has its appeal, but it also has little substance. Life, as the fact of evolution argues, is an often exquisite structure born of the dynamic relations between a biological creature and its environment. That creature must solve its problems, as it were, within its special environmental constraints, and one of the most efficient means of its doing so, as R. I. M.

Dunbar maintains (167), is—to return to our original question now—the construction of a social world.

3

"It is a widely held opinion," writes Konrad Lorenz,

> shared by some contemporary philosophers, that all human behavior patterns which serve the welfare of the community, as opposed to that of the individual, are dictated by specifically human rational thought. Not only is this opinion erroneous, but the very opposite is true. If it were not for a rich endowment of social instincts, man could never have risen above the animal world. All specifically human faculties, the power of speech, cultural tradition, moral responsibility, could have evolved only in a being which, before the very dawn of conceptual thinking, lived in well-organized communities. Our prehuman ancestor was indubitably as true a friend to his friend as a chimpanzee or even a dog, as tender and solicitous to the young of his community and as self-sacrificing in its defense, aeons before he developed conceptual thought and became aware of the consequence of his actions. (246)

I would quibble with some of the phrasing here: "risen above" suggests a kind of transcendence that I don't think Lorenz meant to imply, and "specifically," in the fourth sentence ("specifically human"), begs to be replaced by a more accurate word like "markedly." But, quibbles aside, Lorenz states the case with admirably appropriate force. The British philosopher Mary Midgley, who quotes the passage with approval, adds that, with respect to many animals, whales and wolves as well as human beings, "Social bonds structure their lives." And she italicizes the first of her concluding remarks: *"Communication, and therefore intelligence, develops only where there are these long-standing deep relationships.* It may be possible for it to occur in another context, but if so, nobody knows what it would be like" (*Beast and Man* 275).

The primate evidence in support of this position seems unequivocal to me. The British primatologist Richard W. Wrangham has recently surveyed the behavioral characteristics of humans, modern and "primitive," and their closest primate kin, the gorilla, the bonobo, and the common chimpanzee, in order "to distinguish between aspects of hominoid social organization which are shared, and therefore phylogenetically conservative, and those which are variable" (53). The shared behavior, he concludes, "can be viewed as part of an 'ancestral suite' which, though admittedly hypothetical, offers a logical starting point for behavioral reconstruction at any time during human evolution" (53). In other words, such behaviors will have been exhibited not only by our distant "common ancestor" but also "in intermediate species between the [ancestor] and its living descendants" (53). One of the first and most basic of the similarities is in the "grouping patterns" of those descendants. All four of the species have "social networks" that "share a strong tendency towards closure" (58). Except for the lone traveling male—and, variably and less commonly, female—solitariness is simply not a species-typical trait of the chimp, gorilla, or human being. Which implies strongly, of course, a semiclosed social network, not only for their common ancestor but also for those prerational "intermediate species" that antedated modern man. Rousseau's myth of a "savage" humanity, "with neither a fixed dwelling nor any need for one another, . . . hardly encounter[ing] one another twice in their lives, without knowing or talking to one another" (48), is a vision of no hominid species, at least on this planet, that ever was or probably will be.

For the human primate in particular, the establishment and maintenance of strong social bonds were—and are—of the first importance. The human infant is "altricial," that is, dependent on nourishment, protection, and care for a period longer than that of any other mammalian newborn, and it is because the period of weaning (and the enculturation that accompanies it) is so long that a fast emotional bond between caretaker and child is crucial. This is what Irene Elia has called "the only bedrock of primate association" (232), the necessity dictated by an internal imperative to preserve, in one's infant (or in what one is emotionally seduced into accepting as one's infant), one's own genetic code. Eibl-Eibesfeldt has argued at length that the bond is of such superordinate primacy that all sociability should be attributed to it; in short, "The roots of love," contrary to popular (and much academic) thought, "are not in sexuality [i.e., adult sexual intimacy], although love makes use of it for the secondary strengthening of the bond" (128). The bonding rites of human sexual behavior have originated in infantile or parental gestures that, even in the relations of chimpanzees, have acquired an unmistakably ritualized quality. The kiss, for example, has its probable source in the caretaker's mouth-to-mouth feeding; the "kiss with the nose" in the sniffing of kin; the "love bite" in the friendly grooming nip; the nuzzle in the infant's search for the breast. "In fact, wider sociality in its original essence," Midgley properly concludes, "simply *is* the power of adults to treat one another, mutually, as honorary parents and children" (*Beast and Man* 136).

On reflection, the implications of this are disturbing, though not because of what they may seem to corroborate to the naive disciple of Freud. Eibl-Eibesfeldt is clear on this latter point: "Sigmund Freud, in a strikingly topsy-turvy interpretation, once observed that a mother would certainly be shocked if she realized how she was lavishing sexual behavior patterns on her child. In this case Freud had got things reversed. A mother looks after her children with the actions of parental care; these she also uses to woo her husband" (151). It's this last fact that tends to disturb. The First Bond (as Ibsen's Helmers discover to their despair) lays the foundations for mammalian politics. "Honorary parents and children": as adults, they are ineluctably implicated in emotional power relations—relations that are inevitably exacerbated by the natural inequalities of sex.

For if sex helps strengthen the adult pair bond, it does so in significantly skewed terms. We share with other (though not all) of our fellow primates a noticeably sexually "dimorphic" disposition: like baboons and gorillas (but unlike gibbons and siamangs), humans are sexually differentiated by size, strength, and weight. On the average, men are taller and heavier than women; they also have slightly different anatomical structures. Their limb proportions, skeletal torsions, and muscular densities are such that they excel in competitions of running and throwing, "the archaic specialties of the ancestral hunter-gatherer males" (Wilson 127). Darwin explained the size difference in the sexes as the result of competition for females among those ancestral males, an explanation consonant with what is now generally known of primate anatomy and behavior. Physiological dimorphism correlates with mating patterns across much of the mammalian world: usually the more pronounced the size difference within a species, the higher the average number of females consorting with reproductively successful males.

But dimorphism also correlates with methods of subsistence: a study of the bones of American Indian populations suggested that there was more dimorphism in hunting-dependent tribes than in those that were dependent on agriculture (Elia 219). I raise this point to anticipate objections that may be gathering in some readers' minds. My argument is, of course, moving in the direction of ideological heresy: I'm intent on producing a model of human relations indebted as deeply to primate biology as to historically "constructed" culture, a model that flies in the face (if it flies at all) of the wisdom current in the deconstructed humanities. Gerda Lerner's widely respected *Creation of Patriarchy*, for example, locates the pivotal turn of her title in a "cultural" moment of the prehistoric past. From egalitarian hunter-gatherer origins, when "matrilineal, matrilocal systems abound" (49), humanity suffers a fall into agriculture; "kinship arrangements tend to shift from matriliny to patriliny, and private property develops" (49). (The Marxists can take it from there.)

Quite aside from her indifference to (or ignorance of) the voluminous primate literature, Lerner's reconstruction is weakened, initially and powerfully, by her own rather rueful concessions. However egalitarian hunter-gatherer cultures are—and the existing ones *are*, in fact, more "relaxed and egalitarian by comparison with the majority of economically more complex societies" (Wilson 83)—in none of them do we find political equality, much less a female hegemony. "One must . . . note," Lerner reluctantly observes, "that in all hunting/gathering societies, no matter what women's economic and social status is, women are always subordinate to men in some respects." And she adds: "There is not a single society known where women-as-a-group have decision-making power *over* men or where they define the rules of sexual conduct or control marriage exchanges" (30). Lerner's hypothesized "shift from matriliny to patriliny" seems, moreover, mere fantasy. In the most recent, informed, and sophisticated reconstruction of early hominid society, R. A. Foley and P. C. Lee conclude that "it may be argued that polygynous male family groups *occurring within larger male kin lineages* characterized the social organization of the ancestors and earliest representatives of modern humans" (905, my italics). These conclusions are in accord with the anthropological research of Carolyn Fluehr-Lobban and with Richard Wrangham's primate model, which hypothesizes female exogamy for the so-called ancestral suite.

My point is that cultural, specifically economic, facts alone, at least those derived from the paleontologically recent history of our species, cannot begin to account adequately for its behavioral repertoire. (And to those who know anything about the most recent research in developmental psychology, the Freudian "facts" in which Lerner also dabbles can hardly account convincingly for them at all.) One very important fact in that repertoire—our "moderately polygynous" nature (Wilson 124)—is not only explicable but predictable from the dimorphism that stamps the species. Melvin Konner summarizes the data:

Of 849 human societies in the ethnographic record, George Peter Murdock—one of anthropology's great systematizers—found the marriage form called polygyny (one man to two or more women) in 708 of them (83 percent), these about equally divided between those with usual and those with occasional polygyny. Most hunting-gathering societies have occasional polygyny. . . . Monogamy is characteristic of 137 (16 percent) of the societies, but it must be remembered that in most of these a single individual may have more than one mate in succession, and because of the starkly different reproductive life spans in men and women, men who choose this option are much more likely than their female counterparts to have more than one family. Polyandry—a marriage of one woman to more than one man—occurs in 4 of the societies (less than half of one percent), and in all of these there are special conditions that make the pattern much less than a mirror image of polygyny. The human species can thus be said to be pair-bonding with a significant polygynous option and tendency. (273–74)

In his polygynous disposition (and other respects), the human male, as Alexander and Noonan observe, "is not particularly unusual among primate males, except that he is generally more parental than the males of other group-living species" (436).

The dimorphism of his species is also a clue to his aggressiveness. The greater size and—in Darwin's word—"pugnacity" of the human male (*Descent* 143), relative to that of the female, are both consequences of sexual selection. And they are still very much with *Homo sapiens sapiens*. In one of the most skeptical surveys of gender-difference research, conducted by two "feminists (of different vintages, and one perhaps more militant than the other!)" (12), Eleanor Emmons Maccoby and Carol Nagy Jacklin conclude that "males do appear to be the more aggressive sex, not just under a restricted set of conditions but in a wide variety of settings and using a wide variety of behavioral indexes" (228). The evidence, gathered from a number of different cultures and age groups and supported by both primatological and endocrinological research, is, in Maccoby and Jacklin's words, "unequivocal" (274).

But lest visions of man-the-club-bearing-hunter swim into the inattentive reader's head, I must emphasize that the aggressiveness with which we are concerned here is of an "intraspecific" kind. Almost all zoologists agree today, as E. O. Wilson explains, "that none of the categories of aggressive behavior exists in the form of a general instinct over broad arrays of species" (102). Aggression is neither a universal "drive" demanding "discharge," as a Freudian would have it, nor a universal "will to power," as in the Nietzschean myth. It is a loose rubric for a broad class of behaviors that are elicited by different confrontational conditions and governed by different controls in the nervous system. K. W. Moyer has identified several kinds of aggression, as well as their physiological bases: the former are both interspecific (predatory, fear induced) and intraspecific (maternal, fear induced, territorial, instrumental). The focus of most studies in human behavior has been on "within-species" aggression.

Among the most recent findings are that, first, it emerges early in preschool toddlers; second, it quickly acquires gender-specific characteristics; and, third, it changes complexion in accordance with changes in maturation. In the first years of life, there is a positive correlation among aggression, altruism, and emotionality for boys but no such correlation for girls. "Aggressiveness among girls," write E. Mark Cummings and his colleagues, "is associated with reparation for their own aggressive misconduct, but it is not associated [as it is for boys] with a generally greater sensitivity to another's distress" (184). Between the ages of about five and six, there is a shift from aggression-as-empathy to aggression-as-dominance in boys, and thereafter, at least through late adolescence, their aggressive behavior is positively correlated with their sense of self-esteem (Feshbach and Feshbach 213). That behavior often takes the form of "toughness" in general—of physical and verbal threat and abuse—the acceptance of which has led L. D. Ferguson to speak of a "brutalization norm" (qtd. in Cairns 77). But for the male adolescent who seeks "leadership status," that is, the domination and manipulation of other adolescents, "toughness," as Maccoby and Jacklin observe, may prove an ineffective tool (263). Such a male may turn to

"Machiavellianism," in which he is generally more coercive, more free with direct lies, than his female manipulative counterpart (Maccoby and Jacklin 261). But ontogeny usually recapitulates phylogeny, as it were, the maturing boy's repairing to the social graces with which the males of early hominid societies most likely were endowed—graces that reflect, in Wilson's words, "the necessities of compromise" (86). Wilson quotes the anthropologist Robin Fox: "Controlled, cunning, cooperative, attractive to the ladies, good with the children, relaxed, tough, eloquent, skillful, knowledgeable and proficient in self-defense and hunting" (86): such was—and, omitting the last word, still is—the dominant "alpha" male.

But why strive for dominance at all? The "most parsimonious" answer, writes R. B. Cairns, "is that, for humans, 'Aggression works'" (73). Aggression works to maintain stable hierarchies, and it is in the regressive nature of the human male, especially as he approaches reproductive age, to establish and maintain such hierarchies, particularly among his fellow males. That this tendency has its origins in a hominoid past is suggested by the usual pattern of male aggression. Although, as Maccoby and Jacklin point out, "the same contingencies for aggressors' behavior" are provided by girls as well as boys, the latter "are more frequently selected as the victims of aggression despite the fact that the consequences to the aggressor are more likely to be aversive" (240–41). To explain such behavior by "social conditioning" is to ignore this apparent anomaly, as well as the fact that adults don't seem to reinforce boys' aggression any more than discourage girls'; "in fact, the contrary may be true" (Maccoby and Jacklin 360). "Aggressive expression and inhibition are highly learnable," writes Cairns, "but they are not initially established through specific learning processes" (76). And boys, as Maccoby and Jacklin conclude, are "more biologically prepared" than girls to learn them (361).

They also seem more biologically prepared to learn "alliance" behavior, sharing in this, as in much else, a link with close male primate kin. Although in many Old World monkeys "escalated intergroup aggression is carried out by females as well as by males" (Wrangham 67), in neither gorillas, chimpanzees, nor human beings are females notably active in such encounters. Like their counterparts among the apes, "human females have relationships which may include strikingly friendly aspects, but they rarely involve physical aggression or systematic alliance relationships in which women form predictable alliances against other women" (Wrangham 62). This is clearly not the case with men, young or old. In cross-cultural studies of children's play, the sexes have been reported to segregate in significantly different ways: girls tend to form intimate relationships with one or two "best friends," while boys collect in larger, often competitive play groups, the selections for which are made on the basis of game prowess: "Liking and disliking one's playmates is essentially irrelevant [for boys]. The game," write Maccoby and Jacklin, "is the thing" (207). These patterns have been corroborated by Ritch C. Savin-Williams in a carefully designed and fascinating study of adolescents at summer camp. During "free time" at the camp,

> Boys . . . engaged in sports such as basketball or tennis, usually with fellow cabinmates, or in asocial activities such as reading comic books or sleeping. On the other hand, it was uncommon for girls to spend this time with their cabin group or in organized and competitive activities; rather, they preferred to associate with sisters, cousins, home-town friends, extra-cabin friends, or a close cabin buddy in pairs and cliques, walking and talking. (126)

Savin-Williams concludes that "the greater male proclivity for formulating and maintaining cohesive same-sex groups is empirically congruent with Tiger's (1969) speculations on group bonding and evolutionary theory" (128). It is Tiger's thesis, in *Men in Groups*, that "male-male bonds are of the same biological order for defensive, food-gathering, and social-order-maintenance purposes as the male-female bond is for reproductive purposes" (42).

All of which argues, to quote Maccoby and Jacklin, that "the two sexes may have chosen somewhat different arenas for ego-investment" and that "each sex [has] a higher sense of self-worth in the area of more central . . . involvement" (159–60). The relative structures of their social hierarchies seem to bear this out. Savin-Williams found that although the girls of his study often showed dominance, "Dominance does not appear to have been a highly desirable or discernible trait to them" (126). When his girl campers were asked to identify their most dominant member, they selected the most antagonistic girl, even though counselors had observed that the most "maternally" assertive ("confident, loyal, kindhearted, and manipulative" [115]) had been their true group leader. Power relations were in greater daily flux among the girl campers than among the boys, and dominance was exerted by the girls in less physical and overt ways. For the boys, the dominance-submission order had been worked out very quickly, and the boys that fell into each level were all of a fairly clear "type." The "alpha" boys were (according to their own cabinmates) the handsomest, most athletic, most physically mature, "exhibiting the confidence we have learned to expect from alpha monkeys" (qtd. in Freedman 46); their satellites included a "beta" confidant, who got on well with his superior; a "gamma" bully; a "joker" occupying a middle position; then a boy described as a "quiet" and "submissive" follower, the latter often known as "the nerd."

If such stereotypes smack of Hollywood formula, a kind of cast list for Bill Murray's *Meatballs*, the conclusions are not hard to draw. Maccoby and Jacklin are bold enough to draw them:

> . . . if one sex is more biologically predisposed than the other to perform

certain actions, it would be reasonable to expect that this fact would be reflected in popular beliefs about the sexes, so that innate tendencies help to produce the cultural lore that the child learns. Thus he adapts himself, through learning, to a social stereotype that has a basis in biological reality. (Of course, not all social stereotypes about the sexes have such a basis.) It is reasonable, then, to talk about the process of acquisition of sex-typed behavior—the *learning* of sex-typed behavior—as a process built upon biological foundations that are sex-differentiated to some degree. (363–64)

What exactly those "foundations" are has been the object of much endocrinological research. Aggression in animals has been found to be correlated with levels of circulating testosterone, the male gonadal hormone, although attempts to extend such findings to human subjects have been marred by procedural flaws (see Baucom, Besch, and Callahan for one of the most recent human studies; see Rubin, Reinisch, and Haskett for a survey and critique). What seems the most suggestive endocrinological work to date on gender-related behavior has focused, not on postnatal gonadal steroid effects, but on the prenatal hormonal milieu.

In a 1981 paper in *Science,* Anke A. Ehrhardt and Heino F. L. Meyer-Bahlburg reviewed the research, much of it their own, on the developmental effects of prenatal hormones on sex differences in human behavior. They concluded that while "gender identity" (the "primary identification of an individual with one sex or the other") depends "largely on postnatal environmental influence," and while "sexual orientation" (or "erotic responsiveness to one sex or the other") cannot be given a conclusive etiology, "sex-dimorphic behavior and temperamental sex differences appear to be modified by prenatal sex hormones" (1312). The principal subjects for the latter research have been patients with congenital adrenal hyperplasia or CAH syndrome. Triggered by a genetic defect, CAH results in fetal androgenization and masculinization of the external genitalia, although girls born with the defect can be surgically "feminized" in the first weeks of life. Thereafter, with treatments of cortisone or prednisone, both males and females develop normally, their sexual functioning and fertility unimpaired. Gender identity "typically agrees with the sex of rearing of the child: that is, females with CAH firmly identify as girls and women . . ., provided that sex assignment is clearly female from early childhood" (1314). But "gender behavior" of the CAH female is the reverse of that which is stereotypically associated with her gender roles:

Two studies with a control-group or a sibling-comparison design included genetic females who were surgically corrected and hormonally treated early in postnatal life. . . . In both samples, the behavior of the prenatally androgenized girls differed significantly from that of the controls in that they typically demonstrated (i) a combination of intense active outdoor play,

increased association with male peers, long-term identification as a "tom-
boy" by self and others, probably all related to high energy expenditure,
and (ii) decreased parenting rehearsal such as doll play and baby care, and
a low interest in the role rehearsal of wife and mother versus having a
career. The characteristic pattern was not transient or limited to a brief
phase, but was long-term throughout childhood. (1314)

That these behaviors were essentially uninfluenced by the patients' medical
histories is suggested by similar studies of females whose mothers were treated
with progestogens during pregnancy. Progestogens, like CAH, have an andro-
genizing effect upon the fetus, but the latter is born endocrinologically normal
and is "in no need of medical attention except for surgical correction of an
enlarged clitoris in some cases" (1314). "Most of these girls," write Ehrhardt and
Meyer-Bahlburg, "showed a behavior pattern similar to that of females with
CAH" (1314).

For most scientists it is now irresistibly apparent that not only is human
sex-dimorphic behavior predisposed by hormonal factors—Jaak Panksepp has
argued recently that brain opiods play a key role in various bondings—but the
human brain itself is, in the words of Sandra Witelson, "a sexualized organ"
(295). Witelson, one of the pioneers in work on brain lateralization over the
last ten to fifteen years, has proposed that differences in male and female brain
functioning may result in important differences in behavior. That there *is* a
difference in functioning has been confirmed by James Inglis and J. S. Lawson,
who, in 1981, reported that "lateralized brain lesions produce very different
effects on the intelligence of men and women" (694). Males with left-hemisphere
damage show impairment on the Verbal Scale—and with right-hemisphere damage on the Performance Scale—of the Wechsler Adult Intelligence Scale, but
females show "selective deficits" on neither scale after comparable damage in one
hemisphere or the other. If the sexes are differentiated by degrees of brain
lateralization—and these results strongly indicate that they are—some of the
consequences, as Witelson describes them, may be these: Women would have
a greater ability than men to concentrate on single tasks at one time (or a lesser
ability to perform two or more tasks simultaneously); their habits of perception
and attention would be different from men's, perhaps resulting in different
aesthetic preferences; they would enjoy (or suffer) an overlayering of emotional
responsiveness upon analytic verbal processes (296–98). For none of these conjectures is there firm empirical evidence, but the last is given anecdotal support
by a recent survey of attitudes on computer use. They were collected from over
seventy men and women in various technological fields who had been interviewed
by the Center for Children and Technology of the Bank Street College of
Education in New York. Margaret Honey, the senior research scientist at the

center, told the *New York Times* that "'women in technological fields want their work to be useful, helpful and empower others. . . . Men don't talk that way.'" Asked to "create a perfect technological instrument," women "proposed ways to humanize the computer . . . , while men 'believed the computer has the goods and they want to be connected to it'" (Keegan 27).

4

Honey is speaking (as I have been writing throughout this essay) in a kind of statistical shorthand. "Men" and "women" are population categories, not designations for all same-sexed individuals who should be expected to share the same characteristics. As in all populations, some members—statistically, those of the bell-curve mean—are "more typical" of their sex than others. There is a good deal of overlap between categories, of course, the most aggressive woman being far more aggressive than the least aggressive man, and so on. This is variously expressed in the behavioral literature: Wilson speaks of the "probability" or "capacity" of developing "a certain array of traits" (100, 56); Konner of an expected "range of reactions" (40); Georg Breuer of a "bandwidth" within which a sex (or species) typically operates (20). And it should go without saying that no set of characteristics or behaviors is genetically or biologically "determined." When scientists and laymen inveigh against "biological determinism," they—like Lewontin and company, in *Not in Our Genes*—are simply misrepresenting the issue. "Our species," writes Daniel G. Freedman, echoing scores of his behavioralist colleagues, "is biocultural—100% biological and 100% cultural" (108). Which is to say, as Maccoby and Jacklin imply above, that there is no separating the "innate" and the "learned." Learning, to recite a formula now commonplace in learning theory, can be carried out only by an organism biologically *prepared* to learn, and the "innate" can manifest itself only if environmental conditions allow. My argument, to which I shall return at the end of this essay, is that culture *is* both an expression and a critique of what the species as a "population" (or as a set of sexually differentiated populations) is biologically disposed to do.

That it is disposed to do anything is not even a matter of dispute in many academic quarters: the notion is simply, flatly denied. With the exception of the "maternalist" faction, most feminists, for example, are resolutely set against conceding behavioral differences between the sexes, at least those induced by biology. Those differences that are obvious (and regnant: the "patriarchy") are merely cultural constructions: "I take *masculine* here," writes Ruth Bleier in her introduction to *Feminist Approaches to Science*, "to refer to the set of socially constructed characteristics attributed to men in the patriarchal cultures that are the context for our analyses" (15). In another essay in the same collection, Bleier attacks (how convincingly I must let the enterprising reader decide—after he or she first reads Melissa Hines's article on sex differences in human behavior) the experimental evidence for behavioral differences biologically specific to sex, arguing against the work on aggression, for example, that "'masculinity' is a gender characteristic and, as such, culturally, not biologically, constructed" (150). A biologist herself, she notes at the end of her essay that "biological and environmental factors are inextricable, in ways that make futile any efforts to separate them" (161), but, braving the futility, she concludes with a sentence that shoves biology out the back door: "Rather than biology, it is the cultures that our brains have created that most severely limit our visions and the potentialities for the fullest possible development of each individual" (162–63).

The specific implications of this remark—that culture is wholly independent of biology, that the human brain creates ex nihilo, that constraints are severe limitations of "visions" and "potentialities"—would take more space to address than I have room for, though I will return to the first of them momentarily. What I would like to draw attention to here is the general assumption underlying all three, indeed, underlying most "biophobia." That assumption, very simply, is that the natural is the good. The reasoning—wholly "unconscious," in the most untechnical sense of that word—seems to run this way: If the differences currently observable between the sexes, to which we owe the patriarchy, are "natural," then nature is careless of individuals and their "visions"; but nature is, as the author of those individuals, by definition good; therefore, the differences must be "learned." Never one to betray the heart that loves her, Bleier's "nature" is, like Mohanty's "rationality," the underpinning of a faith (and an idea of culture) that has suffered a wanton perversion. The male-contrived "subject-object split" is the source of all our woe: it is to "harmony" and "holism" (as her colleague Hilary Rose urges [72]) that science must return, but to a holism, I assume, that keeps biology out of the whole. "It seems to me," writes Norman Holland, in the only book of literary criticism I know of to draw upon recent cognitive research, that "the sciences of our age have for many decades outmoded the simple split of subject and object or the simple process of signifiers' signifying. These are flat earth theories that look incontrovertibly commonsensical—until you try to detail them or fit them into other knowledge. We need to get beyond these nineteenth-century models" (175).

In one important respect, at least, feminist criticism has "gotten beyond" the nineteenth century, and that is by exposing, in the "hard" sciences as well as the "soft," the pervasiveness of male bias. In genetic theory, in primatological study, the tendency for male scientists to assume male-centered structures, to build models upon foundations of dominance and overt aggression, has been challenged very provocatively by feminist argument. The feminist historian Evelyn Fox Keller has long championed the work of Barbara McClintock, whose interactionalist account of cellular dynamics offers a radically new perspective upon genomic functioning. The female primatologists, who now number in the scores, have virtually redefined crucial aspects of primate cultures, emphasizing, as Donna Haraway has remarked, "matrifocal groups," "long-term social cooperation," and "flexible process" (231) where their male colleagues had seen little or none. Male bias has typically been given a historical genesis, with Descartes and Bacon as pivotal figures, although the chief defense of this line of reasoning, Carolyn Merchant's *The Death of Nature*, also tracks the bias to the ancient Greeks. But to do so seems to rob "history" of much meaning. There's a more parsimonious explanation for the genesis, I think, an explanation that has an important bearing, not only upon the general argument of this essay, but also upon the nature of human perception and cognition as a whole. I'd like to join the maternalists in proposing that female (and not "feminist") epistemology differs profoundly from that of the male. It does so because of the comparatively different selection pressures that produced that "sexualized organ" the brain.

If we are to take seriously the implications of human evolution, we must acknowledge, as Michael Ruse does (and as Lorenz did before him), that the foundations of human knowledge are to be traced to strategies of survival. That they are rooted in an unmediated apprehension of the world has long been thoroughly discredited. As Mary E. Hawkesworth reminds her readers in a recent and hard-nosed review of feminist epistemological theory, "A fact is a theoretically constituted proposition, supported by theoretically mediated evidence and put forward as part of a theoretical formulation of reality" (550). In Popperian terms, all genuine reasoning is deductive reasoning, in which the truth of the conclusion is implicit in the truth of the premises. Does this therefore suggest that so-called scientific reasoning is a mere shuttling of wisps in the void, the fabrication of a vast skein of meaning that (as a misreading of Thomas S. Kuhn would have it) is displaced by another with each "paradigm shift"?

I think not. The "truth of things" in all of its wholeness and baldness must forever elude the human mind, but that mind has been so constituted by its encounter with those things—it is in fact an emanation of them!—that it necessarily perceives and thinks in adaptively elucidative ways. In other words, the "theoretical mediations" of scientific reasoning, though unable to uncover anything like absolute truth, allow the human thinker to apprehend and manipulate reality in ways advantageous to immediate (but not necessarily long-term) survival. Hence the universality of induction, mathematical logic, the principle of parsimony. Ruse illustrates this idea by proposing scenarios for a typical "proto-human":

A tiger is seen entering a cave that you and your family usually use for sleeping. No one has seen the tiger emerge. Should you seek alternative accommodation for this night at least? How else does one achieve a happy end to this story, other than by an application of those laws of logic that we try to uncover for our students in elementary logic classes. . . .

Analogously for mathematics. Two tigers were seen going into the cave. Only one came out. Is the cave now safe? Again: you have to travel across a plain to get to your hunting grounds. You can only walk a limited distance in this heat. Should you set off now? Should you wait until tomorrow? Should you plan to camp out for the night? And so forth. The proto-human who had an innate disposition to take seriously the law of excluded middle, and who avoided contradictions, survived and reproduced better than he/she who did not. The proto-human who innately preferred "2 + 2 = 4" to "2 + 2 = 5" was at a selective advantage over his/her less discriminating cousin. (162)

In short, the world as perceived is the world *survived*. And it should therefore come as no revelation that the world as perceived by a dimorphic species, whose very dimorphism attests to sexually differentiated strategies of survival, should be a world *differentially* perceived. The male everywhere sees dominance and aggression because, in his distant proto-human past, it was in his adaptive interests to do so.

That his vision, however inimical to female interests, survives robustly today is a perhaps lamentable but inescapable fact about modern life. It is also one of those facts upon which any unsentimental politics (as well as any unsentimental criticism of art) must be founded. The emotionally motivated human animal is a behaviorally conservative animal—though certainly not one impervious to correction. To the politically sensitive I may seem to have been building a case for a kind of quietism here: in the face of a nature afflicted with phylogenetic inertia, we can only fold our hands and wait to declare that *la commedia è finita*. Such, essentially, is the subtext of Steven Goldberg's *The Inevitability of Patriarchy*, a book with which I am, in most points but this, in generally substantial agreement. But neither the politics nor the art that I envisage (and know) is so despairingly passive. I began this essay with a vulgar anecdote; I'll draw toward a close with a vulgar analogy (or homology, to be more precise). No less than much of my behavior is my body the relic of a hominoid past: my armpits give off an acrid stench, my appetite leads me to store more fat than I either want or need, I wake up each morning with a faceful of prickly hair. And every day I meet the politics of my body with resigned but determined resistance: I shave, I diet, I apply Old Spice. In none of this do I deceive myself into thinking that I am "changing" myself (or the world). I am simply muddling through, as best I can, impressed (as I am not when I gape before inner visions of a rosy-hued New Society) with the necessity of *always staying alert*, of living every minute as a reflective labor that cannot ever relax its vigilance. The political life is endless work, grounded, as it is, in certain morally questionable instincts.

So, too, human culture. Breuer offers a crisp formulation: "Instincts in man are . . . emotional tendencies which form the basis for cultural superstructures in specifically human forms" (134). Thus, given my argument: the "patriarchy"— but a patriarchy with the powers of self-criticism. For if rationality is not, as Mohanty argues, the foundation of sociality, it is surely, however weakly, an instrument of (at least) legal equality. Which is not to imply that it is opposed to what Hume called the human "passions." "'Reason' [I quote Mary Midgley now] is not the name of a character in a drama. It is a name for organizing oneself. When there is a conflict, one desire *must* be restrained to make way for the other. It is the process of *choosing which* that is rightly called reasoning" (*Beast and Man* 258). The human desire to form passionate and respectful attachments— to "bond," as an ethologist would say—is as strong as the equally instinctive human desire to dominate. Culture is the record of our complex and shifting allegiances between these imperatives and others.

And it *is* a structure of imperatives, or "inducements," to be more precise. The notion that both culture and the human being are completely plastic "subjects," capable of being bent into any shape that history or language pleases, is a patent absurdity. A tabula rasa mind, Ruse observes, "demands a brain with a great deal of useless capacity"; its "total receptivity" would require a cranial cavity probably "several times larger than the one we now possess"; and it would always be a dangerous instrument, since "one or two wild thoughts could steer [us] straight into maladaptive oblivion" (141–42). It is fortunate that, in Wilson's much quoted and memorable phrase, the human genes "hold culture on a leash" (167). Otherwise, a certain strain of Pauline Christianity, with its loathing of the body and sex, could have put an end to the whole human experiment some two thousand years ago. Wilson and Charles Lumsden have in fact demonstrated that even if a "blank-slate" species were a possibility, natural selection would inevitably favor some genetic types over others, thereby rendering that species, within a very few generations, a genetically directed one (13).

Biology counts. How much it counts has come as a surprise even to the geneticists themselves. Recent studies with twins and triplets have led, write Thomas J. Bouchard and his colleagues of the University of Minnesota, "to two general and seemingly remarkable conclusions concerning the sources of the psychological differences—behavioral variation—between people: (i) genetic factors exert a pronounced and pervasive influence on behavioral variability, and (ii) the effect of being reared in the same home is negligible for many psychological traits" (223). Heritability has been found to be as high as 50 percent—sometimes higher—for traits and conditions including activity level, alcoholism, anxiety, criminality, dominance, extraversion, intelligence, manic-depressive psychosis, obesity, personal autonomy, political attitudes, schizophrenia, sexuality, sociability, values, and vocational interests. Based on the results of his Louisville Twins Study, the late Ronald Wilson hypothesized that "behavioral development is guided by a genetic strategy analogous to that for biological development" (qtd. in Holden 600). Such conclusions are justifying the "quiet revolution" that, in Robert Cairns's words (58), has, since the early seventies, energized the behavioral sciences—a revolution often associated with the word *sociobiology*, though "evolutionary behavioral biology" may be the phrase under which the majority of the revolutionaries would most openly and willingly march. For that phrase acknowledges what E. O. Wilson has called "the philosophical legacy of the last century of scientific research," and it foregrounds, as the manifesto of the revolutionary program, "the essential first hypothesis for any serious consideration of the human condition" (1–2).

To the extent that art as mimesis is a meditation on that condition, the criticism of art has, I think, the responsibility to come to terms with both the legacy and the hypothesis. "No excuse remains," Mary Midgley writes, "for anybody in the humanities and social sciences to evade the challenge of Darwin and treat social man as an isolated miracle" ("Rival Fatalisms" 34). The last fifteen years or so have seen not so much evasion as self-satisfied and self-congratulatory ignorance—have seen, moreover, a willful enthrallment with the notion that *all* foundationalism in the interpretive disciplines is both misguided and corrupt. And so "theory" has drifted blimpishly across the critical landscape, buoyed up by thin hot air (mostly French), nosing this way and that according to whatever politically sanctimonious (foundationalist) enthusiasm seizes the hierophantic pilot of the hour. (An enthusiasm for "antifoundationalist" difference and deferral is of course a foundationalist enthusiasm.) And at all our elbows, as it were, a reproachful little black dog sits. He knows the hierophant for the fraud he is, smelling, in his smell, and sensing, in his moods and more animated accesses, a comrade, a *semblable*, a *frère*. We are all what we are because that little dog knows us, and what he knows should be the beginning of a true account of art.

Works Cited

Alexander, Richard D., and Katharine M. Noonan. "Concealment of Ovulation, Parental Care, and Human Social Evolution." *Evolutionary Biology and Human Social Behavior: An Anthropological Perspective.* Ed. Napoleon A. Chagnon and William Irons. North Scituate, MA: Duxbury, 1979. 421–45.

Barkow, Jerome H. "Sociobiology: Is This the New Theory of Human Nature?" Montagu 171–97.

Baucom, Donald H., Paige K. Besch, and Steven Callahan. "Relation between

Testosterone Concentration, Sex Role Identity, and Personality among Females." *Journal of Personality and Social Psychology* 48 (1985): 1218–26.

Bleier, Ruth, ed. *Feminist Approaches to Science.* New York: Pergamon, 1986.

Bouchard, Thomas J., Jr., et al. "Sources of Human Psychological Differences: The Minnesota Study of Twins Reared Apart." *Science* 250 (1990): 223–28.

Breuer, Georg. *Sociobiology and the Human Dimension.* Cambridge: Cambridge UP, 1982.

Cairns, Robert B. "An Evolutionary and Developmental Perspective on Aggressive Patterns." Zahn-Waxler, Cummings, and Iannotti 58–87.

Crews, Frederick. "The Grand Academy of Theory." *Skeptical Engagements.* By Crews. New York: Oxford UP, 1986. 159–78.

Cummings, E. Mark, et al. "Early Organization of Altruism and Aggression: Developmental Patterns and Individual Differences." Zahn-Waxler, Cummings, and Iannotti 165–88.

Darwin, Charles. *The Descent of Man and Selection in Relation to Sex.* 2 vols. New York: Appleton, 1872.

———. *The Expression of the Emotions in Man and Animals.* 1872. Chicago: U of Chicago P, 1965.

Dunbar, R. I. M. "The Evolutionary Implications of Social Behavior." *The Role of Behavior in Evolution.* Ed. H.C. Plotkin. Cambridge: MIT P, 1988. 165–88.

Ehrhardt, Anke A., and Heino F. L. Meyer-Bahlburg. "Effects of Prenatal Sex Hormones on Gender-Related Behavior." *Science* 211 (1981): 1312–18.

Eibl-Eibesfeldt, Irenäus. *Love and Hate: The Natural History of Behavior Patterns.* Trans. Geoffrey Strachan. New York: Schocken, 1974.

Elia, Irene. *The Female Animal.* Oxford: Oxford UP, 1985.

Feshbach, Seymour, and Norma Deitch Feshbach. "Aggression and Altruism: A Personality Perspective." Zahn-Waxler, Cummings, and Iannotti 189–217.

Fluehr-Lobban, Carolyn. "A Marxist Reappraisal of the Matriarchate." *Current Anthropology* 20 (1979): 341–59.

Foley, R. A., and P. C. Lee. "Finite Social Space, Evolutionary Pathways, and Reconstructing Hominid Behavior." *Science* 243 (1989): 901–6.

Freedman, Daniel G. *Human Sociobiology: A Holistic Approach.* New York: Free, 1979.

Goldberg, Steven. *The Inevitability of Patriarchy.* New York: Morrow, 1973.

Haraway, Donna. "Animal Sociology and a Natural Economy of the Body Politic, Part I. A Political Physiology of Dominance." *Sex and Scientific Inquiry.* Ed.: Sandra Harding and Jean F. O'Barr. Chicago: U of Chicago P, 1987. 217–32.

Hawkesworth, Mary E. "Knowers, Knowing, Known: Feminist Theory and Claims of Truth." *Signs* 14 (1989): 533–57.

Hines, Melissa. "Prenatal Gonadal Hormones and Sex Differences in Human Behavior." *Psychological Bulletin* 92 (1982): 56–80.

Holden, Constance. "The Genetics of Personality." *Science* 237 (1987): 598–601.

Holland, Norman. *The Brain of Robert Frost: A Cognitive Approach to Literature.* New York: Routledge, 1988.

Inglis, James, and J. S. Lawson. "Sex Differences in the Effects of Unilateral Brain Damage on Intelligence." *Science* 212 (1981): 693–95.

Keegan, Patricia. "Playing Favorites." *New York Times* 6 Aug. 1989: A4.

Keller, Evelyn Fox. *A Feeling for the Organism: The Life and Work of Barbara McClintock.* San Francisco: Freeman, 1983.

Konner, Melvin. *The Tangled Wing: Biological Constraints on the Human Spirit.* New York: Harper, 1982.

Kuhn, Thomas S. *The Structure of Scientific Revolutions.* 2nd ed. Chicago: U of Chicago P, 1970.

Lerner, Gerda. *The Creation of Patriarchy.* Oxford: Oxford UP, 1986.

Levy, Robert I. "Emotion, Knowing, and Culture." Shweder and LeVine 214–37.

Lewontin, R. C., Steven Rose, and Leon J. Kamin. *Not in Our Genes: Biology, Ideology, and Human Nature.* New York: Pantheon, 1984.

Lorenz, Konrad. *On Aggression.* Trans. Marjorie Kerr Wilson. New York: Harcourt, 1966.

Maccoby, Eleanor Emmons, and Carol Nagy Jacklin. *The Psychology of Sex Differences.* Stanford: Stanford UP, 1974.

Mandler, George. *Mind and Body: Psychology of Emotion and Stress.* New York: Norton, 1984.

Merchant, Carolyn. *The Death of Nature: Women, Ecology, and the Scientific Revolution.* San Francisco: Harper, 1980.

Midgley, Mary. *Beast and Man: The Roots of Human Nature.* Ithaca: Cornell UP, 1978.

———. "Rival Fatalisms." Montagu 108–34.

Mohanty, S. P. "Us and Them: On the Philosophical Bases of Political Criticism." *Yale Journal of Criticism* 2 (1989): 1–31.

Montagu, Ashley, ed. *Sociobiology Examined.* Oxford: Oxford UP, 1980.

Moyer, K. W. "Kinds of Aggression and Their Physiological Bases." *Communications in Behavioral Biology* 2 (1968): 65–87.

Ortony, Andrew, Gerald L. Clore, and Allan Collins. *The Cognitive Structure of Emotions.* Cambridge: Cambridge UP, 1988.

Panksepp, Jaak. "The Psychobiology of Prosocial Behaviors: Separation Distress, Play, and Altruism." Zahn-Waxler, Cummings, and Iannotti 19–57.

Reiner, Anton. "An Explanation of Behavior." Rev. of *The Triune Brain in Evolution: Role in Paleocerebral Functions,* by Paul D. MacLean. *Science* 250 (1990): 303–5.

Rosaldo, Michelle Z. "Towards an Anthropology of Self and Feeling." Shweder and LeVine 137–57.

Rose, Hilary. "Beyond Masculinist Realities: A Feminist Epistemology for the Sciences." Bleier 57–76.

Rousseau, Jean-Jacques. "Discourse on the Origin and Foundations of Inequality among Men." *Basic Political Writings.* Trans. and ed. Donald A. Cress. Indianapolis: Hackett, 1987.

Rubin, Robert T., June M. Reinisch, and Roger F. Haskett. "Postnatal Gonadal Steroid Effects on Human Behavior." *Science* 211 (1981): 1318–24.

Ruse, Michael. *Taking Darwin Seriously: A Naturalistic Approach to Philosophy.* Oxford: Blackwell, 1986.

Savin-Williams, Ritch C. *Adolescence: An Ethological Perspective.* New York: Springer, 1987.

Shweder, Richard A., and Robert A. LeVine, ed. *Culture Theory: Essays on Mind, Self, and Emotion.* Cambridge: Cambridge UP, 1984.

Tiger, Lionel. *Men in Groups.* 2nd ed. London: Boyars, 1984.

Weeks, Jeffrey. "Questions of Identity." *The Cultural Construction of Sexuality.* Ed. Pat Caplan. London: Tavistock, 1987. 31–51.

Wilson, Edward O. *On Human Nature.* Cambridge: Harvard UP, 1978.

Wilson, Edward O., and Charles Lumsden. *Genes, Mind, and Culture: The Coevolutionary Process.* Cambridge: Harvard UP, 1981.

Witelson, Sandra. "Les Différences sexuelles dans la neurologie de la cognition: Implications psychologiques, sociales, éducatives et cliniques." *Le Fait féminin.* Ed. Evelyne Sullerot. Paris: Fayard, 1978. 287–303.

Wittgenstein, Ludwig. *Philosophische Untersuchungen/Philosophical Investigations.* Trans. G. E. M. Anscombe. New York: Macmillan, 1953.

Wrangham, Richard W. "The Significance of African Apes for Reconstructing Human Social Evolution." *The Evolution of Human Behavior: Primate Models.* Ed. Warren G. Kinzey. Albany: State U of New York P, 1987. 51–71.

Zahn-Waxler, Carolyn, E. Mark Cummings, and Ronald Iannotti, eds. *Altruism and Aggression: Biological and Social Origins.* Cambridge: Cambridge UP, 1986.

Simulacra, or, Vicissitudes of the Imprecise

David F. Bell

Even Science, the strict measure, is obliged to start with a make-believe unit, and must fix on a point in the stars' unceasing journey when his sidereal clock shall pretend that time is a Nought.

—George Eliot, *Daniel Deronda*

The relationship between literary studies and scientific studies has been a difficult one in recent years because it has been a fertile terrain for mutual misunderstanding. The structuralist analyses of the sixties certainly had scientific pretensions, borrowing the notion of homology from mathematics and, in order to justify certain procedures, deferring to linguistics, which was reputed to be the most scientific of the sciences of man. The question of the scientific status of linguistics, however, soon became too thorny for its proponents to continue uncritically promoting linguistics as a potential scientific underpinning for literary analysis. Despite the structuralist episode, for the most part, literary theorists have tended to keep their distance from science, preferring instead to attempt to define a domain in which procedures not governed by scientific principles of analysis are applied. It has been argued that this is an ideologically motivated strategy, one designed to delimit and protect a terrain that would escape the ever more overbearing control of technological experts produced by the relentless invasion of all domains of sociocultural and intellectual life by science in the twentieth century. It has also been argued epistemologically that the object with which literary theory deals is unlike that of scientific study, and therefore that different kinds of procedures are called for in the two different domains.[1]

But whatever the origin of the attitude of suspicion toward science within literary circles and however it is justified in any given instance, it cannot but profit literary theorists to reflect upon certain developments within the sciences, because it is often the case that those developments have had repercussions within literary studies, whether or not literary theorists have been aware of them. The present essay is an attempt to analyze how the notion of the simulacrum became an important one during the sixties and seventies in French philosophico-literary circles by linking its rethematization to scientific developments. Treating in a broad manner the evolution of the idea of modeling within the scientific domain, tracing some of the lines of force along which its history could be written, I shall suggest that the simulacrum returns as a concern in recent French philosophy at the moment when it is simultaneously becoming a fundamental notion in science and, moreover, that interest in the simulacrum within the philosophico-literary domain inevitably raises crucial questions with respect to the validity and significance of simulation as a scientific activity.

It has now become a classic argument to link the beginnings of science, or at the very least one of the major lines of force of any history of its origins, to the act of measuring. A statement attributed to Lord Kelvin provides a succinct formulation of this view: "If you cannot measure, your knowledge is meager and unsatisfactory."[2] The fact that measurement should appear so fundamental to scientific activity is undoubtedly the result of its perceived value as a theoretical gesture. The reasoning goes something like this. As long as measuring is accomplished directly, that is, by physically applying a unit (hand, arm, foot) to a given object, the limits of such an activity are starkly drawn. Only those things which are immediately at hand can be subject to such treatment. Other objects further removed from the observer's immediate vicinity will remain unmeasurable unless the measuring unit can be transported to them. Even this transporting, however, is severely limited: as soon as the object one wishes to measure exceeds certain dimensions, it becomes impossible physically to apply a unit to it. How does one overcome the limitations of measuring as touching? Certain of the central discoveries of the Greek mathematicians are direct responses to this question. Faced with the impossibility of tangibly measuring objects exceeding a certain size or located in excess of a certain distance, the Greek mathematicians looked for means to circumvent this physical restriction. "Geometry is a ruse," as Michel Serres has said ("Mathematics and Philosophy" 85); "it takes a detour, an indirect route, to reach that which lies outside immediate experience."[3] The wording of the preceding remark is particularly suggestive. The indirect is substituted for the direct, a detour for the main road. Unable to walk up to the object and embrace it by touching its entire dimensions (even iteratively), the geometer walks around it, surrounds it even, searching for a mode of reaching it at a distance. What Thales discovers when he considers the problem of measuring the pyramids is a ruse, specifically, the ruse of the model: "the construction of the summary, the skeleton of a pyramid in reduced form but of equivalent proportions" (Serres, "Mathematics and Philosophy" 85). Unable to scale the pyramids with a ladder, Thales invents another kind of ladder, a scale, that is, a model whose proportions are in relation to the actual object.

The distance between the observer and the unmeasurable object that prompts the invention of the proportional model might well be seen, then, as the distance that transforms practice into theory. "For in the final analysis the path in question consists in forsaking the sense of touch for that of sight, measurement by 'placing' for measurement by sighting. Here, to theorize is to see, a fact which the Greek language makes clear. Vision is tactile without contact," contends Serres (86). But we should perhaps not be in such a hurry to make this distinction, for it quickly becomes evident that the distancing implied by the model is not quite the qualitative break it may at first appear to be. Serres again: "As far as I know, even for accessible objects, vision alone is my guarantee that the ruler has been placed accurately on the thing. To measure is to align; the eye is the best witness of an accurate covering-over. Thales invents the notion of model, of module, but he also collapses the visible onto the tangible. To measure, supposedly, is to relate. True, but the relation implies a transporting: of the ruler, of the point of view, of the things lined up, and so on" (86). Vision is an important component of measuring even when no proportional model is necessary, that is, even when the object in question is proximate and small enough to be embraced by iterative touching. The proportional model is only the transporting of touching into a field of vision that is itself anchored in the tactile. The vision implied by theory is in this case still closely attached to practice—perhaps even indistinguishable from it.

The notion of measurement, nevertheless, is often invoked ideologically as one of the guiding principles of scientific thought, as a test of the rationality and theoretical validity of any approach that would qualify itself as scientific. The following statement by Abraham Moles is a recent formulation of the significance it is still perceived to possess:

> The idea of measuring, of a confrontation between the concept of size as man experiences it and as he encounters it in the object that he measures is certainly one of the essential elements of scientific thought. If for the physicist it is first of all the objective implementation of the criterion of size and thus the measure of tolerances in the observation or the domination of the object which has this size, it is, for someone who encounters a phenomenon *in statu nascendi*—in its state of becoming—and who is going to create a new idea, *first* a means of distancing himself from what he encounters, of neutralizing its affective aspect and thus of finding in it a creative strangeness. (*Les Sciences de l'imprécis* 43)

Measurement fulfills a hygienic function for Moles. It allows the thinker to purge himself of the affective charge presented by something that is new and strange and forces him somehow to situate the strangeness of encountered phenomena. In the absence of an attempt to take up the task of describing certain aspects of an unusual phenomenon by the interplay of measurements, the scientist would be able only to speak endlessly in general terms about the object or event in question. There is always a certain distance implied by the act of measuring, but whether that distance is the only possible theoretical one is another question entirely. It would perhaps be prudent to avoid fetishizing the act of measuring: "From measurement as method, we move to measurement as frenzy, and from the frenzy for measurement to the frenzy for precision (the 'frenzy for the rational' is not in itself rationality)" (Moles 44).[4]

One objection to this frenzy immediately presents itself, and it is a weighty one: many phenomena, doubtless even the majority of phenomena with which human beings must deal, are not measurable in the proportional and relational— geometric—sense that the Greeks illustrated so luminously. We do not live in the laboratory with its high-resolution measuring instruments but rather among endless series of perpetually variable situations and vague phenomena. Few of these phenomena are sufficiently isolatable ever to become subject to measurement in the laboratory, and yet we are forced to make decisions, to choose among alternate modes of behavior in the midst of this forest of phenomena. The simplest common sense shows us that we are seldom given over entirely to senseless wandering among these phenomena, that instead we are capable of perceiving patterns, repetitions, regularities that provide us with a basis upon which to decide among optional possibilities for acting. Are we to exclude such patterns and regularities from the purview of rationality, of a certain scientificity, simply because they cannot be measured by proportional models centered upon the notion of transporting relations? Obviously not.

The distinction between what is measurable in the strict sense I have defined above and what is not is too often made to function, nonetheless, as an ideological boundary line between the exact sciences (of which physics is the prime example), on the one hand, and the supposedly inexact sciences of man, on the other. Because instrumental means of measuring patterns and regularities with the requisite geometric precision cannot be devised within the sciences of man, this type of study runs the risk of being relegated to the domain of a less purified type of science. But it quickly becomes apparent that a distinction based upon the notion of precision is a false one and that the differences among various scientific domains are altogether more complex and subtle.

The thesis advanced by Moles is instructive in this context:

Contrary to what the general discourse of the history of science would have us believe, the difference between the exact sciences of nature and the inexact sciences of man and of the living is not a fundamental difference, but one resulting from a choice. At the origin of applied rationalism, . . . the few bold spirits who embraced the adventure of what we have come to call scientific thought could and did *choose* among the paths of knowledge those in which the complexity of what they were studying could be mastered by a mind deprived of powerful instrumental means. (32)

Scientific thought began in a context in which there were very few instrumental means at hand to assist the would-be scientist in his attempts to isolate and measure phenomena (in fact, it could be argued that science itself was necessary to create these means—a feedback loop whose implications are not always evident to scientists). A pressing necessity narrowed the choice of phenomena to those susceptible to study with existing instruments and available materials. The decision to concentrate upon simple phenomena, thus dictated at least in part by material conditions, in turn contributed powerfully to reinforcing a simplified, linear model of cause and effect. What was abandoned by the adoption of such a model was the very possibility of dealing with any truly complex phenomena, those marked, for example, by multicausality, feedback loops, and other nonlinear processes.

Instrumental limitations were not the only conditions militating in favor of confining science to simpler phenomena. A whole cultural and intellectual revolution brought about by statistics and probability in the nineteenth century and by the new types of reasoning to which they gave rise would also be necessary in order to make complex phenomena—those resulting from human interactions, for instance—objects of formal study and analysis: "Scientific investigation according to Newton begins with a complete analysis, yielding general laws that govern the most elementary objects or phenomena. Statistics begins by conceding that individual humans are too complex and diverse to serve as the basis of science, and has recourse instead to numerical frequencies as its elemental data" (Gigerenzer et al. 42). Because of the overawing power the Newtonian synthesis was originally perceived to possess, post-Newtonian developments in the nineteenth century necessitated a rediscovery of the fact that the theoretical and geometrical methods of Newtonian physics were not representative of the whole of the scientific endeavor but only a part of it—and that this had been the case from the beginning:

In contrast to the so-called Baconian sciences—including the early investigations of chemical reactions, electricity and magnetism, of life, and of the earth—the Newtonian tradition of mechanics, astronomy, optics, and, later, theories of heat, electricity and magnetism did not rely predominantly on an extended qualitative study of the phenomena, but rather on mathematical theory and experiment or observation that was informed by that theory. . . . These two characteristic features of modern physics, its highly theoretical character and its geometrical method, have saved it the long and arduous path through natural history that might have required descriptive and inferential statistics and probabilistic methodology in the search for the hidden lawlike order of nature. (Gigerenzer et al. 169)[5]

It is not just that the algorithms of complex, nonlinear systems require powerful instruments to be studied; they require a different perspective on the question of causality as well. It is clear, for example, that when one attempts to study elements of human relations, the issue of the interaction between the observer and the observed becomes immediately troublesome in a way that was not the case in physics until the wide acceptance of relativity theory and the development of quantum theory in this century. One is thus no longer dealing with what Moles terms a causality expressed by "the combination of functions," but with one characterized by "correlations and regressive functions" (33). And by logical extension, a different type of model of the objects to be studied is required. If the relationship between the observer and the object of analysis is one of geometric measurement, then the model required to accomplish the task is one incorporating relations of proportion and transporting: the scale model I briefly described earlier. If, on the other hand, one is attempting to study something that cannot be measured in this way, and, even more, something that is dynamically influenced by the very presence of the observer (human relations, for example), the most fruitful method becomes one in which an attempt is made to build a model whose coherence is based upon certain *correlations* with the phenomena observed, not upon proportional relations with those phenomena. "All the sciences do not use the idea of correlation. Thus, physics is interested in cases (the falling of bodies, etc.) which are accessible in terms of the relation of cause to effect according to tried and true Cartesian methods" (Veuille 37). The Cartesian chain of reasoning in which analysis passes from the simple to the complex by single steps from one element to the next is clearly tied to a traditional definition of science derived from the attempt to limit its scope to fairly simple phenomena. In fact, Veuille's remark obtains only for classical mechanics. With the advent of interest in complex systems characterized by nonlinear behavior—those, for example, which are far from equilibrium—the Cartesian approach to causality has had to be abandoned, in certain cases at least, by physicists as well.[6] This is perhaps more immediately obvious for the sciences of man, where correlations formulated on the basis of probabilistic reasoning have become the norm. Establishing correlations may not permit us to discover causes ("Correlation suffers from a constitutive defect in its nature: the ambiguity of the knowledge it procures when compared to causal explanations" [Veuille 38]), but this does not mean that when our attention turns to phenomena that are more complex than the systems studied by classical mechanics, we can say nothing about them. Even if the nature of correlations is not causal, a model of a given phenomenon constructed from correlations can have predictive power and coherence.

Let me illustrate what the construction of such a model implies by invoking an extremely enlightening example devised by Abraham Moles (50–55). Suppose the sociologist or the anthropologist wishes to record a particular situation of human interaction in order to study it at his leisure. How does he gather his evidence? A seemingly straightforward answer would be that he can photograph or film the scene he wishes to study and use that record for his analytical purposes. A set of problems immediately arises, however. How should the photographs be taken? The sociologist could conceivably enter into the scene that interests him and photograph his subjects directly. But clearly this is a problematic solution, because as soon as the subjects perceive what the sociologist is up to, they will immediately begin posing, and the supposed spontaneity of the scene will be irrevocably lost. The observer is himself observed and the dynamic relations he was attempting to expose are radically altered.

In that case, why not adopt the solution of the hidden camera in which the apparatus and its operator are removed from the scene, out of sight of the intended subjects? Contemporary confidence in the technical means at our disposal causes us immediately to suppose that this solution is attainable without difficulty.[7] Such is not the case, however, for the further away the camera is, the more powerful its magnification must be, and the more resolution will have to be sacrificed. Moreover, the hidden camera will be inherently less mobile, and the angle of its fixed perspective will invariably skew the scene it records. An even more serious obstacle is the fact that the scene that the sociologist wishes to capture will in almost every case be a fleeting one, one that takes place in a locus difficult to predict beforehand, one that cannot therefore be "wired" and prepared with the heavy technical instruments necessary.

Ultimately it may well be that the sociologist will succeed more fully if he *reconstructs* the scene in question and photographs that reconstruction. In other words, he may use his memory of the scene in question by hiring actors and a studio, instructing the actors in their roles, and photographing them as they play out those roles. This solution immediately strikes one as paradoxical. "But, precisely in the difficult domain which consists in seizing relatively subtle and fleeting aspects of the behavior of human beings as objects of science, paradoxical methods of this sort suggest that fiction might well be what best interprets reality when reality is for some reason inaccessible" (Moles 54).

The type of model suggested here is a simulation, a simulacrum. What the researcher does is to pick out what he considers to be significant elements in the scene he has witnessed and to reconstruct that scene by recombining those elements. At stake is no longer simply a question of proportional relations between the model and the object, but an attempt to isolate vital elements and bring them into correlation with one another so that the model functions ("works") in a manner that mimics the original phenomena. Doubtless such a procedure is subject to distortions and tricks, and one must always be vigilant to avoid the kind of scientific kitsch illustrated, for instance, by the innumerable "docudramas" that have become the endlessly repetitive stock of contemporary American television. On the other hand, it is difficult to dismiss this type of procedure out of hand simply because it is fraught with the potential for error. Other types of procedures that are immediately considered to be scientific in nature (measuring, for instance) are also subject to distortions.

Moreover, the fact that such a reconstruction does not treat the question of causality in the same way that a traditional scientific experiment does is not automatic grounds for dismissal. Indeed, the researcher who employs this type of procedure in any useful manner must be as acute an observer and as astute a theoretician as any theoretical physicist. And he must be prepared to constantly compare the reconstruction to the memories of the scene at stake as well as to refine continuously and to criticize the model from the perspective of prior theoretical conjectures and knowledge. That researcher must be someone who is not afraid to err, in the archaic as well as the modern sense of the term, that is, one who is willing to wander and is unafraid to encounter error. Ultimately, the person who remains within the confines of a geometric type of measurement alone is someone who can avoid the risk of the truly new and strange, who can remain within the circle of the known. Measuring is surely useful within the confines of established paradigms of thought, but at the uncertain frontiers of shifting knowledge, other conceptual modes may well be paramount.

The notion of the model as simulation is evidently one that is directly related to the information-processing revolution represented by the invention and refinement of the computer and by the complexity of the algorithms it allows one to study, but its origin lies perhaps more fundamentally in the revolution of statistical and probabilistic reasoning that took place in the nineteenth century: "Apart from error theory, the most important uses of statistics in this period were to model phenomena, and not just to draw inferences about them" (Gigerenzer et al. 55–56). With the refinement of theories of stochastic processes in the early part of the twentieth century and with the later use of the computer, the activity of modeling has taken on a new life.

Rather than further pursue the question from a history of science perspective, however, I would now like to turn to the problem of the simulacrum in another context, that of French philosophical and critical thought in the late sixties and early seventies. The relations one finds between this context and the context of modern developments in the history of scientific thought concerning the notion of simulation are instructive and revealing, not only because the question of the simulacrum reappears in philosophical critique at the very moment when correlational modeling has become a central scientific activity, but also, more significantly, because the treatment of the simulacrum in a certain philosophical circle intersects its treatment in scientific circles at a crucial point, one that engages the very definition of contemporary scientific activity by raising the question of the status of the object of analysis, as we shall see.

Interest in the notion of the simulacrum was evident in French philosophical circles at the end of the sixties and followed on the heels of the structuralist episode, during which, clearly, a notion of modeling based upon correlation had made a massive entry into literary and ethnological studies in France. Fascination with the simulacrum in this context could well be viewed as an attempt to push the idea of modeling to its limit, to exacerbate its tendencies, and thus to use it to undermine itself. For those who wielded the weapon of the simulacrum, it was originally meant to serve as a means of revealing that structuralist analyses were too wedded to a concept of truth purveyed by the sciences and founded upon metaphysics of the Platonic variety. The simulacrum was seen as the pressure point within the Platonic system that could be mobilized to bring down the whole house of cards.

In a short essay on Platonism, Vincent Descombes gives a clear description of the situation of the simulacrum in Plato's thought: "An image resembles the original if simultaneously it somehow illustrates that model and yet indicates that there is a model of which it, as image, is only a copy. . . . But there is another type of imitation, the simulacrum . . . which pretends to a different type of resemblance: to be so similar to the original that the beholder can no longer distinguish between the two" (51). Two things are of interest in these remarks. First, the term *model* is used here to designate the original object or phenomenon of which a copy is made. In a curious way that remains to be explained, modern simulation theory makes the copy the model. In other words, it reverses things— the original phenomenon (here the Platonic idea) is no longer the model; the model is what we construct. Second, the notion of imitation is governed by a hierarchical ordering. There is an original of which a copy is made. That copy is clearly inferior, subordinated to the valorized original, and it is that visible, detectable subservience and the resulting relation of subordination it provokes that maintain order in the hierarchy.

The simulacrum introduces a perversion into this harmonious system and disrupts its functioning, in particular the hierarchy it implies. It threatens, quite simply, to turn order on its head and thereby undo it. Gilles Deleuze, one of the great practitioners of destructive logics during the period in question, remarks: "Copies are possessors who are second in line, well-founded pretenders, guaranteed by their resemblance: *simulacra* are like false pretenders, built on the principle of dissimilarity, implying an essential perversion or misappropriation" (*Logique du sens* 295–96). In a very suggestive manner, Deleuze notes that the

Platonic method of distinction and division is not simply one of definitions and proper classifications, but "a dialectic of rivalry . . . a dialectic of rivals or pretenders" (293). The aim of Platonism is defined as follows: "At the heart of the matter is the attempt to assure the triumph of copies over simulacra, to repress simulacra, to keep them imprisoned in the depths, to prevent them from rising to the surface and permeating everything" (296). If one is to undo this metaphysical organization, one must use the peculiar deviousness and destructive bent of the simulacra themselves: "To deny the primacy of an original over its copy, of a model over its image. To glorify the reign of simulacra and reflections" (*Différence et répétition* 92).

Once again the model appears as the original in these remarks, not as a construction meant to mime the original. More important, however, is the ambivalent valorization of the simulacrum. It is clearly envisaged as a destructive force, but at the same time, the destruction it achieves is viewed as necessary, as a liberation of philosophical discourse. What precisely does the simulacrum undo? A certain notion of the truth. The simulacrum is not employed to attain another type of truth, rather, to empty the ideal Platonic hierarchy of all operational validity. Once simulacra are unleashed upon the world, there will be no going back, no return to safe haven, only a kind of endless circulation of images, each a pretender but none capable of ending the strife of ideas by establishing an origin and founding point. We are not far from the notion of Derridian undecidability here. The oscillation between or among meanings that is characteristic of certain Derridian notions (*hymen, tympan, pharmakos*) reproduces an effect that is typical of the simulacrum in Deleuze's analyses. Other philosophico-critical themes of the period are also waiting in the wings: the labyrinth, for instance, which one can find illustrated in the novelist Michel Butor's work or in the work of the Argentine writer Jorge Luis Borges, widely read and appreciated in French intellectual circles during the period in question. The defining element of the labyrinth is precisely the fact that every path within it resembles every other—no path distinguishes itself sufficiently enough to guide one to an exit, no path can be found and thus reveal an itinerary.

One must insist once again upon the equivocal status accorded the simulacrum in the preceding analyses: it is simultaneously destructive and liberating. Freeing thought from the shackles of Platonic hierarchies and distinctions, it allows a circulation of images, concepts, and notions that would be impossible without it. To accomplish that circulation, however, the founding elements of metaphysics are attacked, and the idea of truth in a Platonic sense is put into question. The destructiveness of the simulacrum will come back to haunt those who unleashed it—it is clearly a Pandora's box for certain of the thinkers who participated in its contemporary rethematiziation.

This threat and its accomplishment can be graphically illustrated in the work of another thinker of the period, Jean Baudrillard. Baudrillard wrote a book on the subject, *Simulacres et simulation*, which I shall discuss in a moment, a book that marks a turning point in the appreciation of the simulacrum after the euphoria of the sixties and early seventies. He encounters the notion of the simulacrum earlier, however, in the context of an essay devoted to the idea of seduction, when he explores the trompe l'oeil in painting. Traditional approaches to the trompe l'oeil have emphasized the idea that it is a realist device, one that increases the measure of reality in painting: "Absurd. The increased level of reality is never where the miracle takes place, but, inversely, in the sudden powerlessness of reality and the giddiness of being engulfed by this movement" (*De la séduction* 89–90). Baudrillard continues:

> When the hierarchical organization of space which privileges the eye and vision, when this perspectival simulation—for this is nothing but a simulacrum—is undone, something else surges forth, which, in the absence of a better term, we express as a kind of *touch*, a tactile hyperpresence of things "as if we could touch them." But this tactile phantasm bears no relationship to our sense of touch, it is a metaphor for the "seizure" [shock, seizing in the mechanical sense] which results from the abolition of the scene and space of representation. (90)[8]

Instead of playing on the real and reinforcing it, the trompe l'oeil, by miming it, throws a shadow of radical doubt upon it. The space of the real collapses. The distance and depth that are supposedly characteristic of the real are perverted by the trompe l'oeil when it succeeds in producing the illusion of depth upon a surface. Baudrillard sees in this hyperrealization of the superficial the beginning of the sphere of appearances where there is nothing to see (perspective implies depth, something behind what is immediately and superficially visible, and, therefore, a structure of meaning), where, instead, "things see you" (91).

The simulacrum finds itself aligned with seduction in *De la séduction*, and both are arrayed with a certain irony and pleasure against the preponderant structures of meaning and signification. Seduction works toward freeing certain tendencies that are imprisoned in a civilization weighed down by symbolicity and meaning—it is a foil to desire, just as the simulacrum is a foil to the drive for signification and depth of meaning. There is a certain playfulness to simulation in the context of Baudrillard's essay, a sentiment of emancipation, a reveling in the superficial circulation permitted by seduction and simulation: "Trompe l'oeil, mirror or painting, it is the charm of this *one less dimension* that bewitches us. It is this one less dimension that composes the space of seduction and becomes a source of giddy bewilderment" (95).

The contrast with *Simulacres et simulation*, which followed shortly on the heels of *De la séduction*, is striking. What is remarkable in the transition between the two essays is not only a change in tone but Baudrillard's desire from the outset of *Simulacres* to turn the debate away from the philosophico-literary context in which he found it and to which he contributed in *De la séduction* and back toward the scientific backdrop of the problem that I developed in the first part of the present analysis. *Simulacres* begins with the recounting of an incident that is quickly elevated to the status of a paradigm for the proliferation of simulacra in the contemporary world and, in particular, in contemporary science. The incident in question is the decision made by the Philippine government in 1971, at the behest of anthropologists themselves, concerning the primitive Tasaday society, a decision that, in effect, sent the Tasaday back to their primitive life. Faced with the disintegration of that society provoked by its contact with contemporary societies and with anthropologists attempting to study and analyze it, the decision was made to protect it by cutting it off from tourists, anthropologists, and other inhabitants of the Philippines (18). In a manner whose paradoxical nature quickly becomes the object of Baudrillard's irony, the scientists are forced to lose their object in order to gain it, to take a distance from it in order not to devastate it, in short, to sacrifice their contact with it to the higher goals of science. Comments Baudrillard, "In any case, the logical evolution of a science is to become ever further removed from its object until it finally can do without it entirely: the autonomy of science is thus all the more fantastic, it attains its pure form" (19).

    The energy of Baudrillard's critique of the Tasaday incident lies in its perverse interpretation of the anthropologists' gesture. Schooled in ecological thinking, embracing any attempt to "protect nature," the typical reader of this narrative might at first be tempted to laud the ascetic, seemingly eminently ethical decision made by the anthropologists to give up this potentially fascinating object of study for the sake of protecting a primitive culture. For Baudrillard, however, the anthropologists' concession is not simply an isolated incident to be chalked up to the credit of the ethical conscience of a group of researchers, but a veritable paradigm of contemporary science. The anthropologists can easily afford such a gesture of apparent self-sacrifice and self-effacement because, he claims, science is reaching a stage in which the object of analysis will be more and more often abandoned in favor of its simulation. Thus the apparently disinterested decision concerning the Tasaday becomes instead an exemplary incident illustrating the cynical manipulation that is beginning to be the order of the day in contemporary scientific activity generally. In the absence of its object—and thus of the control supposedly exercised upon it by that object—science becomes pure simulation. With no barrier to its proliferating theory, it invades the whole of reality and transforms us into just so many Tasaday, just so many far-removed and thus infinitely interchangeable—and ultimately useless—objects of its purified, pervasive, and arcane activity.

With this critique we have reached the crux of the matter. The accusation that chides science for giving up any contact with its object is a thinly veiled attack upon its tendency to turn away from "facts" and "reason." It is not long before Baudrillard lays all his cards on the table:

What happens is that we are in a logic of simulation which no longer has anything to do with a logic of facts and an order of reason. Simulation is characterized by a *privileging of the model,* of all models over the smallest fact. Models are there first, their circulation . . . constitutes the true magnetic field of the event. Facts no longer have their own trajectory; they are born at the intersection of models. A single fact may be engendered by all models simultaneously. (31–32)

Taking his key from contemporary theories of modeling and simulation, Baudrillard, unlike Deleuze and Descombes before him, calls *model* not that which is the original event, fact, or idea but, on the contrary, that which is constructed by theoretical artifice and which positions itself in the locus of origin. In short, he claims that for contemporary science, there is no fact or event at the origin. There is no object that provokes scientific theorizing, there are only models that, in effect, produce the facts in as many ways, by as many causal sequences as the theoretician cares to imagine. In the Platonic schema, the original event functions as a model to which all copies conform. In simulation, according to Baudrillard, the model is not an originary event; rather, it is a construct to which all events must conform. Worse, it is not *a* construct, but *any number* of competing possible constructs.

It is evident that Baudrillard privileges the "logic of facts" and the "order of reason" in the preceding statement, in other words, that he is much more at home with what Veuille called "les bonnes vieilles méthodes cartésiennes," "tried and true Cartesian methods" (37). This criticism of simulational methods, however, obscures the fundamental point, the very problem that gave rise to them. It is not possible to apply Cartesian reasoning about causes to phenomena that are not simple in themselves. One cannot really compare the creation of simulacra and models to the causal reasoning of classical mechanics, for example, because the causes of phenomena in domains such as human relations are so complex, so tied to feedback loops of all sorts, that causal explanations quickly become too heavy-handed to be of any use. Baudrillard would simply banish such phenomena to the realm of ignorance or, more perversely, claim that since a simulacrum of a phenomenon of this sort can always be replaced by another and different simulacrum, simulational models can tell us nothing about the phenomenon at stake: they are merely proliferating fictions.

We have clearly come full circle here in the debate concerning the status of the simulacrum within the circle of French philosophical analysis of the sixties and seventies. From the valorization of the simulacrum as a method of destroying "outdated" philosophical categories and distinctions, we finish with an exemplary argument making manifest a fear that the proliferation of simulacra will provoke a crisis of the real in which we shall no longer be able to distinguish between our own artifices and what is supposedly "out there." And this crisis of the real formulated in Baudrillard's argument spills over from the philosophical domain, where Baudrillard found it, into the scientific domain. The (quasi-paranoid) horror of the simulacrum is ultimately, however, a function of a willful misunderstanding of what it claims to accomplish. A simulation does not pretend to explain a phenomenon in a causal manner but to offer a model that permits us to grasp certain repetitive structures and thereby to gain some predictive power. It is subject to modification rendered necessary by the most astute and theoretical judgment possible of its capacity to incorporate in a sufficiently persuasive manner as many of the elements of the event it is meant to explain as possible. Only by obscuring fundamental aspects of the notion of simulation in theoretical (scientific) contexts is Baudrillard able to condemn it as a dangerous fiction. Only by holding it accountable to a simplifed, Cartesian notion of causality is he able to disqualify it.

There is, moreover, a further dimension to the problem at stake here that Baudrillard chooses to ridicule rather than to consider seriously. Let us return for a moment to the incident concerning the Tasaday—that parable of modern science, according to Baudrillard. Indeed, it is a parable of modern science in more ways than he chooses to recognize. The rise of scientific thought can also be seen as the rise of an ideology of interventionism. The confidence inspired by the early discoveries of science left the pioneers in the domain with an increasing confidence not only in their capacity to understand nature but also in their ability eventually to intervene in its processes, to master it. Relations of mastery are also invariably relations of violence and destruction. The ravages of technology, which are becoming altogether too evident around us, are the ultimate result of the destructive interventionism that is characteristic of the classic scientific method. Can we continue to pillage nature even as nature seems to turn its forces back against us? The request of the anthropologists to spare the Tasaday can, in fact, be read in a less perverse manner as the potential beginning of a recognition that the scientist might well have to construct a new type of relationship with natural phenomena. "We must therefore change directions and abandon the course imposed by the philosophy of Descartes. Because [the structure of nature is marked by] multiple interactions, mastery endures for only a short term and turns into servitude" (Serres, *Le Contrat naturel* 61). It is possible to envisage the request of the anthropologists not as a ruse to extend the powers of science by isolating it from its object and turning it into an all-permeating and proliferating fiction, but as a realization that a different method of analysis is necessary: not one that runs amok amid natural phenomena and is possible only by means of destructive interactions with nature, but one that results from a new respect for natural phenomena and from an attempt to study them with a minimum of violent intervention.[9] "In every domain which is closely or even remotely connected with the living (and especially with man), experimentation is encountering—or is going to encounter—increasing obstacles, a warning not to touch. This would perhaps be a regression or, rather, a displacement of an occidental philosophy based on the domination of nature—which remains the basis of technology—toward a philosophy based on the contemplation of this nature as a given and intangible object. . . . To the question 'How can we replace experimentation?' the answer will be 'By constructing signification'" (Moles 188–89). Simulation could thus be viewed as a method for respecting the autonomy of the real, for entering into a less destructive relationship with nature, for *constructing meaning* instead of *destroying nature* (or, to put it another way, destroying the object).

Baudrillard's argument presents us with a dilemma of conflicting alternatives in deciding upon the significance of simulation: its valorization in certain quarters of the sciences of man or its pejorative position in Baudrillard's argument. The crux of the matter is that the notion of experimental control has undergone a radical reassessment in the context of simulation, and Baudrillard raises a valid question when he wonders how that control can be reinstituted in a theoretically satisfying manner in such a context.[10] It is certainly easy as a polemical gesture to push things to extremes and to claim that in simulation, anything goes. On the other hand, one certainly cannot accept the Baudrillardian critique of it without reservation, since Baudrillard steadfastly refuses to distinguish between simple causal models and correlational models that do not attempt to identify causes—thereby vitiating his own criticism. It should now be apparent, in any case, that the appearance of a debate concerning the simulacrum in French philosophico-critical circles in the sixties and seventies was linked to the growing importance of simulational methods in the sciences. Discussion of the simulacrum in one context thus invariably led—with Baudrillard functioning as a mediating figure—to reflection upon its use in the other. Whether or not Baudrillard's critique is significant, it certainly touched upon a crucial point: does simulation really mean that the relation between scientific theory and its object has changed? And if so, how are we to theorize this change?

The lessons of this confrontation between a certain school of philosophical thought prevalent in France in the sixties and seventies and the reformulation of the notion of the simulacrum in light of its use in the sciences over the last few decades should not be lost on literary studies. The action of the simulacrum in its role as destroyer of a metaphysical conception of hierarchical truth stands in an obvious relationship with the so-called philosophico-literary approach to criticism prevalent in the seventies and eighties, which emphasized the notion that there was no ultimate meaning or truth in the literary text and that the interpreter's job was to turn the pretended truth of the literary text against itself in order to undo it. The usefulness of this activity was that it allowed traditional ideologies concerning the literary text to be challenged—perhaps unfortunately on shaky grounds, however. Ultimately, the proliferation of interpretations which this approach welcomed occulted the flip side of simulation, that is, its theorization in scientific fields, the attempt to make of it a formal modeling activity destined to construct meaning, not to destroy it. We are perhaps poised on the threshold of a new attempt, different from its structuralist predecessor, to theorize modeling in literary studies. It remains to be seen whether and eventually how the ideology of the construction of meaning that underlies the goal of scientific simulation can have an impact upon literary theory.

Notes

1. This argument is one that I reject in large part, as will become progressively more evident.

2. Kuhn (178) claims to be unable to find such a remark in Kelvin's writings but concurs that it is representative of Kelvin's attitude. See also Ian Hacking 60.

3. Serres (84–85) indicates that this point of view is shared already in the nineteenth century by Auguste Comte in his *Cours de philosophie positive* and by Paul Tannery in his *Géométrie grecque*, and that it is part of the traditional explanation found in the ancient texts themselves when they deal with the origins of mathematics.

4. Kuhn argues iconoclastically that measurement is not even a particularly good heuristic device: one can rarely, if ever, proceed from measurements to a theoretical proposition. Measurement almost invariably comes after a hypothesis in an attempt to confirm that hypothesis, and even if measurement does not succeed in offering confirmation of what has been posited, this is often far from a definitive reason to jettison a hypothesis altogether. The scientist will tend to fault the measurement instead and to search long and hard to make measurement conform to the hypothesis. Moles himself is not absolutely clear on the function of measurement in discovery in the passage just quoted. In particular, it is not apparent that what is "hygienic" really possesses any heuristic value other than to permit an unspecified distancing.

5. See also Hacking 60–63; and Kuhn.

6. For a clear presentation of the impact that the study of systems

far from equilibrium has had upon thermodynamic theory and thus upon the views espoused by classical mechanics, see Prigogine and Stengers.

7. One cannot but think in this context of the technological boasting of the United States' military establishment in the context of the Persian Gulf crisis, when its proponents claimed to have spy satellites so powerful they could, for instance, spot a glove lying on a table or, more pertinently, distinguish between real enemy weapons and decoys (unfortunately, they had not counted on advances in decoy technology which quickly forced a return in some cases to the more brutal technique of "carpet bombing"). In a less somber vein, one could invoke Francis Ford Coppola's film *The Conversation*, in which the technological means at the disposal of the main character pose more problems than they resolve.

8. Note the ambiguous position of touch in this analysis, which has a parallel within the problem of the scale model treated above.

9. Let us not forget, to give a simple example, that a particle accelerator, that fetish of modern physics, requires the ravaging of acres of land to be constructed and used.

10. But this criticism conveniently ignores, it must be noted, the complex theoretical work that has been accomplished in attempting to define correlation since the advent of the notion in the nineteenth century. See Gigerenzer et al. for an account of that work.

Works Cited

Baudrillard, Jean. *De la séduction*. Paris: Galilée, 1979.

———. *Simulacres et simulation*. Paris: Galilée: 1981.

Deleuze, Gilles. *Différence et répétition*. Paris: PUF, 1972.

———. *Logique du sens*. Paris: Minuit, 1969.

Descombes, Vincent. *Le Platonisme*. Paris: PUF, 1971.

Gigerenzer, Gerd, et al. *The Empire of Chance: How Probability Changed Science and Everyday Life*. Cambridge: Cambridge UP, 1989.

Hacking, Ian. *The Taming of Chance*. Cambridge: Cambridge UP, 1990.

Kuhn, Thomas. "The Function of Measurement in Modern Physical Science." *The Essential Tension: Selected Studies in Scientific Tradition and Change*. By Kuhn. Chicago: U of Chicago P, 1977. 178–224.

Moles, Abraham A. *Les Sciences de l'imprécis*. Paris: Seuil, 1990.

Prigogine, Ilya, and Isabelle Stengers. *Order out of Chaos: Man's New Dialogue with Nature*. New York: Bantam, 1984.

Serres, Michel. *Le Contrat naturel*. Paris: Bourin, 1990.

———. "Mathematics and Philosophy: What Thales Saw..." *Hermes: Literature,*

Science, Philosophy. By Seres. Ed. Josué V. Harari and David F. Bell. Baltimore: Johns Hopkins UP, 1982. 84–97.

Veuille, Michel. "Corrélation: Le concept pirate." *D'une science à l'autre: Des concepts nomades.* Ed. Isabelle Stengers. Paris: Seuil, 1987. 35–67.

Poststructuralism and the Pragmatic Test:
Theory in the World of Art and Criticism

From Text to Work

Paisley Livingston

Over twenty years ago, Roland Barthes published an essay in which he concisely and forcefully set forth some ideas that have remained central to poststructuralist tendencies in literary studies. Entitled "De l'oeuvre au texte," Barthes's 1971 essay promoted a shift from the classical category of the literary work to the modern (and now one is supposed to say "postmodern") category of the "text." In what follows, I shall describe and evaluate some of the main ideas that were involved in the program for this "textual revolution." My central claim will be that the kind of shift Barthes evoked is by no means as practicable or as desirable as many critics seem to think. I support this claim by describing aspects of the notion of the "work" that it would be very difficult and costly to do without. Yet what I am advocating is not a complete return to the kind of literary scholarship Barthes and others wished to replace, and I shall propose ways in which *some* of the textualist's intuitions may be reframed in a reasonable and constructive manner.

Barthes develops his binary opposition between texts and works in terms of seven topics, which I shall not recapitulate in detail here. The themes are by now quite familiar: works fit nicely within static classificatory schemes, while texts are paradoxical and defy all taxonomies. Works have stable identities and can be located in space and time, whereas texts are open-ended activities and processes. Works have stable meanings, but texts are plural and demonic. "My name is legion, for we are many," says the text, while works are associated with, and belong to, individual human subjects—the authors who created them. Discrete and stable social roles and identities are dissolved in textuality, where there are no judges, teachers, confessors, and analysts, just a depersonalized play of signifiers. In the world of the work, reading and writing are distinct activities of particular agents, but in textuality they are part of a single, symmetrical process. Barthes wanted the distinction between work and text to carry a number of sociological and political connotations: if the world of textuality is not exactly a social utopia, it is at the very least a linguistic one, for in the open field of intertextuality the final transparency of signifying relations has been achieved: no more stable institutions, no more private property, no fixed rules, categories, and distinctions. Every text is the intertext of another text, and hence belongs to the intertextual as such; it can be indefinitely subdivided, just as it can connect up with other parts of the textual network, in a kind of partouze of signifiers. And so if the work can sometimes give pleasure, it is the text that brings the total release of *jouissance*.

Thus ran Barthes's motifs. He framed his presentation of them with some important disclaimers, beginning with the admission that his remarks were not meant to be taken as arguments but merely as metaphors, and ending by saying that there could be no theory of textuality because the text, as such, defies all metalanguages and cannot be the object of any form of knowledge. Strictly speaking, textuality is supposed to be sublime and unknowable, so Barthes can hardly pretend to have accurately situated it in opposition to the category of the work. Yet he nonetheless presents the overall transition from work to text as being part of a larger epistemological shift, which is itself said to belong to a genuine historical mutation. Barthes seems to be sincerely asserting that the category of the work has really been overturned and replaced by the play of textuality, just as, in his opinion, all Newtonian concepts have been completely replaced by Einsteinian ones—a cliché of framework relativist approaches to science. And even if Barthes was only just playing around and not making any serious historical assertions, as he seems to admit, many are the literary scholars who have taken his remarks very seriously. Thus Josué V. Harari included a translation of "De l'oeuvre au texte" in his influential poststructuralist anthology *Textual Strategies*, writing in the introduction that Barthes's essay manifests a fundamental change of perception of the literary object (39). Barthes's main themes have indeed found many echoes in contemporary literary theory, where it is often taken for granted that concepts of text and discourse are superior to such outmoded categories as author and work.

At first glance, the notion of textuality seems to have the virtue of recognizing and promoting a maximum degree of interaction and freedom. This impression is directly connected to the anticlassificatory and holistic bent of the critical tendency that Barthes expresses. Not only are the unity and integrity of the individual work of art disrupted, but the multiple fragments of the work-turned-text are themselves brought into a multiplicity of relations with all other texts. We are meant to contrast this sort of claim favorably to the repressive categorial systems of librarians and old style literary historians, who impose the pigeonholes of discipline, genre, period, and Library of Congress classifications onto the open field of textuality, where everything interacts with everything else. Shouldn't we all prefer the latter, more liberating framework, privileging a realm of maximum semiotic freedom over the disciplinary regime of the work, with its name, rank, and serial number? Yes, of course, on the surface of it, one wants to agree with such liberating ideals, but when we begin to think more carefully about the situation, the inadequacies of the textual revolution come to light.

To start with a very basic point, it seems to me that critics who advance the concept of intertextuality certainly promise a maximum of freedom and interaction, but that promise can only be kept by means of a radical weakening of the kinds of interaction and freedom that are in question (for background and useful clarification of the notion of intertextuality, see Hermerén). In such a context, what "interaction" really means is this: every textual item X is "somehow related to" every other textual item Y. And the "freedom" that is offered is a matter of literary critics being allowed to think of ways in which any textual item X is somehow related to any other textual item Y. Now, "somehow related to" is about the most vague and overly general predicate one can think of; and the claim that every linguistic utterance or inscription is somehow related to every other linguistic utterance or inscription is trivially true and totally uninformative. By the way, there is no reason to limit this sort of claim to texts: as a matter of principle, every item in the universe is similar to every other item in an infinite number of respects, just as every item in the universe is different from every other item in the universe in an infinite number of respects. So if we are going to champion an intertextual revolution in which the multiple segments of all possible works are brought into interaction, we need to have a more interesting sense of the kinds of relations that are to be explored and invented in this manner. Although it is no doubt true that we can take pleasure from juxtaposing different textual items in our minds, what is the cognitive value and importance of a critic's reports about such *correspondances générales?* It may be humorous, and even riotously transgressive, to compare passages from works by Hegel and Jean Genet, but what is learned from the juxtaposition? My claim in what follows will be that such an approach is ill suited to teach us anything about either the aesthetic or the sociopolitical issues that lead us to take an interest in texts in the first place.

It is logically possible to conceive of semiosis as an infinite field of multiple, open-ended, purely textual relations, but this idea conflicts with any number of deeply entrenched practices and discriminations that are respected even by those critics who claim to be in favor of a totally unconstrained form of textuality. Although such critics may systematically stop using the words *work,* "*oeuvre,*" "*ouvrage,*" "*Werk,*" and "*opera,*" replacing them with such terms as *text, discourse,* and "*unité discursive,*" the ways in which these latter terms are employed continue to be oriented by some of the most basic categories associated with the former list of terms. In short, in many cases the revolution is in actual practice more terminological than conceptual. A telling example can be found in Barthes's own essay. According to the literal content of his theoretical proclamations, Barthes advocates severing all relations between texts and authors, the implicit formula being, text equals work minus author, which may be taken to imply that the way to get from the work to the text is to forget the author. But in practice,

Barthes continues to rely on such filiations in a fundamental way, designating textual unities and pertinent textual systems by means of proper names. He also categorizes textuality in terms of periods, speaking of "The Middle Ages," the classical period, and modernity, which means that texts are still being situated— however schematically—in a context determined by the time and place of the author's activity. It is hard to see how any of this talk is compatible with the wilder claims about the dissolution of all classificatory notions in the sea of textuality: if the concept of textuality is one that severs all anchorings to individual agents and authors, as Barthes himself claims, it is a misnomer to speak of "Bataille's text" because the latter expression assumes that a text or corpus of texts can accurately be referred to as a single writer's work. Barthes contradicts himself here, just as his own writerly practices necessarily correspond to the practical category of the work more than to the ideal theory of limitless textuality: the essay is signed Roland Barthes, has a beginning and an end, and thus stands as a work that is clearly delimited from the other works printed alongside it. The same basic point is what is being exploited when people cattily remark that for all of their talk of an impersonal *écriture*, poststructuralists still insist on having their names, and in some cases, photographs, on the cover of their books, and no doubt would complain vehemently should their royalty checks be paid to the order of Monsieur LeTexte.

What would be required for such performative self-contradictions to be avoided, or in other words, for the critic's writerly practice to live up to the theoretical program of a complete intertextual revolution? What I want to argue is not that the move from work to text is impossible, but that the price that would have to be paid to achieve such a revolution is very high, for it is a matter of discarding a number of basic conceptual constraints that are the enabling conditions of many valuable practices. To grasp this point, let us try to imagine a world of textuality devoid of the "author function." Imagine, then, a new textual institution, or system of institutions, in which all of the world's written documents have been thoroughly scanned and stored in the vast memory of a central computer. All of the old printed and written documents, being at once dangerous and obsolete, have been locked away somewhere. But this is no oppressive regime: everyone has access to computer terminals and can call up to the screen the electronic version of any document or documents. What is more, everyone can freely type in any new text, which will automatically be added into the computer's memory, becoming available to all other users. No text is inaccessible, then, and there are no constraints on publication: no overbearing editors, anonymous readers, evaluating committees, and so on.

The signifiers are already getting pretty emancipated, but we have not yet imagined Barthes's completely impersonal textual society, or the anonymous murmurings that Michel Foucault fancies at the end of "What Is an Author?" (for background and a valuable critical discussion of Foucault's essay, see Chartier). To do that, we have to make a few changes as we create our textual data bank. We have to strip away all the proper names, as well as all the dates and any other information that could possibly have the function of anchoring the different morsels of textuality to a particular agent and particular context of production. Once this has been done, the resultant string of sentences would no longer be interrupted by "illusory" connections between authors and texts, and readers would no longer have any way of reliably linking chunks of text with knowledge about individual or collective authors. Someone who had just typed a string in would, presumably, be momentarily in a position to recognize that unit of text as his or her own work, but in general, textuality would be anonymous and decontextualized, and therefore—or so the theory goes—open to an endless array of liberating readings and pleasant new connections, in short, the maximum of interaction between texts.

But even if we wanted to go this far, there is a technical problem here of some interest, for it is not clear what method could be used to catalog and access different segments of the endless string of textuality. Should units be numbered to make possible reiterated access of a single document without a lengthy search, and if so, what would the pertinent unit be—sentences, paragraphs, or something else? Should sentences or larger chunks typed in at a particular time by one user be indexed with a single number? But that would have the effect of reinforcing the concept of the work, for a single textual unit would be identified by reference to a single producer: calling up textual unit number 1,332, for example, I would at least know that some one agent had entered, if not composed, this string, so there would still be a sense in which the text would also be someone's work, and I might have the misfortune of starting to associate attitudes or even a personality with what I read. How could texts be cataloged and accessed without in any way relying on the categories of author and work?

One solution would be to take all the world's books and articles and break them down into strings of randomly numbered, interspersed sentences. That way, readers would not be in any danger of reading sentences in the order some author had intended them to be read. If I called up sentences numbered 15,000 to 16,000, the 1,000-sentence-long chunk of text on the screen could in principle be a kind of surrealist *cadavre exquis* to which one thousand different writers had unwittingly contributed. It would be impossible for me to have access to the string constituted by all the texts George Bataille ever wrote, for his sentences would not be consecutively numbered or identified in any other way. And if I typed in a three-hundred-page monograph, the machine would automatically give each sentence a random number (not a Becker number, but a "Mallarmé" number), and then distribute these numbered sentences randomly within the vast intertext. Given such a textual institution, what Barthes called the "myth of filiation" would at last be definitively extirpated. One might imagine that certain subversive activities would emerge, such as typing in monstrously long sentences in the hope that something like the integrity of a work or statement could be preserved and made public; but the machine could no doubt be made to parse such a work and break it down into anonymous texts.

The point of my little thought experiment is to suggest that we do not really want to bring about a situation where all works are transformed into texts in Barthes's demonic sense. There are important ways in which works are identified and individuated that would be lost in an impersonal field of textuality. One way to understand what would be lost along with the category of the work is to explore the implications of one of Jorge Luis Borges's most famous stories (philosophers who have discussed this example include William E. Tolhurst, Samuel C. Wheeler, Gregory Currie, and David Davies, whose views on this topic may be contrasted to those of Nelson Goodman and Catherine Elgin; Currie presents a different example in his "Work and Text"). Borges's narrator describes a twentieth-century Frenchman, Pierre Menard, who has composed a fragment of Cervantes's *Don Quixote*. Let us imagine instead that Menard goes on to complete his task, composing, word for word, the text of Cervantes. Although the two texts are identical, our response to the two works that they instantiate differs. As Borges's narrator remarks, "The archaic style of Menard— in the last analysis, a foreigner—suffers from a certain affectation. Not so that of his precursor, who handles easily the ordinary Spanish of his time" (53). Menard's work has a relation to Flaubert's *Salammbô* that Cervantes's does not; and so on.

The texts are the same, that is, they are semiotically identical tokens of the same type of text, but they constitute different works. How can this be? It would seem that the conclusion that needs to be drawn is that the very notion of a work is not reducible to a string of sentences that is a token of a certain semiotic text type, for if that is all a work is composed of, then Cervantes and Menard wrote the same work, an idea that is, as Borges's narrator correctly points out, quite wrong. And if works are not reducible to text types, that means the identity of a work essentially involves such factors as the time of the text's composition and the identity of the agent or agents who created the work.

The upshot of this analysis can be put more precisely by adopting some basic notions from the mathematical theory of functions (see Levy for background). As I would like to make my point in a manner that will be at once accurate and comprehensible, I must risk boring my readers by sketching in a few elementary notions. Let A_1 and A_2 be two sets, neither of which is empty. The product (also known as the Cartesian product), $A_1 \times A_2$, of A_1 and A_2 consists of all the pairs (a_1, a_2), such that the first element, a_1, is a member of the set A_1, and the second element, a_2, is a member of A_2. A simple example would be a case where the set A_1 is composed of only two elements: $A_1 = \{0,1\}$. A_2 has three elements: $A_2 = \{x,y,z\}$. The product of the two, $A_1 \times A_2$, contains six pairs: $\{(0,x),$ $(0,y),$ $(0,z),$ $(1,x),$ $(1,y),$ $(1,z)\}$. A simple literary example runs as follows. Take the set of (extant) novels by Marivaux, $A_1 = \{Le\ paysan\ parvenu,\ La\ Vie\ de\ Marianne\}$, and the set of (extant) novels by Apuleius, $A_2 = \{The\ Golden\ Ass\}$. The product of these two sets, $A_1 \times A_2$, equals a set having two pairs: $\{(Le\ Paysan\ parvenu,\ The$ $Golden\ Ass),\ (La\ Vie\ de\ Marianne,\ The\ Golden\ Ass)\}$. Now, a relation R is simply any subset of $A_1 \times A_2$, where A_1 is called the domain of R and A_2 is called the range of R. When we specify a relation where the domain and the range are the same set, e.g., A, we then say that R, a member of the product $A \times A$, is a relation on A. A total function is a type of relation, defined as the subset of a Cartesian product, $A_1 \times A_2$, consisting of all pairs (x,y), where each x in A_1 occurs exactly once and each y in A_2 occurs at least once. Such a function is often called a mapping of A_1 on A_2; it may be conveniently thought of as an operator that associates a value (from A_2) with points in the domain A_1. A function is written $f:A \to B$, and is the set of all pairs (a,b) where a is a member of A, b is a member of B, and $b = f(a)$. Think of a function as reaching into a set A, taking one of its members, and finding the unique member of set B, $b = f(a)$, that is associated with it. If for all elements of the set A, the function is defined, that is, there is a $b = f(a)$, then the function is said to be a "total function $A \to B$." If f is not defined on all elements of A, then the function is said to be partial. A total function $f:A \to B$ is said to be "onto" if for each b in B, there exists an a in A such that $f(a) = b$; the function is one-to-one if it maps unique elements of A to unique elements of B. A function that is both onto and one-to-one is called a bijection.

To illustrate these notions and to demonstrate their pertinence in the present context, let us imagine that the elements of set A are "texts." More precisely, they are semiotically equivalent (that is, identically spelled) text types. All identically spelled instances of the present sentence—be they in handwritten, typographic, or electronic form—then, would be tokens of a single text type and hence a member of the set A.[1] So would an infinite number of larger chunks or textual strings. Let us imagine also that another set, B, is composed of all "literary works of art." (Readers will of course have scruples about the idea that literary works constitute a well-delimited class, but let them, for the sake of the argument, concentrate on whatever items they deem it highly reasonable to call literary works.) We then construct the Cartesian product of these two sets and ask whether there are any interesting relations defined by subsets of it. Are there any functions—even partial ones—that map texts onto works, or works onto texts? This question is crucial insofar as the concept of functionality is basic to the idea of deterministic computation.

The answer is that no semantic function, not even a partial function, maps all text types onto literary works. Some types of textual inscriptions (indeed an infinite number of them) are not correlated with works at all. Some text types may be correlated with more than one work (as in the extended case of the works of Pierre Menard and Cervantes). Nor is there a total or partial function mapping works onto types of inscriptions: some works may be correlated with more than one type of inscription, as in cases where there are different textual versions of the same work (thus in the list of Pierre Menard's works, Borges includes a symbolist sonnet that appeared twice in the same literary journal, but with slight variations). More generally, the identity of a given literary work is usually not held to be destroyed as a result of minor variations of spelling, although of course there are cases where changing a single character would entail massive differences.

The situation can be visualized, then, as follows:

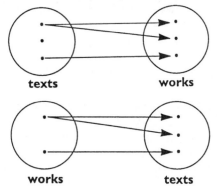

The pair of sets on the left illustrates the fact that there is (at least) one member of the set of texts that is not correlated with a member of the set of works; also, there is (at least) one text that is correlated with more than one work. The pair of sets on the right shows that (at least) one work is correlated with more than one text. Is this meant to imply that relations between texts and works are simply chaotic? Not at all, but the argument does have some revealing implications concerning the ways in which we actually do pair off literary works and their textual instantiations. If for any literary work there is no one text type with which it may be associated (and which may be said to instantiate it), how are works effectively identified? This question is not readily answered, but one strong hypothesis that may be proposed in response to it runs as follows: in practice, particular correlations between text types and works are guided by pragmatic factors involving aspects of the attitudes (beliefs, motives, plans, etc.) of the agent responsible for the creation of the textual artifact in a given context. If the two variants on the symbolist sonnet are taken to be instances of one work, this is at least in part because Menard intentionally published both variants under the same title, proposing them to his readers as variants of the same literary work. The reference to authorial intention may be more external and global than this example allows, as in the case of the multiple and highly divergent editions of a single (unfinished) work by Marcel Proust. Our knowledge that Proust believed himself to be elaborating a single work while writing the disparate manuscripts militates against the decision that any two of the many different possible editions would in fact constitute "different works," and this in spite of the fact that we can surely identify significantly different aesthetic properties in the different editions. The plurality of aesthetically different manuscript variations and editions does not warrant the conclusion that Proust wrote more than one work.

These observations about the individuation of works entail some important constraints on literary appreciation, which is revealed to depend on the "author function" in ways that textualists hardly suspected. Reference to pragmatic factors may be needed to determine the assignment of a text type to a particular genre, as in cases where a text may be read as fantastic fiction, as a hoax, or as earnest supernaturalism. Reference to the author's context can determine the nature of a work's stylistic properties: textual features recognized as highly innovative and unconventional in one context could be viewed as archaic and imitative in another, for example, should it be learned that the inscription was a twentieth-century work and not a reprint of an eighteenth-century original. Reference to the author's intentions is even necessary in determining some of the most basic features of the text, as in cases where the only reasonable reading is one based on the decision that the author has unintentionally committed a spelling or typographical error. We often read texts that have been corrected or modernized and do not reasonably doubt that they can offer us access to the work's aesthetically relevant properties. We also deem it a mistake to correct the capitalization and spelling in poems by ee cummings, a decision that also involves an individuation of a work's features in terms of beliefs about authorial intention.

The upshot of all this is that our framework for understanding and individuating literary phenomena relies heavily on action descriptions and related assumptions about agency. Bringing these assumptions into the foreground reveals the inadequacy of prevalent ideas about a totally impersonal domain of textual process. It does not follow from these points, however, that one must subscribe to an extreme version of intentionalism (e.g., the untenable idea that all meaning is the speaker's meaning; for background on intentions and varieties of intentionalism, see Livingston and Mele, and Mele and Livingston).

So far I have stressed the kinds of deeply entrenched aesthetic intuitions and practices that run contrary to the program for a textualist revolution, and one may anticipate the objection that the framework of aesthetic ideas is only a "bourgeois" construct that deserves to be replaced in favor of sociopolitical analyses. If the shift from works to texts disrupts the framework of aesthetic concepts, so much the better—or so the objection would run. The "textual revolution" may seem appealing to many because it is at least ostensibly animated by emancipatory ideals: the cult of art and individual genius, an expression of the values of one class and culture, is to be replaced by a transgressive and transdisciplinary exploration of the open fields of textual practice. But even if one were to grant that rather sweeping thesis, the shift to the context of a pragmatic, deaestheticized approach to literary history only brings to light other crippling weaknesses of the textualist revolution, namely, the complete absence of anything remotely resembling a responsible, informed, and plausible framework of sociopolitical analysis. This point is fairly obvious when it is a matter of someone proposing to substitute *jouissance* for justice and carnival for emancipation and equality. But it also holds for a number of critics who at first glance appear to be engaging in an alternative form of literary historiography but whose textualist antics in fact distance their work from genuine sociohistorical explanations. Again and again, the crippling shortcoming is the idea that spinning out transgressive textual associations can somehow promote historical understanding and emancipatory values, when in fact neither of those goals can be advanced in the absence of the right sorts of conceptual tools. In what follows, I shall support this contention by arguing that one of the most important pragmatic categories that is lost in a field of impersonal textuality is the strong concept of interaction. This—and not a purely textualist "interaction"—is the notion that is needed by critics who want to distance themselves from what they take to be the "individualist" bias of classical aesthetics.

What is this concept of interaction, and how is it to be distinguished from the weak sorts of interaction that may be attributed to texts and discourses? The kind of interaction I have in mind can be introduced in a number of different ways, but I think it best in the present context to begin with a literary illustration. One of the finest examples I can think of is Edgar Allan Poe's "The Purloined Letter," a story in which Poe's narrator stresses the detective Dupin's ability to outthink both the chief of police and the villainous Minister D——. Dupin explains his superior manner of reasoning by recounting the success of a schoolboy at the game of "even and odd," which consists of a series of guesses as to whether one's opponent has chosen to conceal an even or an odd number of marbles in his closed fist. The schoolboy wins all the marbles because he is able to identify his opponents' reasoning: the one alternates from even to odd and is easily beaten; the next swerves away from that obvious pattern but in a way that is itself obvious, so that the schoolboy outwits him as well. In the same way, Dupin manages to fathom and to surpass the Minister's strategic rationale: the Minister knows that the police chief will assume the purloined letter is hidden away carefully in some nook or cranny and will conduct the search for the letter in keeping with that idea; thus the Minister leaves his home open to the policemen's protracted search, tricking them into believing that their search has been exhaustive. But Dupin, having grasped the trick of hiding the letter in a conspicuous place, cleverly deceives the Minister and, by means of a diversion, steals it away.

Poe articulates his intuitions in the somewhat limited framework of a drawing room detective story, but the more general concept of interaction to which he points is by no means restricted to such a context (for a compilation of post-structuralist commentaries, none of which articulates the basic game-theoretical concepts, see Muller and Richardson). The basic idea is that there are situations in which the consequences of each individual's actions depend directly on what the others do: in the game of odd and even, the success or failure of my guess about the marbles depends on what the other player has decided, just as the other player's decision will be successful or not depending on the nature of my guess. This interdependence of outcomes can be either known or unknown to the parties who are part of such a situation; when the interdependence of outcomes is known to at least one of the parties, a particular type of interactive reasoning becomes possible. In its strongest form, both parties are aware of the crucial interdependence, in which case each party tries to base his or her decision about what to do by reasoning about what the other party is going to do, the extra twist being that one can also be aware that the other is aware of one's awareness of the interdependence. The player does not simply try to make an accurate guess; instead, his or her reasoning is a matter of trying to outguess the other party, who is also engaging in an effort to out-outguess the other, and so on. This kind of reasoning is referred to as reciprocal expectations and is at the heart of so-called game-theoretical models of social interaction, which many take to be foundational for all social science (for background, see Harsanyi and Selten, Schelling). A point that needs to be stressed here is that although the Poe example involves a situation of bitter rivalry and conflict between the parties involved, game-theoretical models of the role of reciprocal expectations in interaction do not make any such general assumption, for the claim is that such expectations are also involved in situations of cooperation and in situations where the players' interests partly coincide and partly diverge. An example of a game-theoretical application of this notion of interaction to a cooperative situation is David Lewis's famous analysis of conventions, his claim being that it is a network of reciprocal beliefs that makes it possible for two or more parties to solve a particular variety of coordination problems (for a discussion and literary-historical application, see my "Convention and Literary Explanations").

The notion of reciprocal expectations makes possible a very strong conception of interaction because in such situations the influence that one agent can have on another agent's activity can take the form not only of a direct, causal intervention but also of mere projection and anticipation: one agent's belief that another agent is going to do something suffices to reorient the first agent's plans—a process that can be at work simultaneously for each agent in the interaction. Here we have a real *Wechselwirkung*, or strong form of simultaneous reciprocity. A particularly interesting variety of bootstrapping may be the result of this sort of process: John expects Jack to perform some action, and when Jack gets wind of this expectation, Jack decides to do that very action because of John's expectation, the result being that John's expectation works as a self-fulfilling prophecy. Following the basic insights of John Maynard Keynes, André Orléan and others have used an interactive pattern of this form to develop rigorous mathematical models of the dynamics of financial markets: expecting other parties to sell, an agent may then decide to sell a certain commodity, which sends the signal to the others that its value is going to fall; when these parties sell so as to cut their anticipated losses, they provide an apparent confirmation of the first party's expectations. Soon everyone is selling. This kind of interactive mechanism can produce either a radical convergence or a radical divergence of belief and action; when expectations converge and the agents know it, there can be the strong type of consensus known as mutual belief or common knowledge, which for some theorists is the key to successful communication because it guides and sustains common patterns of inference and reflexivity in a community. When reciprocal expectations diverge, false consensus and pluralistic ignorance become possible, as do diverse forms of competition, radical uncertainty, and crisis.

What has this got to do with literature? I have suggested above that texts cannot engage in the strong form of interaction that I have just described, for the simple reason that they lack the kinds of cognitive and practical capacities that are required to form expectations and decisions. Texts are symbolic artifacts, types of semiotic inscriptions or utterances that, once created by sentient agents, lack the kinds of causal powers required to engage in action or interaction. But texts do serve as forms of mediation in interactions between actual agents, especially when those agents think of them as works and not as depersonalized texts. Thus a theory of reciprocal expectations and strong interaction is directly pertinent to our understanding of important aspects of literary history. The relations between writers and other writers, between writers and readers, and between readers and other readers can involve interaction in both a weak and a strong sense. The strong sense holds, for example, whenever a reader, in thinking about the meaning of a work, considers not only that the meaning depends on what the writer had in mind but also that what the writer had in mind involved specific expectations about what the reader would expect, and so on. Similarly, writers form expectations about the public's background beliefs and modes of response, but they also can anticipate ways in which the reader will be trying to take into account those very writerly expectations, and this higher-level expectation can shape the writer's strategy. This sort of process can contribute either to shared understanding and communicational coordination, or to deception, misunderstanding, and ambiguity. It can reinforce conventional modes of literary exchange, or be part of innovative and transgressive modes of writing and reading. Thus reciprocal expectations do not constitute any simple, deterministic mechanism; instead, they designate a process that is open to contextual influences and historical contingency, which is an additional reason why this is a model of interaction that is of particular value in the context of literary research.

What I am suggesting, then, is that the notion of interdependent decision making guided by reciprocal expectations is the strongest concept of interaction available to us ("strongest" in the sense of most "specific" and far-reaching in its applications, implications, and explanatory power). As such, this concept ought to be employed by scholars who insist on the importance of a pragmatic and sociohistorical turn in literary studies. Yet the tenets of a textualist revolution run contrary to these intuitions, for there is no way texts or discourses can plausibly be said to engage in reciprocal expectations. Thus we ought to abandon the textualist tenets, for not only do they fail to square with the basic discriminations of literary aesthetics, but they are also too weak to support the project of a political and historical approach to culture.

Notes

I am grateful to David Davies and Gregory Currie for valuable discussions of the issues taken up in this essay. I discuss their views in "The Wolves and the Manger" and in "Texts, Works, and Literature."

1. It follows that text types are not particulars localizable in a single space-time, and the same is true of works. In this regard, Barthes makes an especially egregious error, for he contends that unlike a text, a literary work is a concrete, physical object: "L'oeuvre est un fragment de substance, elle occupe une portion de l'espace des livres (par exemple dans une bibliothèque)" (226). It is simply false to say that a literary work is a physical object that can be located on one's bookshelf. There can be multiple copies of the text of a work, and no one copy or token is identical to the work.

Works Cited

Barthes, Roland. "De l'oeuvre au texte." *La Revue d'esthétique* 3 (1971): 225–32.
Borges, Jorge Luis. "Pierre Menard, Author of Don Quixote." Trans. Anthony Bonner. *Ficciones*. By Borges. New York: Grove, 1962. 45–56.
Chartier, Roger. *L'Ordre des livres: lecteurs, auteurs, bibliothèques en Europe entre XIVe et XVIIe Siecle*. Paris: Alinea, 1992.
Currie, Gregory. *The Nature of Fiction*. Cambridge: Cambridge UP, 1990.
———. *An Ontology of Art*. New York: St. Martin's, 1988.
———. "Work and Text." *Mind* 100 (1991): 325–40.
Davies, David. "Text, Context, and Character: Goodman on the Literary Artwork." *Canadian Journal of Philosophy* 21 (1991): 331–45.

Foucault, Michel. "What Is an Author?" *Textual Strategies: Perspectives in Post-Structuralist Criticism*. Ed. Josué V. Harari. Ithaca: Cornell UP, 1979. 141–60.

Goodman, Nelson, and Catherine Z. Elgin. *Reconceptions in Philosophy and Other Arts and Sciences*. Indianapolis: Hackett, 1988.

Harari, Josué V. "Critical Factions/Critical Fictions." *Textual Strategies: Perspectives in Post-Structuralist Criticism*. Ed. Harari. Ithaca: Cornell UP, 1979. 17–72.

Harsanyi, John C., and Reinhard Selten. *A General Theory of Equilibrium Selection in Games*. Cambridge: MIT P, 1988.

Hermerén, Göran. *Art, Reason, and Tradition: On the Role of Rationality in Interpretation and Explanation of Works of Art*. Stockholm: Almqvist, 1991.

Keynes, John Maynard. *The General Theory of Employment Interest and Money*. London: Macmillan, 1973.

Levy, Leon S. *Discrete Structures of Computer Science*. New York: Wiley, 1980.

Lewis, David K. *Convention: A Philosophical Study*. Cambridge: Harvard UP, 1969.

———. "Languages and Language." *Language, Mind, and Knowledge*. Ed. Keith Gunderson. Minneapolis: U of Minneapolis P, 1975. 3–35.

Livingston, Paisley. "Convention and Literary Explanations." *Rules and Conventions: Philosophy, Literature, Social Theory*. Ed. Mette Hjort. Baltimore: Johns Hopkins UP, 1992. 67–94.

———. "Texts, Works, and Literature." *Spiel* (forthcoming).

———. "The Wolves and the Manger: Analytic Aesthetics and the Dogmas of Poststructuralism." *Poetics Today* 13 (1992): 369–86.

Livingston, Paisley, and Alfred R. Mele. "Intentions and Interpretations." *Modern Language Notes* 107 (1992): 931–49.

Mele, Alfred R., and Paisley Livingston. "Intention and Literature." *Stanford French Review* 16 (1992): 173–96.

Muller, John P., and William J. Richardson, eds. *The Purloined Poe: Lacan, Derrida, and Psychoanalytic Reading*. Baltimore: Johns Hopkins UP, 1988.

Orléan, André. "Mimetic Contagion and Speculative Bubbles." *Theory and Decision* 27 (1989): 63–93.

———. "Mimétisme et anticipations rationelles: une perspective keynésienne." *Recherches économiques de Louvain* 52 (1986): 45–66.

Poe, Edgar Allan. "The Purloined Letter." *Collected Works of Edgar Allan Poe*. 3 vols. Ed. Thomas Olive Mabbott. Cambridge: Harvard UP, 1978. 3:972–96.

Schelling, Thomas C. *The Strategy of Conflict*. Cambridge: Harvard UP, 1960.

Tolhurst, William E. "On What a Text Is and How It Means." *British Journal of Aesthetics* 19 (1979): 3–14.

Tolhurst, William E., and Samuel C. Wheeler III. "On Textual Individuation." *Philosophical Studies* 35 (1979): 187–97.

Play, Mutation, and Reality Acceptance: Toward a Theory of Literary Experience

Nancy Easterlin

Why do we bother with literature? This is not merely an interesting question for literary theory but a fundamental one, because with it speculation begins about what actual social or psychological purposes are served by the writing and reading of literary texts. Yet many current literary theorists, perhaps because of their disaffection with what is now called "the subject," largely avoid this question. In so doing, they neglect, from the pragmatist's point of view, one of the major obligations of the theorist: to mediate between speculation and the cumulative picture of available reality which we derive from our experience.

I am not convinced, for instance, by the materialist critic who insists that literature requires no definition beyond being another form of work, because he or she cannot tell me why Hawthorne wrote *The Scarlet Letter* after finding employment in the Custom's House, where he in fact earned a living, as he had not done at his writing. The predictable rejoinder that Hawthorne imbibed the ideology of his culture, which "valorized" literary production, is not supported by the facts of the historical case. The arbiters of nineteenth-century American culture were rather more suspicious than supportive of literary enterprises; moreover, the tendency of that culture to judge texts according to primarily ideological criteria militated against a positive appraisal of Hawthorne's work. It is inaccurate, then, to say that Hawthorne's decision to pursue a career as a writer was motivated primarily by either monetary or ideological reasons.[1]

As this single example indicates, theories that evade questions about the origin and function of art suffer from a fundamental inadequacy. A demonstrable number of individuals will withstand substantial personal and economic sacrifices to engage in artistic activities even when such activities are held in low regard by the culture at large. Since literary texts are produced by individuals, and since some but not all "subjects" throughout history have elected to be writers (usually in spite of numerous hardships), one of the questions a legitimate theory must take into account is why, in fact, they've bothered. By the same token, we need an idea of why people read literature, an activity without monetary remuneration for most and, I need hardly add, with less than entirely encouraging remuneration for the professor of literature.

The recent compartmentalization of literary theories into ideological and other categories—feminist, Marxist, reader response, and the like—is counterproductive to a sophisticated inquiry into what literature might do and be, fostering through false categorization the sort of intellectual oversimplification I alluded to above. Consistent with their singularity of focus, poststructuralist theorists tend to offer rigid formulations of the ideological relations between writer, text, and reader and of the correlation between political stances and specific literary modes, genres, and forms. Such formulations result in the seemingly contradictory phenomena of false specialization and overgeneralization. On the one hand, many current critics deem it contemptibly naive to consider both authorial intention and reader response during the interpretive process; on the other, they offer totalizing definitions of particular modes (e.g., fictional realism) and of specific forms (e.g., iambic pentameter).[2]

The desire for strict definitions and universalizing interpretations which motivates much poststructuralist theory runs counter to our available knowledge of literary activity. The production and use of literary texts represents a complex, multifaceted, and continually transforming phenomenon; it has an evolutionary basis but is both highly determined and continually transformed by cultural factors. Theoretical constructs that ignore the complexity and variety of authorial purposes, final texts, and reader responses, and that divorce social factors from biological and psychological ones, misconstrue grossly the relationship between individuals and texts and suggest increasingly that literature and all the activity surrounding it is essentially meaningless.

To demonstrate the kind of theoretical oversimpification pervasive throughout poststructuralist theory, I will discuss some of the assertions of Catherine Belsey's *Critical Practice*, giving special consideration to Belsey's definition and analysis of expressive realism. I have chosen this popular introduction to materialist criticism not because it represents a particularly egregious example of current theory but because it is representative of the current tendency to make universalizing claims from within a narrow perspective. In fact, the view I wish particularly to address here, that mimetic literature indoctrinates readers in a prevailing bourgeois ideology, is not at all restricted to Belsey's critical denomination but accepted by a number of poststructuralist schools, including so-called French feminism. While many critics who adopt this antirealist stance consider questions of reading outside the domain of their chosen perspectives, the antirealist position nevertheless rests on an implicit characterization of the reader as passive and manipulated. Such a problematical assumption should not go unchallenged. Poststructuralist criticism has made an extremely valuable contribution in its insistence that literary critics and theorists investigate their assumptions; now that the directives of poststructuralism represent a dominant discourse in literary studies, it is logically necessary that the assumptions and assertions of these related schools of critical thought invite honest critique.

The alternative Marxist approach Belsey sketches in *Critical Practice* is recommended as a replacement for what she conceives of as the traditional attitude in criticism, defined by her as "the commonsense view of literature" (1). According to Belsey, the traditional approach endorses and promotes a dominant aesthetic—expressive realism (7). Both the presumed traditional critical approach and its corresponding mode are unfavorable from the materialist perspective because their underlying assumptions about subjectivity and causality reinforce a belief in individualism, which in turn reinforces capitalist ideology. Thus, in keeping with other poststructuralist critics who draw on Saussure and Foucault, Belsey assumes that literature has a direct and powerful ideological influence.

Because Belsey is making such extraordinary claims for the power of literary texts, her definitions of the presumed hegemonic critical approach and the literary mode require careful inspection. Citing a scene from David Lodge's *Changing Places* in which the English professor Philip Swallow and a student discuss a projected novel, she comments that

> professor and student share an assumption that novels are about life, that they are written from personal experience and that this is the source of their authenticity. . . . Common sense assumes that valuable literary texts, those which are in a special way worth reading, tell truths—about the period which produced them, about the world in general or about human nature—and that in doing so they express the particular perceptions, the individual insights of their authors.
>
> Common sense also offers this way of approaching literature not as a self-concious and deliberate practice, a method based on a reasoned theoretical position, but as the "obvious" mode of reading, the "natural" way of approaching literary works. (2)

Ironically, Belsey offers no theoretical, philosophical, or pedagogical source for this definition of common sense, a point to which I'll return in a moment. A more immediate question arises with respect to her interpretation. What person either in the literary profession or outside of it assumes that all works of literature are "about the world in general or about human nature" in anything like the literal-minded way Belsey suggests here? The implication of her statement is that the "commonsense view of literature" puts an absolute premium on literary realism. Yet in the example she herself gives, the student and professor assume only that the novel *under discussion* is realistic, not all literature. Wily Smith, a white student writing a novel about a black child growing up in the ghetto, tells Swallow, "Like the story is autobiographical. All I need is technique" (67). Smith himself, then, defines the novel as not only realistic but autobiographical. Given a set of cultural assumptions about what constitutes an autobiographical novel, Swallow is understandably perplexed by the logical impossibility of Smith's project. While a great number of canonical texts do indeed correlate with what Belsey terms "the commonsense view of literature," a brief moment of reflection on the canon alerts us to the absolute senselessness of such a critical stance. Spenser's *Faerie Queene*, Sterne's *Tristram Shandy*, Byron's *Don Juan*, Joyce's *Ulysses*, Nabokov's *Pale Fire*—these works have surely not been included in the canon on the basis of the literal-minded critical values that Belsey considers dominant.[3]

Moreover, common sense, implicitly defined in Belsey's discussion as the license to take for granted unarticulated and narrow views of art, emerges from her discussion as a sorely abused concept. Sophisticated theorizing about common sense began in the eighteenth century with a group of philosophers who sought to understand how the human mental apparatus interprets data from the outside world and negotiates our relationships with it. Commonsense philosophy, then, provided significant impetus for all subsequent researches in psychology and cognition. Writing at the end of the nineteenth century, William James describes it thus:

> . . . *our fundamental ways of thinking about things are discoveries of exceedingly remote ancestors, which have been able to preserve themselves throughout the experience of all subsequent time.* They form one great stage of equilibrium in the human mind's development, the stage of *common sense.* Other stages have grafted themselves upon this stage, but have never succeeded in displacing it. . . .
>
> In practical talk, a man's common sense means his good judgment, his freedom from eccentricity, his *gumption,* to use the vernacular word. In philosophy it means something entirely different, it means his use of certain intellectual forms or categories of thought. Were we lobsters, or bees, it might be that our organization would have led to our using quite different modes from these of apprehending our experiences. . . .
>
> . . . All our conceptions are what the Germans call *denkmittel,* means by which we handle facts by thinking them. Experience merely as such doesn't come ticketed and labelled, we have first to discover what it is. . . What we usually do is first to frame some system of concepts mentally classified, serialized, or connected in some intellectual way, and then to use this as a tally by which we "keep tab" on the impressions that present themselves. (75–76)

Hence, philosophically defined, common sense represents our essential capacity to adapt and survive, which entails the application of common forms of conceptualization—identification, definition, comparison, causality, and so on—to the world around us (James 76). Thus, the ways of thinking that Belsey describes as the product of an outmoded discourse are, in the evolutionary and developmental view, basic yet flexible structures that enable us to orient ourselves in the world; they are, therefore, not a product but a *precondition* of language.

Strictly speaking, then, it is common sense, in addition to more refined systems of understanding that have evolved over time, which informs us that a great number of literary works conform to the definition Belsey attributes to the commonsense view of literature. By this we would mean that our rudimentary forms of analysis reveal that numerous literary works share a range of characteristics. In making discriminations of this kind, we rely on more specialized conceptual structures that have evolved over many centuries, through the influence of rudimentary common sense, variable real-world influences, and cultural factors. Such an understanding of common sense is humanist, as Belsey points out, but it is a far cry from the simplistic notions she attributes to the proponents of the commonsense view of literature. Strictly speaking, common sense informs us that while there are ways in which we can talk about the relationship between literature and life, and while for some texts there is a closer relationship between fictive and real events than in others, absolutely *no text* is indistinguishable from life.

Implicit in Belsey's description of the traditional approach to literature, then, is an exceptionally literalistic view of what literary activity entails. Her definition of expressive realism and the classic realist text, which dovetails with her critique of the commonsense view of literature, extends this literalism to the reader-text dynamic, and it is in her discussion of the classic realist text that serious questions emerge about the materialist conception of imaginative experience. In Belsey's rendition of Althusser's argument, the use of consistent characterization and plotting in the nineteenth-century novel "'interpellates' the reader, addresses itself to him or her directly, offering the reader as the position from which the text is most 'obviously' intelligible, the position of the *subject in (and of) ideology*" (57). The word "interpellates," designating governmental interrogation, is instructive here: according to the materialist view, the reader is effectively cross-examined and indoctrinated by the text itself. Notice also that Belsey asserts that the reader is a position *in the text*, not that as readers we align our own values with those of specific characters. Again, in her brief discussion of *Jane Eyre*, she asserts that this text "interpellates the reader as subject, as the 'you' who is addressed by the 'I' of discourse. This interpellation (address) in turn facilitates the interpolation (inclusion) of the reader in the narrative through the presentation of events from a specific and unified point of view" (76). In short, the device of direct address to the reader by the main character in *Jane Eyre* dictates subjectivity to the reader while simultaneously dictating the reader's perception of events.

For Belsey, then, the ultimate evil of expressive realism is that, in creating the semblance of a world in which standards of plausibility and probability apply, it allows us to think of others and ourselves as coherent subjects, as individuals, and thus perpetuates what to the materialist is a capitalist illusion.[4] (It is not within the parameters of this essay to take up the issue of subjectivity, but here, I think, the burden of proof rests with the materialists. History, biology, and experience all support the conviction that individuality is a long-standing rather than recently invented phenomenon; there have been shifts in ideological emphases between the individual and the collective, but there is no evidence whatsoever that either can survive without the other.) I wish to address two things in Belsey's definition of expressive realism: first, her failure to raise or acknowledge questions pertaining to the reader's knowledge of discursive practices, a failure that rests on an insupportable assumption about how human beings relate to literary texts; and second, her refusal to consider the specific content of individual texts, and her correspondingly exclusive concern with linking a particular mode or form with a specific ideology.

Now there are well-informed readers and less well-informed readers, but there are no readers in any given modern culture as poorly informed as Belsey suggests. That is, at a very basic level we all make distinctions between the kinds of activities and the kinds of discursive practices that are continually conflated in current theory. In her discussion of post-Saussurian linguistics, Belsey includes an analysis of the various signs and representations in three perfume advertisements. At the conclusion of this analysis, she asserts:

> These advertisements are a source of information about ideology, about semiotics, about the cultural and photographic codes of our society, and to that extent—and only to that extent—they tell us about the world. And yet they possess all the technical properties of realism. Literary realism works in very much the same kind of way. Like the advertisements, it constructs its signifieds out of juxtapositions of signifiers which are intelligible *not as direct reflections of an unmediated reality* but because we are familiar with the signifying systems from which they are drawn, linguistic, literary, semiotic. This process is apparent in, for instance, the construction of character in the novel. (49, my italics)

One of the assumptions underlying this passage, evident in the compunction Belsey feels to assert that language does not directly reflect an *unmediated* reality, and also evident in the passage cited earlier that announces the placement of the reader in *Jane Eyre,* is that we have been duped, psychologically and cognitively, into accepting the illusion of realism as reality itself. This is simply untrue. Not only do we distinguish reading about Jane's marriage to Rochester from the experience of witnessing a real marriage, and not only do we distinguish reading a perfume ad from actually buying perfume, but we also distinguish reading advertisements from reading novels. Very unsophisticated readers, in fact, make such distinctions; as Howard Gardner points out, a normal child has the ability to respond to art by the age of seven or eight (qtd. in Dissanayake 52).

The implication that we are made to believe that our literary experiences are unmediated, and that we do not distinguish discursive modes from one another or from direct experience, constitutes, I believe, the major underlying fallacy of much recent theory. I wonder how Belsey would respond to James Gorman's "Mother Goose Biology," in which the humor of the author's feigned outrage against the taxonomic inaccuracies of E. B. White's *Stuart Little* depends entirely on overlooking such distinctions:

> In *Stuart Little* a human family gives birth—or perhaps I should say gives rise, since this is more like speciation than reproduction—to a mouse. . . . he Littles (who are actually full size) take the mouse to their bosom, being careful not to crush him, and he becomes a valued, if small, member of the family. I can't say it's not a good story. I ended up rooting for the mouse, as I'm sure everyone does. But I can't help wishing that Mr. Little, when he was first presented with a rodent in swaddling clothes, had been as honest as my nephew, and had said to the nurse, or Mrs. Little, or whoever was around, "I don't know, it looks an awful lot like a rat to me." (31)

If we didn't distinguish between the hypothetical experiences of literature and real-world experiences, we would be as enraged by *Stuart Little* as Gorman suggests we should be. Much to our surprise, we'd find rats living beneath the subway tracks rather than in houses with human beings. But the fact is that even quite small children may imbibe tale after tale where assorted animals consort with human beings and still never make the mistake of expecting to find badgers in their Sunday finest taking tea next door.[5]

Of course, there are always exceptions that prove the rule. As Jerome Bruner points out in his recent discussion of the centrality of narrative to human cognition, since both fact and fiction gain meaning through plot, all narratives demonstrate a shadowy epistemology (52–55). Certainly the nineteenth-century readers of *The Sorrows of Young Werther* who committed suicide were victims of too close an identification with the protagonist (not to mention, poor readers of Goethe's irony). And certainly John Hinkley made no distinction between the fictional and the actual when he confused the actress Jodie Foster with the character she played in *Taxi Driver*. But just as certainly such episodes are generally viewed, within modern cultures where realistic narrative forms are common, as instances of psychopathology. Our judgment that such confusions of real and hypothetical experiences are pathological rests on a perception that imaginative experience constitutes a vital mode of relation to the actual; to conflate the real and the hypothetical, therefore, signifies the individual's failed perception of reality. As Bruner puts it, the person who acts on beliefs or desires without taking into account the outside world is "folk psychologically" insane, because his or her actions are inconsistent with the culture's shared understanding of human motivation and behavior (i.e., its folk psychology) (40). This is the waxwing sailing full flight into the image of the sky reflected in an unyielding pane of glass.[6]

As individuals, our relations with the actual—that is, the world outside ourselves—are always mediated by our cognitive apparatus and by a variety of conceptual structures, and whether or not we have consciously considered or theorized those conceptual structures, they continue to mediate for us. James includes among the basic structures of common sense the ability to distinguish fantasy from reality, but over the course of our social evolution we have developed more elaborate means of categorization, not incidentally related to advances in technology and to the proliferation of both means and modes of communication. Thus, when Belsey tells us that the perfume ads contain all the technical properties of realism, and that literary realism works in basically the same way as advertising, she is being disingenuous. The ads she is discussing rely heavily on four-color photographic art, as stories and novels do not; they contain very little text; their narrative content is simple rather than complex; and they are included in colorful, glossy magazines rather than hardback books. All of these features help us place them as a separate sort of phenomenon, one that tries to lure us into believing that we will all metamorphose into some sort of idealized female type if we go out and buy a certain brand of perfume. By comparing the features of the novel to those of the ads, Belsey is implicitly suggesting that all kinds of representational forms have a sales agenda, and that, correspondingly, all readers have a single mode of response to the broad range of discursive and representational forms she calls realistic. But her analogy rests on a failure to make distinctions we make automatically every day, on an exclusive focus on presumed latent over manifest content, and on a convenient refusal to consider the origin and function of advertising. The proliferation of advertising in the twentieth century is directly related to the proliferation of consumer products, and advertisers as well as consumers are quite aware that the explicit aim of advertising is to sell products. In the analogy made by the materialists, the realistic novel arose in the eighteenth century to sell us capitalist ideology and a concomitant belief in autonomous selfhood. Since neither writers think they write nor readers think they read for this reason, acceptance of such an analysis becomes a sheer act of faith.[7]

In short, how we perceive a product of our culture depends very much on how we have agreed as a culture to construe it within our culture. Advertising serves a different function than the reading and writing of literature, and the stated purpose of any mode of communication cannot be ignored if we are going to theorize broadly about specific forms or analyze specific outcomes. People are motivated to produce advertisements because they believe advertising helps sell goods, and is therefore materially profitable. But what motivates people to write and read stories? Individual writers and readers will give various answers to this question—a writer might say she had a specific moral, philosophical, or political point to make, or that she hoped to write something entertaining; a reader would be likely to give compatible answers. But very few imaginative works are produced strictly for monetary gain or for political indoctrination—which is not at all to say that they are free of ideological content. Moreover, if one wishes to make a particular moral, philosophical, or political point, why should this be framed within a fictional narrative, and why would readers be interested in reading it in this form, when it's likely they could find the same point made quickly and concisely in a nonfictional text? And if brainwashing is the aim, there are more direct and effective means of accomplishing that as well.

In thus ignoring the sets of conventions that we use to distinguish various modes of discourse, Belsey's materialism, and many other poststructuralist theories like it, result in distorted explanations of the function of literature. This is to some extent ironic, since poststructuralist theories are preoccupied with conventions and constructions; in fact, it is to the credit of recent theory that it has directed attention away from what literature *is* and toward what it *does*. The trend away from seeking the essence of art—a holdover from the Platonic tradition—and toward describing its function has been gaining impetus in a number of other disciplines concerned with art theory, including philosophy and cognitive psychology.[8] As George Dickie indicates, traditional theories of art are all contextual in some sense, but they fail to describe the context of art with appropriate complexity (7). Belsey's theory of expressive realism fails on the same grounds, in part because it does not give an account of the origin of literary art. Such an account is imperative for a full description of literature's context.

There is a fuller and more accurate explanation than Belsey's of why we bother with literature, an explanation that accounts for the origin and function of literary and other aesthetic activities. Over the past century, a consensus has developed in anthropology and psychology which places such activities under the broad rubric of play and which suggests the centrality of all such activities to human adaption and survival. In his seminal text on the function of play, Johan Huizinga defines it thus:

Summing up the formal characteristics of play we might call it a free activity standing quite consciously outside "ordinary" life as being "not serious," but at the same time absorbing the player intensely and utterly. It is an activity connected with no material interest, and no profit can be gained by it. It proceeds within its own proper boundaries of time and space according to fixed rules and in an orderly manner. It promotes the formation of social groupings which tend to surround themselves with secrecy and to stress their difference from the common world by disguise or other means.

The function of play in the higher forms which concern us here can largely be derived from the two basic aspects under which we meet it: as a contest *for* something or a representation *of* something. These two functions can unite in such a way that the game "represents" a contest, or else becomes a contest for the best representation of something. (13)

In Huizinga's analysis, play is not an outgrowth of culture but vice versa, since play includes various types of ritual and contest that, while not in and of themselves serious, have outcomes that are. A spear-throwing contest among our human ancestors might have determined who the next tribal leader would be, for instance. Thus, in terms of primitive cultures, the distinction between play and seriousness is exceedingly fine; contests whose purpose it is to establish the social organization of the group might easily result in the death of one of the contestants. Needless to say, these more life-threatening forms of play no longer predominate in modern culture, although they are hardly nonexistent; one thinks of various professional and recreational sports, including boxing, football, skydiving, and the like. According to Huizinga, "Civilization gradually brings about a certain division between two modes of mental life we distinguish as play and seriousness respectively, but which originally formed a continuous mental medium wherein civilization arose" (111).[9]

Huizinga's analysis of the phylogenetic function of play raises a vexing question: does the greater and greater distance between play and seriousness—the fragmentation of what Laura Thompson calls "logico-aesthetic integration" (qtd. in Dissanayake 46)—over the course of human evolution suggest that all play has become increasingly trivial, a residual cultural phenomenon whose adaptive purpose has been superseded by refinements in cultural organization? This would mean that all forms of aesthetic activity—including the production and interpretation of literature, music, painting, drama, film, and so forth—are trivial, without adaptive or cognitive value. Doubts about the validity and purpose of aesthetic activities are certainly not new, dating back to the beginning of our cultural history; in fact, the sense of crisis among scholars, critics, and writers regarding this issue is hardly as new as many of us like to think, dating back at least to Wordsworth's revisions to the preface for the third edition of the *Lyrical Ballads* which insist on the high office of the poet.[10] It seems that no one in the past several hundred years has made a particularly effective or long-standing case for the value of literature, which only makes it more curious that these highly sophisticated forms of play have not only survived but proliferated. As a species, we have made significant gains in controlling our environment, but our position in the universe is nowhere near secure enough for us to waste enormous amounts of energy on trivial activities, unless, of course, we are blindly pursuing a self-destructive course (again, not a new idea).

If certain forms of play no longer have the cultural significance they had in earlier stages of our culture—for instance, tests of physical strength and skill no longer function exclusively and ubiquitously as initiation rites for adolescent males—there is little reason, given the vast array of imaginative phenomena within our culture, to assume that *all* forms of play exist merely for the purpose of entertainment. For while our need to adapt as a species is perhaps less pressing now than it was thousands of years ago, the individual effort to adapt to a culture of great complexity has become more and more of a challenge. Our adaptive capacity is now increasingly cognitive and psychological rather than physical. In keeping with this, much of the research of the past several decades which posits an adaptive and cognitive value for play activities approaches them from a psychological perspective and focuses on their ontogenetic function. D. W. Winnicott, a prominent child psychologist and theorist of the psychological function of play, insists that child's play is not simply a diversion but a learning process in which toys (called by Winnicott "transitional objects") serve as instruments for reality testing. Through repeated play activities, the child gradually learns to distinguish between her subjective existence and external reality. Moreover, play is perceived as fun by the child because of "the precariousness of the interplay of personal psychic reality and the experience of control of actual objects" (47). Thus, through elementary forms of play, the child begins to learn about the complicated nature of her interactions with the world while simultaneously experiencing a beneficial illusion of control.

Recent research in cognitive psychology supports Winnicott's theory that play serves a cognitive and developmental function. In Andrew Whiten's example, a child who speaks into a banana as though it were a telephone is holding two representations of the world in a precise relationship (Whiten and Byrne 269).[11] This capacity for metarepresentation is linked to the development of mental state terms, and thus to the child's increasing ability to predict the behavior of others (a mental function referred to, somewhat unfortunately, as "mindreading" in cognitive literature). The capacity to form representations that allow the child to predict human behaviors fosters, in turn, the ability to reason from pretend premises. Thus, the manipulation of objects and their meanings in play ultimately enables the manipulation of concepts, which allows the child to vary her responses to and effect upon her world. The illusion of control the child experiences in play, then, is part of a process in which the child learns to become an effective agent in her environment.

Needless to say, child's play and works of art, including literature, stand at opposite ends of the spectrum of play phenomena, the one representing rudimentary activities with simple parameters, the other representing a wide variety of artifacts created and interpreted according to complex yet variable sets of cultural practices and aesthetic rules. But the play activities of child and adult are ultimately continuous rather than disparate, for the fundamental source of imaginative behavior remains consistent throughout human life: never, as individuals, are we fully assured of our position in the world; never is adaption complete. In Winnicott's words,

> It is assumed here [in this analysis of play phenomena] that the task of reality-acceptance is never completed, that no human being is free from the strain of relating inner and outer reality, and that relief from the strain is provided by an intermediate area of experience (cf. Riviere, 1936) which is not challenged (arts, religion, etc.). This intermediate area is in direct continuity of the small child who is "lost" in play. (13)

In short, we do not outgrow the need for play but rather progress to more-sophisticated forms of imaginative activity. Because of the ambiguous and shifting relationship between the individual and reality, play phenomena have both an epistemological value, since they help us to determine or redetermine the relationship of self to world, and a protective value, since they consist of experiences in which the individual has a greater degree of control than he or she has in normal daily interactions. This is to say that play activities, including literature, serve two essential yet contradictory functions: they allow us to act out novelty within an arena that ensures control and safety. What is implicit in Winnicott's discussion of the problematic nature of reality acceptance is an insight into the fundamental insecurity of human existence. James also had a profound sense of our fundamental insecurity, and of the human drive to deny it: "Experience is mutation, and our psychological ascertainments of truth are in mutation—so much rationalism will allow; but never that either reality itself or truth is mutable" (108). Whether we are consciously willing to admit to it or not, we feel the changefulness of our existence every day; since birth and death constitute the only absolute facts of our existence, it follows that our strategies for coping with the anxiety attendant upon mutability in the face of an increasingly complex reality would be fairly elaborate.

This suggests that literary fictions, while offering us a temporary break from the discontinuity and uncertainty of daily life, provide hypothetical frameworks that ultimately bring us into a more satisfactory relation with external reality.[12] Now since it is precisely the question of unknowns that stimulates the creation of fiction, it follows that our modes, forms, genres, and styles will change with the course of history; logically, there should be a greater variety of aesthetic practices as well as a greater abundance of artifacts in a complex society than in a simple one. We have, simultaneously, a greater need to experience novelty and a greater need for control than our ancestors of even a few centuries ago.

The implication of this evolutionary view of art for literary theories that promote particular modes, forms, and genres while stigmatizing others is profound, for such theories ask us, ultimately, to narrow our potential range of creativity and response. Belsey does this by insisting that the postmodern novel liberates while realism enslaves, but in this she reveals her affinities with rather than differences from the New Criticism, which promoted the short lyric and the imagist aesthetic in poetry as well as realism and structural perfection in the novel.[13] It is possible that the desire for control outweighs the appreciation of novelty in critical approaches that attempt to narrow the range of formal and aesthetic possibilities. Given that it is in the nature of critical work to exert control and influence over literature, it would perhaps be worth our while to try to distinguish more carefully between personal preferences and aesthetic judgments.

It is not possible within an essay of this length to speculate about the various adaptive advantages of diverse genres and modes of literature, but I would hope that ensuing studies in literary theory might take such a pluralistic course. The current showdown between postmodernist and realist aesthetics seems to me largely beside the point, since it's likely that the two modes offer different adaptive advantages. Because realism is consistently disparaged in contemporary narrative theory—either because it is viewed as the purveyor of bourgeois ideology or because it is deemed aesthetically anachronistic—I would like in closing to treat it as a brief case in point.

It must be kept in mind that distinctions between realism and postmodernism, or realism and experimentalism, or realism and satire are extremely difficult to make with any degree of certainty. (Is Lodge's *Small World* realistic? Or Michael Malone's *Handling Sin?*) As Wayne Booth points out, throughout the nineteenth century and the first half of the twentieth century, writers whose aesthetic practices were actually quite diverse took pains to assert the realism of their methods (53–60). The ongoing attempt to represent reality in fiction is, I think, an indication of the intensity of the modern struggle with reality acceptance; that is, if so many writers still find it a challenge to represent the real, and if readers are compelled to read works that claim to represent the real, we are a long way from overcoming the feeling of crisis that has plagued us since the collapse of the Enlightenment. The medieval vision of a heavenly paradise as the ultimate reality located somewhere above us and in the future no longer significantly available, so we are compelled to formulate the real from the limited ground of our own human knowledge. Materialist theory, in its urgent contempt for representational art and for the individual, reveals its belated rationalism and utopianism; all we need do is free ourselves from capitalist discourse and the task of reality acceptance will be complete, since individuals will no longer exist. The problem is that such thinking rests on a basic contradiction, according to which it is possible to have a world populated by human bodies but free of individuals. I do not see how we can ever begin to understand anything about ourselves and our creations unless we first acknowledge that our dealings with reality are essentially difficult and problematic.

For those of us in America who are women and minorities, reality acceptance is even more difficult and problematic than it is for white males, because our marginal status constantly conflicts with the basic human need for acceptance and security. This being the case, it is hardly a wonder that experimentalist and postmodernist fictional texts are predominantly the productions of white males. Just as *Jane Eyre* traces the attempt of a female orphan to establish a safe and secure existence in nineteenth-century English culture, *Their Eyes Were Watching God* relates a black female orphan's difficult struggle for identity and independence in 1930s America, a culture both sexist and racist. One of the things I—and, it seems, great numbers of my students and colleagues—experience when we read these books is an appreciation for the suffering and perseverance of the characters, whose experience we analogize to the real world. These books do, in an indirect way, teach us something about life, and they are critical of cultures that make the intertwined phenomena of self-possession and reality acceptance unduly difficult. Thus, the manifest content of these novels contains implicit but obvious social criticism—criticism Belsey would have us overlook in light of a theory that asserts the latent capitalist hegemony of realist texts.

Even more striking cases arise if we broaden the parameters of this investigation a little: How can Belsey's assessment of expressive realism provide a responsible account of African fiction? In Nadine Gordimer's *July's People*, Maureen Smales's loss of self is a deformation resulting from her own participation in a society warped by institutionalized injustice. Maureen's inability to see a coherent reality in the veld to which she has been abruptly relocated mirrors her loss of self and foreshadows her final act: abandoning her husband and three children, she runs toward the sound of a helicopter somewhere in the bush. Faced with such realistic accounts of what it means to struggle with one's reality or to lose it, materialist criticism and all other brands of poststructuralism that seek annihilation of the individual and promote theory over content become not only untenable but also dangerous. The refusal to recognize individuals destroys the basis upon which individual rights are founded, and thus provides an implicit justification for infringements of individual rights.

For the most part, women, minorities, and inhabitants of oppressive cultures—and, I would add, white men in great numbers—do not have the luxury of taking the world less seriously than they do; adaption at the individual level being more problematic, meaning and the contingent ability to establish one's identity become pressing issues. As Gordimer tells us, in Africa the theme picks the writer (qtd. in Cooke 22). Literary theories that view literary realism as anachronistic refuse to acknowledge the essentially problematic and insecure nature of human existence, and unwittingly enforce a bias against those groups and individuals for whom a secure and consistent relation to reality is not an option.[14] As Thomas Pavel points out,

> Since we [like others living in earlier periods of uncertainty] live in a world of transition and conflict, the temptation arises to let indeterminacy take over our fictional worlds. Avant garde strategies consist in fully assuming incompleteness and indeterminacy, and in pushing them to their extreme textual consequences. But this is not the only way left open to us and, as with the fictional strategies of Marlowe and Cervantes, contemporary writers have the option of building worlds that resist the radical workings of indeterminacy. In order to construct fictional systems accounting for the difficult ontological situations in which we find ourselves, we do not need to opt for maximizing incompleteness and indeterminacy. An important choice left to contemporary writers is to acknowledge gracefully the difficulty of making firm sense out of the world and still risk the invention of a completeness-determinacy myth. (112)

Ultimately, then, it does not make much sense to pronounce the death of literary realism, for we continue to live in an uncertain relation to a reality that becomes increasingly difficult to know. Moreover, contemporary realistic writing does not simply repeat the models and techniques of the last two centuries but introduces both innovative techniques and new perceptions, for aesthetic techniques necessarily alter along with social change. For instance, Anita Brookner's novels are hardly iterations of the novels by James, Wharton, and Mann to which they consciously allude. In Brookner's presentation of blameless women, isolated by their propriety within the casual and fluid atmosphere of modern social life, the contemporary novel of manners confront its own belatedness. Brookner's tendency to use an excess of summary and description provides a technical correlative to the enclosed lives of her characters and marks the enormous difference between her realism and Jane Austen's, where quantities of glittering conversation establish the continuity between the individual's social training and her social reality.

In sum, works of literature deserve to be judged on an individual basis, not according to broad generic categories and sets of a priori assumptions about the aesthetic or political merits of those categories. For such categories only represent critical tools of limited validity and use; they are, in fact, critical constructions, which by their very nature cannot account for the source of our ongoing interest in literature—its diversity and variety. According to the theory I have proposed here, literary art, like all forms of play throughout the course of human history, has an ongoing adaptive and cognitive value. As individual readers and writers, we experience gradual and subtle expansions of perception and awareness that are indirectly advantageous in our dealings with reality.

Although I am making a claim for the power of literature and the source of our interest in it, I would like to distinguish my claim from Belsey's. In asserting that realism provides indoctrination of individuals, Belsey presupposes, along with many poststructuralist critics, that literary texts exert an enormous, direct influence over human cognition and behavior. If this were in fact so, I suspect that materialist critics could easily prove the point with a sociological study; but no such study has been done, for the quite likely reason that there is no evidence that individuals respond to literature as Belsey suggests. In its anxiety—an anxiety we all share—to establish the relevance of literary texts, materialist criticism participates in a wish fulfillment that manifests itself as vulgar romanticism. When Wordsworth and Shelley made great claims for poetry, they were reacting to their own anxious awareness that literature, especially poetry, was undergoing a cultural devaluation in the face of science. Given that the romantics lived in a culture that was just beginning to devalue art; given that they did not have access to sophisticated arguments about the value of art; and given that their theoretical propositions were intended as much as rhetorical gestures as literal statements, their claims for the power of literature are understandable. Claims of this kind today, however, constitute a willed denial of historical reality. Any literary critical theory that counsels that generic transformation will result in social liberation so misconstrues the function of literature that it ultimately endangers the case for the value of literary studies. For as long as theorists continue to insist that literature serve a revolutionary function, they will continue to confront their own sense of literature's failure.

Notes

1. The conditions nineteenth-century American authors confronted were discouraging in the extreme. Because there was no international copyright law for much of the century, it was less expensive for American publishers to pirate English works than to publish the works of native authors; Hawthorne himself was unable to publish his first two volumes of tales. In addition, the disproportionate influence of the clergy on critical standards early in the century served to perpetuate puritanical evaluations of literary works (see Charvat for a complete discussion of early critical principles in America). Judging from the

zeal with which poststructuralists have embraced moralizing views of art, it appears that American criticism remains extremely loyal to its theocratic origins.

2. I will discuss Catherine Belsey's totalizing definition of literary realism in this essay. Anthony Easthope makes a similar case against iambic pentameter in *Poetry as Discourse.* According to Easthope, iambic pentameter creates the illusion of transparent texts and thus fosters a belief in subjectivity. In his words, "English poetic discourse is rooted in the pentameter. Through it certain ideological meanings and a subject position are 'written into' the discourse. Pentameter defends the canon against the four-stress popular metre, which foregrounds the poem as poem; it promotes the 'realist' effect of an individual voice 'actually' speaking" (76). Easthope, then, finds in the development away from the ballad and toward the more frequent use of pentameter throughout the ages of English literature a force assisting the rise of capitalism. I find it something of a wonder that "Tintern Abbey," the sole poem in blank verse in the first edition of *Lyrical Ballads,* serves as a prominent example—the rest of the poems in Wordsworth's volume, of course, being adaptions of the ballad form (i.e., "the four-stress popular metre"). The canon, it would seem, is not particularly well defended.

3. Moreover, in borrowing from a fictional text to prove a point about critical values in the real world, Belsey confounds her own assertion that the commonsense view of literature is based on a number of naive suppositions. Content to treat a scene from a satiric fiction as evidence of actual critical values, she demonstrates that the simple equation of literature with life is certainly ill advised.

4. Although materialists continually connect linear plots and consistency of character with bourgeois capitalist ideology, it was in fact Aristotle who introduced criteria of probability and possibility into the critical lexicon many centuries before the development of capitalism.

5. Lest it should seem that I am taking liberties with Belsey's theory, she herself includes fantastical texts under the rubric of classic realism, asserting that "speaking animals, elves, or Martians are no impediment to intelligibility and credibility if they conform to patterns of speech and behaviour consistent with a 'recognizable' system. . . . The plausibility of the individual signifieds is far less important to the reading process than the familiarity of the connections between the signifiers" (51–52). In other words, according to Belsey, because *Stuart Little* is organized according to the recognizable system of realistic narrative, it reinforces capitalist illusions as surely as *Jane Eyre.*

6. Additionally, the ambiguity underlying all aesthetic experiences concerning degrees of reality and fictionality is a product of the dynamic relationship between societies and their discursive forms. In Thomas Pavel's words, "Fictionality is in most cases a historically variable property. Fictional realms sometimes arise through the extinction of the belief in mythology; in other cases, conversely, fictionalization originates in the loss of the referential link between the characters and events described in a literary text and their real counterparts" (80–81).

7. This characteristic poststructuralist habit of insisting that things are never what they appear robs skeptical critics of any ground for objective assessment. Both the recent influence of Foucault and the rather more prolonged influence of Freud are responsible for the current tendency of one critic or another to assume his or her higher authority and level of insight. The question is, why should we defer to any critic's claims of privileged insight into a psychological or cultural subtext when those claims can't be subjected to proofs?

8. For instance, recent studies in cognitive psychology and philosophy point out that since classes of things do not have precise boundaries, we should not look for typical members or defining features of a class (Dissanayake 58). Findings of this kind reinforce the belief of theorists that art can only be defined according to its function. Functional definitions of art are not particularly recent; in his 1968 book *The Languages of Art*, Nelson Goodman asserts that emotion functions cognitively in art, whose "primary purpose is cognition in and for itself." (258).

9. Dissanayake's recent discussion of art from an ethological perspective somewhat modifies Huizinga's thesis by describing play as central to but not solely responsible for the development of the arts. Dissanayake stresses the importance of what she calls "making special," that is, the propensity to elaborate beyond the everyday in an effort to impose a human, civilizing order on nature (74–78). In her view, "making special" arises from a number of human characteristics and cannot be reduced to a single origin (108). Although Dissanayake's concept of "making special" may, in its breadth, provide a more inclusive theory of all the arts than the theory I propose here, Huizinga's emphasis on play has particular relevance to a discussion of literary narrative. Cognitive psychologists increasingly suggest that our primary mode of mentation is narrative; it follows, then, that diverse behaviors that follow a sequential organization may have particularly strong epistemological affinities.

Morse Peckham's *Man's Rage for Chaos* also takes a functional and evolutionary approach to art. Peckham, borrowing primarily from game theory and role theory, asserts that the purpose of art is to break up patterns of behavioral response that have become too rigid. Although I think his theory is an important attempt to place art within the larger context of human behavior, his account is troublesome on two points. First, the analogy between general human behavior and game theory is limited, in that normative patterns of behavioral response are not nearly as highly structured (or simple) as game responses. Second, when Peckham asserts that "[the artist's] purpose is to reduce the tension elicited by the disorienting effects of a problem," he gives art a defensive characterization (11). Yet recent psychological theory generally follows Martin Seligman's seminal study, which asserts that humans and animals *seek stimulation* in their environment as a means of establishing control (145–55). In keeping with this idea, models of the self, whether called "interactionist" (Bruner) or "transactional" (Csikszent-mihalyi and Rochberg-Halton), stress the feedback relationship between individuals and their environment. Thus, while Peckham ardently disavows an alliance with behaviorist psychology, his model of artistic behavior is ultimately tied to a classical stimulus-response model of human behavior. Ironically, in that it drastically reduces the possibility of individual agency, this mechanistic account of man's engagement with his environment aligns Peckham with recent theorists like Belsey who see all the discursive forms of a society as means of social policing.

10. Gerald Graff's remarks on the defensive and contradictory posture we have inherited from the romantics are particularly cogent. As Graff comments,

The ultimate futility and impotence of art was implicit in the very terms with which romantic and subsequent modernist writers attempted to deify art as a substitute for religion. The concept of an autonomous creative imagination, which fabricates the forms of order, meaning, and value which men no longer thought they could find in external nature, implicitly—if not necessarily intentionally—concedes that artistic meaning is a fiction, without any corresponding object in the extra-artistic world. In this respect the doctrine of the creative imagination contained within itself the premises of its refutation. (35)

11. Whiten indicates that this development in pretend play takes place at about the end of the child's second year. Thus, while children do not learn to distinguish fictional from real stories until the age of seven or eight, an understanding of pretense, evident in pretend play, is exhibited at a much earlier age.

12. In her analysis of *The Golden Bowl,* Martha Nussbaum points to the ethical value specific to the hypothetical experience provided by novels:

When we examine our own lives, we have so many obstacles to correct vision, so many motives to blindness and stupidity. The "vulgar heat" of jealousy and personal interest comes between us and the loving perception of each particular. A novel, just because it is not our life, places us in a moral position that is favorable for perception and it shows us what it would be like to take up that position in life . . . it does not seem far-fetched to claim that most of us can read James better than we can read ourselves. (187)

13. Graff identifies the combination of a formalist view of literature, in which the literary work is autonomous from reality, with the visionary view, in which literature appropriates objective reality, as underlying critical theory from the New Criticism onward. His definition of the visionary attitude as "a kind of formalism on the offensive" is an apt characterization of the sort of theorizing in which Belsey engages.

14. In *Beyond Feminist Aesthetics*, Rita Felski discusses the bias against women's fiction which arises specifically from within contemporary French feminist theory. Like new historicists and poststructuralists of other schools, French feminists draw a connection between disruptions of normative discourse and social liberation, so that female writers who construct realistic narratives are viewed as participants in the hegemonic (now patriarchal rather than capitalist) discourse.

Works Cited

Belsey, Catherine. *Critical Practice*. London: Routledge, 1980.

Booth, Wayne. *The Rhetoric of Fiction*. Chicago: U of Chicago P, 1961.

Bruner, Jerome. *Acts of Meaning*. Cambridge: Harvard UP, 1990.

Charvat, William. *The Origins of American Critical Thought, 1810–1935*. Philadelphia: U of Pennsylvania P, 1936.

Cooke, John. *The Novels of Nadine Gordimer: Private Lives/Public Landscapes*. Baton Rouge: Louisiana State UP, 1985.

Csikszentmihalyi, Mihaly, and Eugene Rochberg-Halton. *The Meaning of Things: Domestic Symbols and the Self*. Cambridge: Cambridge UP, 1981.

Dickie, George. *The Art Circle: A Theory of Art*. New York: Haven, 1984.

Dissanayake, Ellen. *What Is Art For?* Seattle: U of Washington P, 1988.

Easthope, Anthony. *Poetry as Discourse*. London: Methuen, 1983.

Felski, Rita. *Beyond Feminist Aesthetics: Feminist Literature and Social Change*. Cambridge: Harvard UP, 1989.

Goodman, Nelson. *Languages of Art: An Approach to the Theory of Symbols*. Indianapolis: Bobbs, 1968.

Gorman, James. *The Man with No Endorphins*. New York: Viking Penguin, 1988.

Graff, Gerald. *Literature against Itself: Literary Ideas in Modern Society*. Chicago: U of Chicago P, 1979.

Huizinga, Johan. *Homo Ludens: A Study of the Play Element in Culture*. 1950. Boston: Beacon, 1955.

James, William. *Pragmatism and Other Essays*. 1913. New York: Pocket, 1963.

Nussbaum, Martha Craven. "'Finely Aware and Richly Responsible': Literature and the Moral Imagination." *Literature and the Question of Philosophy*. Ed. Anthony Cascardi. Baltimore: Johns Hopkins UP, 1987.

Pavel, Thomas G. *Fictional Worlds*. Cambridge: Harvard UP, 1986.

Peckham, Morse. *Man's Rage for Chaos: Biology, Behavior, and the Arts*. Philadelphia: Chilton, 1965.

Seligman, Martin. *Helplessness: On Depression, Development, and Death*. San Francisco: Freeman, 1975.

Whiten, Andrew, and Richard W. Byrne. "The Emergence of Metarepresentation in Human Ontogeny and Primate Phylogeny." *Natural Theories of Mind: Evolution, Development, and Simulation of Everyday Mindreading*. Ed. Andrew Whiten. Oxford: Blackwell, 1991.

Winnicott, D. W. *Playing and Reality*. New York: Basic, 1971.

The Crisis of the Literary Left:
Notes toward a Renewal of Humanism

William E. Cain

1

Sequestered in the academy, the literary Left is intolerant and, perhaps, irrelevant. Its practitioners believe that they are in touch with the social and political issues of the day and are forceful agents for change. But they are dogmatic and self-absorbed, unwilling, it seems, to accept dissenting voices or to query the failure of their work to create significant differences in American culture as a whole. Since, for better or worse, I count myself a member of the literary Left, I find this situation a painful one to face. But the truth has to be acknowledged, and the inadequacy of the Left's contribution addressed.

A single slight but revealing case in point. Recently a friend submitted an essay on the "literature of imperialism" to a prestigious journal. In it he maintained that several important late nineteenth- and early twentieth-century British writers did not wholly subscribe to the prejudiced discourse about the native population that most writers, administrators, and historians employed. They were hardly as enlightened as one might wish, but the language of their texts displays nuances, hesitancies, and forms of sympathy that break with the usual harsh colonialist framework. My friend's essay seemed to me to make a worthwhile point, but it was rejected—not because it was poorly written, researched, or argued, but because it failed to adopt the proper political line about the pervasiveness of imperialist brutality and exploitation.

In their letter of rejection, the editors stated that they in fact admired the essay themselves. However, they said that before making a final decision, they had felt obliged to send the essay to a "subaltern feminist" for her response. The feminist critic reported back that exceptions to the rule do not matter, for "no one cares" whether a few writers departed from the imperialist pattern. The dominant tendency was unequivocally racist, and this, she concluded, is what a scholarly piece should stress. An essay that intimated otherwise should not be accepted for publication. The editors of the journal went along with this report, apparently unable to see that they were denying their own judgment in order to accommodate a political position.

This type of censorship occurs all too frequently. If you challenge or fail to repeat the Left's formulations about race, class, and gender oppression, then you will likely experience difficulty in getting your essays published. It is deemed acceptable to present an argument that is *more* "Left" than someone else's, but not acceptable to qualify or refute a popular leftist claim. For years, the hallmark of ideological narrowness was the journals of the literary and cultural Right— the *New Criterion, Commentary,* and their kin. Compared to them, the journals of the academic Left once seemed models of intellectual openness. But no longer. I fear that the Left knows what it wants to hear, just as the Right does: its conclusions about writers and texts are known in advance and recapitulated as if they came straight from a manual.[1]

To me, being on the Left means believing in and striving to achieve the shared progressive goals of social justice and economic freedom. But it should also imply dissent, self-scrutiny, and criticism. It should not lead to a doctrinaire reliance on code phrases, or to an impatience with analyses and opinions that fail to jibe with the prevailing Left consensus. Yet such a straitjacketing of the mind has become common today, as advanced, liberationist rhetoric serves to muffle opposing voices.

Many on the Left surely must recognize that something is askew, but they are afraid to say the wrong thing, or else, if they do venture to say "wrong" (i.e., disconcerting, troublesome) things that disrupt the usual categories, they are denied a fair hearing by those in positions of influence and power. Too many on the Left are eager to pounce on those who presume to diverge from orthodoxy; and lots more in the liberal and moderate camps fret about being painted as reactionaries, and so they cave in to arguments and demands that they know are faulty.

But it is not just a question of censorship and suppression of undesirable ideas. The problems of the literary Left go deeper than this. In America the literary Left has prospered and extended its sway in academic circles during the very period when conservatism has intensified its hold in the public sphere. It would be heartening to think that the academic Left has kept alive the progressive spirit that American society has temporarily renounced. But the real point at issue is that the extraordinary amount of leftist scholarship and pedagogy has not influenced the general political atmosphere. It has not made much difference.

Critics on the Right have been asserting for some time that the Left has damaged the humanities by seeking to indoctrinate students and that in this respect it has indeed affected the general culture. But in reply one wants to say that if the Left has aimed to do this, it has failed. The majority of college students in America are conservative. They supported Ronald Reagan and George Bush in the 1980, 1984, and 1988 presidential campaigns, and they have little, if any, interest in socialism or even liberalism. On the whole, they know next to nothing about political life and social policy. In fact, according to one recent study, Americans between the ages of eighteen and thirty (nearly half of whom attend or have attended college) know less about public affairs than any other generation of Americans in the past fifty years. Not only has the Left been unable to propel young people in a radical direction, but it has not even managed to convince them that they ought to be interested in politics.

There is no denying that the Left has accomplishments to its credit, the most important of which has been the discovery and celebration of artistically impressive texts by women and minorities. Readers can now enjoy and value, for example, Nella Larsen, Zora Neale Hurston, Ann Petry, and other African-American women authors; and scholars have begun to incorporate these women in studies of American and African-American literature. But the Left's error has been to suppose that the admirable capaciousness of the new reading lists, buttressed by a highly politicized pedagogy, inevitably produces some sort of political awakening. So far, there is no sign that it has done so. There has been a glaring *lack* of result from the Left's years and years of politicized criticism and teaching.

One might have wagered that the literary Left would find this situation disturbing and would seek to examine what it suggests about its theories and practices. But the relationship between the labor of the literary Left and the conservative, even depoliticized, public sphere remains unexplored. Men and women on the Left go about their scholarly business, apparently unconcerned about the failure of their work to have consequences for life outside the academy.

Let me be even more specific. During the past decade, perhaps the most vital new field for research has been African-American and Caribbean literature, theory, and criticism. Much fine work has been done, and more is under way, especially in the area of postcolonial studies.[2] But this work has occurred alongside a terrible deterioration of American race relations and an alarming rise of racist incidents on college and university campuses.

Consider the following facts:

The infant mortality rate for black babies is 17.9 for every 1,000 births, which is twice the rate for white babies.

The rate of low birth weight among black infants is more than twice the rate for white infants: 127.1 for blacks, 56.8 for whites.

Black babies are twice as likely to die before their first birthday as white babies.

Nearly half of the total number of black children under the age of six are in families that live below the poverty line.

Fewer than 30 percent of minority children (this figure includes Hispanics and Native Americans as well as blacks) take courses that prepare them for a four-year college or university.

The college participation rate for blacks during the period from 1976 to 1988 fell by 12 percent, whereas for whites it increased by 3.6 percent.

Blacks make up only 3 percent of college faculties.

Nearly one of every four black males between the ages of twenty and twenty-nine is on probation, in prison, or on parole, and the rate is even higher in some inner-city neighborhoods.

Approximately 50 percent of young blacks are unemployed, and 25 percent under the age of twenty-five have never held a job. In Milwaukee, to take a single example, the overall unemployment rate is 5 percent, but it is 25 percent for blacks.

Nearly one-third of all black Americans live in poverty.

The median income for blacks in 1987 was 57.1 percent of that for whites.

As of 1984, the median net worth of black households was $3,397, which is 9 percent of the white average.

While whites can expect to live 75.5 years, life expectancy for blacks is 69.5, and for black men it is 65.1. Men in Bangladesh, one of the world's poorest countries, have a better chance than men in Harlem of living past the age of 40.

Blacks have a death rate from AIDS that is three times higher than whites, and nearly 50 percent of the infants born with AIDS are black.

The situation is growing worse. According to one report, the total appropriations for subsidized housing, health services, social services, job training, and related programs declined by 54 percent from 1981 to 1988. There were also substantial cutbacks in food stamps and aid to families with dependent children. Most of these programs served to expand opportunity, and as has been shown time and again, they saved money in the long run even as they enabled poor people—so many of them blacks—to lead somewhat better lives. But there is little public anger about poverty and racism in America, and most people seem only vaguely aware of the depth of the nation's social crises. The literary Left has minimal influence on public debate (what little there is of it), and it has shown no ability to convert people to progressive causes and reverse the momentum of the Right's social policies.

The 1960s were different. That decade saw the transformation of America by the women's movement, the campaign for civil rights, and the protests against the war in Vietnam. A good deal of this left/liberal activity occurred on college and university campuses, and it involved faculty and students whose reading lists, it should be noted, rarely included texts by blacks or women. These faculty and students, furthermore, were not yet dedicated to a radical criticism and pedagogy—they had not even begun to ponder what a full-fledged Marxist or socialist literary studies might look like. To be sure, they indicted the academy and exposed the shortcomings of the "humanism" that literary studies upheld. But at the same time, it was their humanistic training that impelled them to perceive the cruel conditions of social and political life. And—in a nice paradox— it was this training that alerted them to the gaps in what they had learned in school: it highlighted for them the values, interests, and needs that humanistic literary studies had typically neglected to consider.

This is exactly the observation that Richard Ohmann makes, without dwelling upon its implications, in *English in America*, his lively Marxist analysis of academic professionalism and the New Criticism, the method of "close reading" the "text itself" that reigned supreme from the 1930s through the 1960s. Ohmann's major thrust is against the hypocrisy and corruption of New Critical humanism, yet he notes in passing that "the very humanism we learned and taught was capable, finally, of turning its moral and critical powers on itself." Ohmann admits that this "humanism saw the inhumanity of the society outside the university" and aided in making "*visible* the war on Vietnam and, at home, racism and poverty" (90–91). It is sobering to realize that Ohmann has here defined a relationship between the New Criticism and radical action that is far more powerful and persuasive than anything he and others on the Left have said about their current scholarly work and today's sociopolitical scene. Whatever its faults, the New Criticism, Ohmann implies, was a source of humane, critical illumination for students: it enabled them to see—that is, to "read"– and feel intensely the injustices in American society and foreign policy, and spurred them to take action.

Why does the Left refrain from confronting its failures and the limits of its positions? Why the absence of self-criticism? It is all well and good for leftist scholars to hold conferences and launch journals for fellow leftists, and for similarly inclined teachers to espouse radical analytical methods to captive stu- dent audiences. But where are the public consequences of this earnest inquiry? Will the future usher in more leftist scholarship and pedagogy while the state of the society—quite oblivious to the literary Left—continues to deteriorate?

The Left has erroneously assumed, I think, that the kinds of teaching and criticism now in vogue will awaken readers and students to radicalism and prompt them to fight against unfairness and intolerance in America. I would argue instead that the Left's cause is far more likely to be served by encouraging students to be skeptical and open-minded, and by subjecting to stringent criticism the political conclusions that most people on the Left have come to accept— that the traditional canon is intrinsically repressive, that classic texts must be demystified in order to expose the biases of their authors, and finally, that radical forms of scholarship and pedagogy (deconstruction, Marxism, new his-

toricism, feminism) will directly translate into acts of social and political radicalism in the public sphere. These assumptions are proving to be an obstacle to
truly forward-looking thought, however firmly the Left may wish to cling to
them. When orthodoxy starts to take shape in literary studies and everybody
seems content with the positions that have been established, then it is time to
go the other way. It is one of the responsibilities of the critic and intellectual
to be dialectical, to feel discontented at the prospect of certainty, and to take
apart assumptions that have become habitual, automatic.

2

This seems to me an especially important point to keep in mind in the midst of
the heated debate about the literary canon, a debate in which neither side has
distinguished itself. Conservatives and traditionalists are, in my view, wrong to
wish that they could limit the canon to the great books of the past, for in practice
this argument leads to an undue emphasis on white male writers and an unwillingness to make room for women and minority writers. It is not simply a matter of
giving all parties equal representation, but rather of ensuring that the literary
and artistic achievements of women and minorities are recognized. Frederick
Douglass, W. E. B. DuBois, Richard Wright, and Zora Neale Hurston do not
belong on reading lists for American literature courses *because* they are African-
Americans; they belong there because they have written important, innovative,
absorbing books that the general culture has customarily ignored or neglected
because the authors of these books were black. It is therefore misleading in the
extreme to suggest, as do many conservatives, that opening up the canon means
the end of standards and the addition of texts to reading lists solely on the basis
of gender and race. The canon has to be expanded because the gender and race
of good writers often prevented their good and great books from being studied,
taught, and included in literary histories and anthologies.

Opening up the canon is, then, more than a matter of remedying past
injustices. It is a proper means for making criticism and teaching richer, more
informed and accurate. By including, for example, Hurston and Wright in courses
on the modern American novel and realism and naturalism, it is possible to
enlarge the scope of literary knowledge. Hurston and Wright should appear on
the reading lists of courses like these, for giving them the attention that they
merit *adds* something important to the study of the novel as a genre, the specific
evolution of the American novel as a form, the range of resources of language
and idiom and imagery that American writers have invoked, and the complex,
multiple traditions in which we can view the work that American writers have
done—and in which they located themselves.

But literary radicals who have proposed the expansion of the canon have not made a wholly persuasive case. They have done part of their job well, rediscovering and calling attention to many undervalued writers. But the mistake they make is to focus above all on the *differences* between these writers and the familiar roster of white, male masters, as though there has not been (and should not be) commerce between them. There are differences, of course. It is perfectly defensible to describe and construct separate traditions of writing by women and minorities, and to stress the particular themes and strategies that such traditions, grounded in race, gender, or ethnicity, embrace. But a truly dialectical form of criticism and teaching should also work to view all texts in relationship to one another. The aim, in short, should be to update and extend T. S. Eliot's insistence, in "Tradition and the Individual Talent," that the whole of literature "composes a simultaneous order" (38). The connections, relationships, and resemblances, as well as the differences, between writers and texts should bear upon the inquiry that teachers and students undertake. And this same sense of difference *and* sameness, multiplicity *and* commonality, should also inform the courses that teachers design.

This begins to express what I mean by the term *humanism* in my title. It does not mean the denial of differences: these have to be perceived and talked about; but it does suggest that men and women of different races, religions, and backgrounds might nevertheless share values and interests. Nor does such a renewed humanism presume that all persons will feel the same way, or answer the important questions about their lives exactly as do others. It simply proposes that critics and teachers encourage one another and their students to risk breaking through the divisions of gender, race, and class that the literary Left has so heavily stressed and, apparently, has come to regard as insurmountable.

In making this proposal, I am led to cite a crucial passage from the opening chapter of Lionel Trilling's *Sincerity and Authenticity*:

> Generally our awareness of the differences between the moral assumptions of one culture and those of another is so developed and active that we find it hard to believe there is any such thing as an essential human nature; but we all know moments when these differences, as literature attests to them, seem to make no difference, seem scarcely to exist. We read the *Iliad* or the plays of Sophocles or Shakespeare and they come so close to our hearts and minds that they put to rout, or into abeyance, our instructed consciousness of the moral life as it is conditioned by a particular culture—they persuade us that human nature never varies, that the moral life is unitary and its terms perennial, and that only a busy intruding pedantry could ever have suggested otherwise. (1–2)

In the wake of poststructuralism, it may seem naive to refer to an "essential human nature," yet the phrase as Trilling employs it carries a considerable appeal. He is concerned here with the power of literature to cross differences in cultural background, gender, race, class. Literature does not always succeed in doing so; and there is ample reason to believe from the record of critical history that the claims of an "essential" human nature have often masked more pointedly particularized, narrowing values. But limited, badly dated conceptions of "human nature" have been demystified repeatedly by contemporary theorists. By now it should be possible to perceive differences—accepting and even rejoicing in them—while asking if these can be bridged in the name of a recuperated humanism, one that is wiser, more self-aware and self-critical than the older humanism that left women and minorities unrecognized.

Trilling states his position with so much conviction that his counterstatement to it feels almost hurtful:

> And then yet again, on still another view of the case, this judgment reverses itself and we find ourselves noting with eager attention all the details of assumption, thought, and behaviour that distinguish the morality of one age from that of another, and it seems to us that a quick and informed awareness of the differences among moral idioms is of the very essence of a proper response to culture. (2)

Trilling's sensitivity to moral complexity and cultural difference shows that he cannot be simply categorized as elitist or reactionary. And this part of Trilling's account would probably meet with the assent of many in literary studies today. The emphasis at the present time falls on historical and cultural distinctiveness, and on the particularity of specific groupings of texts and literary and cultural traditions. On one level, this has proved extremely valuable, as I have indicated, and represents a vital kind of canon revision and revaluation not all that different from the challenges to orthodoxy and academic custom that T. S. Eliot, F. R. Leavis, and the New Critics launched during the 1920s and 1930s. It is, in addition, faithful to the continuing transformation of America into a multi-cultural society.

Yet it is precisely the lesson of the dialectic that Trilling encourages that we would want to return from his second point to his first, appreciating the flexible movement of thought that he expresses. Reading literature can make us intensely responsive to the idea of a human nature that transcends cultural differences; but we know how important these differences are and the challenges they raise to any quick appeal to commonality among persons; yet still one wonders whether we can nevertheless get back to that impulse of feeling bonded to others, however different from ourselves, as though we were at one with them.

3

What should be the business of literary studies, particularly in the classroom? It should be to put into· practice the dialectic that Trilling describes, a form of response to texts that is mobile and modulated, and that is sensitive to the simple but profound possibility that persons might be both different and the same. To follow this course would be to give up the purity of leftist ideology; it would mean contesting the political attitudes that the Left has fostered, and being skeptical about the link between scholarship (as well as pedagogy) and social transformation that the Left has taken for granted.

To exemplify this renewed humanist enterprise, I might focus on a passage from Emerson's "Self-Reliance":

> I ought to go upright and vital, and speak the rude truth in all ways. If malice and vanity wear the coat of philanthropy, shall that pass? If an angry bigot assumes this bountiful cause of Abolition, and comes to me with his last news from Barbadoes, why should I not say to him, "Go love thy infant; love thy wood-chopper; be good-natured and modest; have that grace; and never varnish your hard, uncharitable ambition with this incredible tenderness for black folk a thousand miles off. Thy love afar is spite at home." Rude and graceless would be such greeting, but truth is handsomer than the affectation of love. Your goodness must have some edge to it,—else it is none. (262)

Emerson describes here the hard, cold impact of "rude truth" and is especially concerned to expose the falsity of a person who indulges in charitable sentiment toward those far away yet remains unloving toward his or her own family and neighbors. Emerson is not attacking philanthropy as such but rather the motives that may disfigure it. Philanthropy must be assailed when the philanthropist bases his or her words and deeds on a desire for self-approval—one sign of which is a determination to convert others, to make them into replicas of oneself. Emerson names abolition as a "bountiful cause": he is not dismissing it in itself but castigating those who misuse it by seeing it as an opportunity for self-advertisement and self-righteous display.

But Emerson's language is intense, even exaggerated, and may intimate more than he knows. His angry voice in the imagined dialogue he conducts with the Abolitionist conveys a feeling of personal offense, as though he is repelled by the moral claims that the Abolitionist has made, claims that would oblige Emerson to think about charity beyond his own personal sphere. Once he attends to love of family and neighbor, is he obligated then to love the "black folk a thousand miles off," and if so, is some appropriate action incumbent upon him? When Emerson decries the "incredible tenderness" that the Abolitionist shows toward the blacks of Barbados, he means to shame the Abolitionist. Yet he may also unwittingly cast shame upon himself, in implying that there is something incredible, intrinsically unbelievable and unimaginable, about charity that seeks to span distances. From this point of view, the "edge" that Emerson ascribes to truth cuts two ways, humbling the Abolitionist and protecting Emerson from taking the moral inventory that his passage would seem to insist upon: he does not see the mote in his own eye.

There are three figures cited in this passage—Emerson, the Abolitionist, and the blacks of Barbados—and the relationships among them can be profitably discussed and debated in the classroom by students. In what it says and does not say, the passage dramatizes white speech about enslaved people, and the complicated, morally problematic degree of urgency whites feel or do not feel for groups different from themselves. But while the context within which Emerson sets the moral issue is suggestive and historically important, the issue itself can also be stated so that it fastens, more generally, on the nature and necessity of "rude truth." Is truth always "rude"? Must it inevitably be sharp-edged? What might be the forms of self-interest that accompany the fervor by which a man or woman voices truth?

This passage from Emerson thus has a specific relevance to the antebellum crisis over slavery and abolitionism, and to the distant place that blacks occupy when whites address the question of their freedom. But it is also a passage that one could use to talk about the kinds of revelations—not always intended—that are made by persons determined to speak truth. Emerson's account has a wider moral bearing; it lives beyond the precise terms in which he frames it, and it offers opportunities for readers to think about other contexts in which his disquieting moral drama could be enacted.

Next, compare Emerson's passage from "Self-Reliance" to one from Douglass's *My Bondage and My Freedom*, in which Douglass describes the prohibitions that his white abolitionist friends place upon him:

> During the first three or four months, my speeches were almost exclusively made up of narrations of my own personal experience as a slave. "Let us have the facts," said the people. So also said Friend George Foster, who always wished to pin me down to my simple narrative. "Give us the facts," said Collins, "we will take care of the philosophy." Just here arose some embarrassment. It was impossible for me to repeat the same old story month after month, and to keep up my interest in it. It was new to the people, it was true, but it was an old story to me; and to go through with it night after night, was a task altogether too mechanical for my nature.

"Tell your story, Frederick," would whisper my then revered friend, William Lloyd Garrison, as I stepped upon the platform. I could not always obey, for I was now reading and thinking. (361)

Douglass studies here the limited rights accorded him as the narrator of his own story. His white colleagues know his place, the role that he should perform in their campaign for black freedom. He is to speak the facts and not presume to move beyond the literal details of his past life. He is to remain pinned down, as though he were piñioned by reincarnations of the slavebreakers from whom he thought he had escaped, or as though he were some kind of rare exhibit that had lost its life. But Douglass chafes against the sameness of the part that the abolitionists have scripted for him. He feels both the desire for autonomy and the impossibility of mechanizing his consciousness. His irony is fairly restrained but piercing nonetheless—"my *then* revered friend, William Lloyd Garrison" (my italics). And it serves to intensify the momentum of his yearning for personal liberation—"I could not always obey," suggesting that he could not oblige his keepers even if he wished.

Here, as in Emerson's passage, there is a dialogue—actually two of them, one between Douglass and Foster, the other between Douglass and Garrison. But the term *dialogue* is in fact not quite accurate, because Douglass himself does not speak. His duty is to listen to the commands that the white folks issue, and the language through which he portrays the scenes, especially the one between himself and Garrison, connotes his perception of white guilt and embarrassment. Garrison whispers his words to Douglass, not wanting to make known the nature of the control over the black man that he seeks to exercise. Douglass wants to illuminate the fact that the whispering Garrison does dimly apprehend the ugliness of the coercive advice he gives. He seems not to trust Douglass, who needs to be reminded of his responsibility to speak only "the facts" before each turn at the podium.

Of course, the abolitionists judge that they are acting in Douglass's own best interests. They are concerned about him, care for his people, loathe slavery. But the revelation that Douglass brings home is the punitive quality of the abolitionists' conception of what freedom for the black man involves. It means the end of literal enslavement and the passage into another form of bondage. Douglass's agency is still denied. His white friends are not ready for it—and no doubt have concluded that neither is Douglass.

But as Douglass continues he makes clear that the momentum of freedom cannot be forestalled:

New views of the subject were presented to my mind. It did not entirely satisfy me to *narrate* wrongs; I felt like *denouncing* them. I could not always curb my moral indignation for the perpetrators of slaveholding villainy, long enough for a circumstantial statement of the facts which I felt almost everybody must know. Besides, I was growing, and needed room. "People won't believe you ever was a slave, Frederick, if you keep on this way," said Friend Foster. "Be yourself," said Collins, "and tell your story." It was said to me, "Better have a *little* of the plantation manner of speech than not; 'tis not the best that you seem too learned." These excellent friends were actuated by the best of motives, and were not altogether wrong in their advice; and still I must speak just the word that seemed to *me* the word to be spoken *by* me. (361–62)

Douglass grants the good intentions of his friends even as he quotes the words through which they degrade him. His consciousness is expanding: he is feeling the energy of independence and therefore desires to reflect upon the lessons that his story teaches. But it is that ever-expanding self, impelled to select its own words, that the abolitionists cannot abide. What the abolitionists want is all the more grotesque because it is so detached from their sense of themselves and their sense of their fine intentions: they essentially insist that Douglass relocate himself in slavery, make himself sound like the slave he was, and, in effect, must remain even when no longer so identified as a slave. Douglass needs, they say, to color his speech so that it conforms to the expectations of the abolitionists and their audiences.

The longer Douglass lives in the free North, the more keenly he perceives his isolation and the bitter restrictions on the freedom he has won. In this respect, as with the passage from "Self-Reliance," Douglass's words both are tied to and gesture beyond their immediate context of the slavery crisis. The context matters crucially, as it focuses powerfully the dramatic differences between black and white, the balked hopes of the black man, and the condescension and insult dispensed by the whites. But here once more I would want to extend the moral issue that Douglass's account dwells upon, so that it poses the problem of how an identity is earned. For most people, black or white or other, forging an identity is a matter of working against resistances, some of which are cruel and overt, and others of which are more subtle and sly. Black students may feel a special force as they read and respond to Douglass's passage, but its force can be felt sharply by other students as well. This passage is a memorable one precisely because it both speaks to the historical conditions of life for black Americans and relates a challenging insight—liberation as a form of imprisonment—in which all persons can find some share of common truth.

My point in treating these examples from Emerson and Douglass is to suggest a type of criticism and teaching that highlights differences but that also details a moral inquiry at work in literary texts that does not depend on race, gender, or ethnicity to make itself meaningful. This does not mean that everybody will agree about how passages like these should be understood; but the debate conducted about what Emerson and Douglass say in them will not be formulated exclusively in racial terms. Conceivably a black student might be repelled by Emerson's comments on the blacks of Barbados yet still confess an affinity for the view that truth must be rude, must have an edge, just as a white student might grasp exactly the burden that Douglass experiences when he tells of the models for good behavior that are imposed upon him.

But how does this dialectical method address the crisis of the literary Left with which I began? And what is its relationship to the cruel facts of life for many black Americans and for America's poor that I surveyed? How, in short, does what I have proposed bring about social change? These are, of course, questions that my essay inevitably raises, but I am not convinced that they are the right questions. In my view, the mistake that the literary Left has made, and continues to make, is to assume that its politicized criticism and teaching should and will produce changes in the society. I see no evidence for this. If anything, the evidence goes in the other direction, suggesting that the more widespread politicized criticism and teaching are, the more reactionary and uncaring grows the society. If change for the better does eventually come, it will come from other sources, other struggles, aided perhaps but not caused by what students have absorbed in their literature courses. This strikes me as the right, limited, somewhat humbling point with which to conclude. Yet I would be willing to offer one last distinction, making my wager that progressive change is more likely to be advanced by a humane, moral criticism and teaching than by a politicized program that never doubts its rightness.

Notes

1. The debates about scholarship, pedagogy, and higher education have been growing steadily more intense, even polarized. For exemplary instances, see the contributors to special issues of *South Atlantic Quarterly* 89 (Winter 1990) and *Partisan Review* 58 (Spring 1991), both of which focus on the politics of education and the university. See also John Searle, "The Storm over the University," and the letters published in subsequent issues of *The New York Review of Books*.

2. See, among many examples, Selwyn Cudjoe, *V.S. Naipaul;* and Cudjoe, ed. *Caribbean Women Writers.*

Works Cited

Cudjoe, Selwyn. *V.S. Naipaul: A Materialist Reading.* Amherst: U of Massachusetts P, 1988.

————, ed. *Caribbean Women Writers.* Amherst: U of Massachusetts P, 1990.

Douglass, Frederick. *My Bondage and My Freedom.* 1855. New York: Dover, 1969.

Eliot, T. S. "Tradition and the Individual Talent." *Selected Prose.* By Eliot. Ed. Frank Kermode. New York: Harcourt, 1975. 37–44.

Emerson, Ralph Waldo. "Self-Reliance." 1841. *Ralph Waldo Emerson: Essays and Lectures.* New York: Library of America, 1983.

Ohmann, Richard. *English in America: A Radical View of the Profession.* New York: Oxford UP, 1976.

Searle, John. "The Storm over the University." *New York Review of Books* 6 Dec. 1990: 34–42.

Trilling, Lionel. *Sincerity and Authenticity.* Cambridge: Harvard UP, 1972.

When No Means No and Yes Means Power: Locating Masochistic Pleasure in Film Narratives

Carol Siegel

As a woman who entered the university already considering herself a radical feminist, I have often had cause to feel grateful for the steady increase of respect in my field for feminist scholarship and gender studies, which has made possible my work as a critic and my career as a professor of literature. However, I have gradually come to believe that a major source of prestige for much gender-oriented literary theory—its heavy reliance on ideas taken from psychoanalytic writings—can have a detrimental effect on the work of the feminist critics whom it has seemed to enable, alienating us from other feminist communities and pushing us into positions that are necessarily opposed to the most fundamental feminist goals. Focusing on one small and still-developing area of gender studies, I hope to reveal some of the dangers of basing feminist criticism on psychoanalytic theory by pointing out ways that the latter can conflict with the premises underlying some of the last two decades' most-successful movements to effect immediate social change to save the lives of physically endangered women.

Although gender theory often seems indistinguishable in attitude from the best known feminist theories, recent discussions of male subjectivity have made apparent some deep disjunctions between gender studies and feminism as it is commonly understood. One such disjunction is evident in most recent discussions of masochism in film. Following Freud, these discussions blur the line between voluntary and involuntary suffering. Such blurring should be profoundly troubling to feminists, since it implicitly undercuts the claims about pleasure and volition upon which feminist action in opposition to the violent enforcement of traditional sex roles is predicated. Locating masochistic pleasure in relation to a film's manifest content is difficult but necessary to the recognition of that film's negotiation with and possible resistance to patriarchal law. In order to illustrate the importance of representations of volition to narratives of masochism, I will discuss two films in which eroticized torture scenes are central. In arguing for a return to attention to the stories about choice told within

141

films, as well as to the discourse in which they are told, I will also be arguing for a more careful and consistent attention in feminist criticism to the narratives about sex- and gender-related suffering that have been formulated by more directly politically active feminisms.[1]

Feminism as a political movement has shared with legal and ethical discourses a preoccupation with consent in sexual matters, to which category masochism is popularly considered to belong. The alignment between these discursive modes is evidenced by the instrumental role feminists have played in redefining rape in the last ten years so that two previously naturalized exercises of male privilege—"date rape" and "rape within marriage"—have emerged as new forms of illegal sexual assault. These redefinitions were possible because both the legal profession and the general public treat consent and refusal as separable states. The precise delimiting of tacit consent is important because of the emphasis law places on consciousness and intentionality.[2] Such attitudes can come into conflict with poststructuralist theories that read individual choice as a bourgeois myth to be deconstructed. Feminists outside the university have raised more-pragmatic objections to the general legal practice of reading "yeses" as assent.

Mariana Valverde seems right to suggest that the majority of feminists, fearing that many women are coerced into accepting unpleasurable sexual experiences, have been moving for many years toward the development of an ethical community that would "deprivatize the process of establishing consent" (250). One way in which consent has already been legally deprivatized to some extent is that some states now routinely prosecute in domestic violence cases whether or not the injured spouse presses charges. This policy reflects the feminist view, now current among therapists, that a dependent or severely emotionally damaged woman may not be able to voice her unwillingness to be subjected to violence and thus society must speak on her behalf. As a legal position, this is consonant with the laws that forbid citizens to sign away their legal rights or to sell themselves into slavery.

Of course, all feminist activists do not share the same definitions of rights and consent. Whether women can participate willingly in sadomasochistic rituals —or the production of more-ordinary pornography—has been for some time a topic of passionate feminist debate. Disagreements between feminists about what constitutes consent have been intense enough to cause rifts in some communities of women. The threat of division was perhaps most succinctly expressed with the emergence of an aggressively propornography periodical for women entitled *On Our Backs* in explicit resistance to the antipornography slant of the radical feminist *Off Our Backs*. Bitter as they can be, these disagreements are useful to the formulation of feminist theory in that they bring up important questions about female identity and subjectivity within a culture. They may ultimately push us beyond our present conflicting answers to such questions as whether one can make choices *as a woman*.

However, the threat to feminist theory posed by psychoanalysis is much more extensive than that posed by "rebel" feminists asserting their right to act on their own masochistic and exhibitionistic desires. Self-styled feminist sexual outlaws and their opponents disagree about the meaning of a woman's "yes," but agree that a major goal of feminism is to ensure that a woman's "no" be taken seriously. Linda Williams rightly points out that while the idea of voluntary "masochism strikes the wrong note with certain feminisms," Freud poses "problems for [all] feminists" in describing the unconscious as the locus of unqualified affirmation, because this description might be interpreted as implying that unconscious masochistic pleasure is always the response to forced sexual experience and pain (16–17).

Masochists, as they have been most frequently described, enjoy a paradoxical relationship to power. While enacting a painful submission to cruelly imposed punishments, masochists are actually receiving sexual gratification. If masochism is consciously chosen, it includes access to power. Not only do masochists often manipulate and even control the others who act in response to their desires, they also always satisfy their desires in defiance of the law that would coerce or constrain them. Their pursuit of pleasure is also an exercise of personal power— as long as yes and no have separable meanings. But when, as Freud asserts in his analysis of Dora, no means yes not as part of a consciously chosen game but at a level of the psyche readable only by the analyst, then the term masochism defines powerless suffering rather than powerful play.

On the problems inherent in the psychoanalytic use of the term *masochism*, William Grossman writes, "In practice, when considering particular instances of clinically observed behavior, it may be difficult to distinguish between realistically endured suffering and covertly sought pain, or between deliberate self-injury and poor judgment" (382–83). The double bind of the traditional romanticization of the feminine role in love and the modern insistence upon individual responsibility holds many women in a position that is difficult to describe fairly yet in accordance with Freudian definitions of masochism. In a keynote address delivered to a symposium on masochism, Arnold M. Cooper unwittingly made clear the dangers of these definitions when he attempted to answer feminist objections to the use of masochism as a diagnostic term by explaining that such films as *"The French Lieutenant's Woman*, depicting a man led to his ruin by a mysterious woman, seem to confirm the idea that men are also prone to masochistic depravity." His interpretation of the film does go against the misogynist tendency to gender masochism as feminine, but by equating doomed love and "depravity," it also authorizes the practice of blaming the victim against which feminism has consistently struggled. The wrong of misnaming the sufferer a masochist is hardly likely to be redressed by doing it to men as well as women. Yet this seems to be the practice, though not the intention, of some of the most prominent commentators on male subjectivity and film.

Kaja Silverman is one of the most influential of these critics. Her frequently cited essay "Masochism and Male Subjectivity" set a high standard for knowledge and analysis of theories of male masochism. In essays on Fassbinder and T. E. Lawrence, she focuses on ways their well-known masochistic tendencies can be seen reflected in their works. But in an earlier essay, on Frank Capra's film *It's a Wonderful Life*, she enters more problematic territory by assigning the masochism she scrutinizes to a fictional character, the protagonist, George Bailey. She sees his experience as challenging "the distinction between male and female subjectivity." She argues, like Lacan, that all subjectivity entails suffering because it depends upon acceptance of lack, debt, and pain ("Male Subjectivity" 16). Consequently, the "exemplary" male subject is the masochist who accepts his castrated condition within society as a source of pleasure (18). To Silverman, George becomes a masochist "exemplar" when, near the end of the film, he revels in the return of all his problems and "embraces most enthusiastically" the restored signs of his defeats because they signify his return to human existence (21). The trouble with calling George's joyful acceptance of his bereft and tormenting condition "masochism" is that he is not shown to have come to value suffering for its own sake. He values it because the only alternative to suffering seems to be nonexistence. To call his attitude masochism is analogous to calling the desire to keep living a passion for growing old.

Particularly troubling about Silverman's reading of this film is that her ostensible purpose seems to be to critique "Freud's account" of masculinity (18) and to replace it with a more politicized understanding informed by Althusser; however, her acceptance of psychoanalysis's standard confusion of submission with pleasure in pain undercuts her thesis that cultural subjectivity is a "compulsory," cruel violation (18). If George Bailey has actually become a masochist at the end of the film—and we might pause to ask if one can *become* a masochist or whether one can only become aware of one's masochism—then we must ask, can his forced interpellation have done more than fulfill his deepest desires?

I will turn briefly to a "strange scene" observed by Theodor Reik to clarify what is at stake when no distinction is made between an enthusiastic acceptance of pain as the sign of one's presence in the world and the pursuit of pain as an end in itself. Reik's description of the scene is as follows: "A boy of six years, who had early shown himself to be backward and unruly, was chastised by his young and irascible father. My intervention had been rejected. And while the boy was severely beaten he kept screaming, 'I am laughing, I am laughing!'" According to Reik's interpretation of what he has seen, "The boy wished to prove to his father, as well as to me, that he did not care about hard blows, that on the contrary he enjoyed them." And we might add that the child apparently also wished to assert his independence as an actor in the drama of his own life. But

Reik cautions his readers, "This example is not to be taken for infantile masochism. Obviously the child was in no mood for laughing" (144). There can be little doubt that this unusually commonsensical diagnosis is correct, and as enemies of child abuse, we might admire both Reik's attempt to interfere and his insistence that the child's pain rather than his defiant assertion of pleasure be taken seriously. But we might also ask what interests would have been served had Reik taken a more conventionally psychoanalytic view of the case.

Elaine Scarry's analysis of the structure of political torture suggests some answers. Scarry points out that extreme pain causes a sense of disintegration of self in the sufferer. She explains that interrogation functions as an essential part of political torture even when no information is needed from the victim because it consolidates the victim's loss of power by creating the illusion that he, not the torturer, is "the cause of his loss of self and world" (35–36). But rather than emphasizing pain, she argues, the torturer "denies the pain," and instead stresses agency in order to effect "the conversion of the enlarged map of human suffering into an emblem of the regime's strength" (56–57). These two strategies are intended to reduce everything the victim experiences to endless reaffirmations of the regime's power. If we apply this portion of Scarry's theory to the situation Reik describes, we can see how a conventionally psychoanalytic interpretation— and intervention—could work to negate the child's pathetic self-assertion and reinforce his father's power as patriarchy has authorized it.

Psychoanalysis teaches us that the child in this case is neither heroic, as he himself probably feels, nor purely a victim, as the sympathetic observer thinks, but is complicitous, owing to Oedipal guilt, in the father's violence. Analysis could bring the child, in his later years, to such an understanding of the incident. Rather than simply recording that the son suffered, the analyst is likely to ask questions designed to make him feel implicated in his own suffering. The son might also learn that what was important in the experience was neither his pain nor his defiant claim that his father's disciplinary efforts amused him but rather his struggle with a paternal power that he was mistaken in fighting because he could acquire it himself as a man. That he already loves this power and desires the one who wields it is a commonplace of Freudian theory.[3] Thus all revolt becomes an expression of masochism, and the best the boy can hope for is to forget his own pain and abandon rebellion in the promise that he will someday be allowed to refuse a response to the pain of others by reinterpreting such pain as a masochistic attempt to engage with the power of the fathers. The problem for feminists in offering such a reading of suffering is obvious. Yet the frustrating tendency of human beings in everyday life, as well as characters in films, to assert illogically that they have the control that they obviously lack and to exult foolishly over their actual situation as sufferers can tempt us to label them masochists without considering the political implications.

Films that more generously indulge the viewers' fantasies of escape from the demands of everyday life lend themselves even more easily to sweeping interpretive equations of suffering and masochism. In an article on Clint Eastwood, Paul Smith begins by discussing how action films eroticize the male body in such a way as to provide the viewer with sadistic pleasure or a partially pleasurable masochistic identification when the protagonist undergoes the obligatory beating or wounding, but soon Smith is referring to "male masochism" as if such pleasure were depicted within the narrative of the film (102–4). No distinction is made between scenarios of male suffering and representations of men's masochistic pleasure. In fact, although Smith mentions that the villain in *Dirty Harry* "is marked as effeminate and perverse in many different ways," he does not comment on the scene in which this villain pays for a beating and receives it with apparent pleasure (96).

This omission seems notable because the scene functions narratively to problematize male masochism as a psychological attribute. The scene's context suggests that behaviors that appear pitiable to the liberal gaze are really simply stratagems. First, we are led to believe that the villain is obeying one of his sick compulsions when he gleefully urges his contracted (and attractive) black assailant to hit him harder. Then, we are shown that the source of his pleasure is his knowledge that the hero, Harry Callahan, will be blamed for the beating. In effect, masochism is parodied rather than represented in this scene; it is revealed as a sham, not used as a trope. The problem in this case occurs in the intersection of definition, which must perforce be based on interpretation, and identification. As viewers, we may identify with the character who is beaten and derive masochistic pleasure through our identification with him. However, the narrative explicitly, diegetically opposes our interpretation of the beating scenes as causing their victims pleasure. Therefore, to speak of male masochism as if it were located within the story seems wrong.

Tania Modleski, usually scrupulously attentive to the intricacies of viewer identification, occasionally elides male suffering and masochism when discussing film plots. For example, she describes the identification of *Vertigo*'s protagonist with women as "masochistic" because it is a source of agony to him and, ultimately, forces him to recognize his own powerlessness. Although it is easy to see as sadistic the protagonist's retreat from this painful identification with women into cruel control of them, it is less clear why we should consider masochistic an identification that he never seems to enjoy. If psychoanalytic theory demands that painful identifications always be read as masochism, a psychoanalytic definition of masochism seems ill suited to feminist goals.

Some critics even leave identification out of the equation. Passage after passage in Gaylyn Studlar's book on "the masochistic aesthetic" in von Sternberg's films demonstrates a tendency to define suffering as masochism. We are told that La Bessiere in *Morocco* and Don Pasquale in *The Devil Is a Woman* are depicted as masochists because each is shown to remain in love with a woman who treats him badly. There seems little reason to argue with Studlar's detailed analyses of the cinematic techniques used to suggest that these characters, and others in von Sternberg's films, are experiencing disavowed sexual pleasure while they suffer. But a love that persists despite adversity and even in the face of the beloved's apparent indifference cannot be considered masochistic per se without a complete reassessment of the majority of the art products of both Western and Eastern culture.

Such reassessment may be necessary, yet it will serve little purpose for anyone struggling against oppression if it moves toward categorically defining victims—whether of individuals, societies, or love—as masochists. I do not believe that is the intention of any of the critics I have discussed so far. Nonetheless, their allegiance to a particular critical approach nudges their theories in this direction. Because of the impact these critics have already had on film theory in the growing area of scholarship on masochism and male subjectivity, I think their work may reasonably be regarded as representative of the new directions such academic thought is taking. At the risk of seeming antitheoretical, I would like to propose that rather than continuing on this track, we would do better to return to a more careful consideration of what specific film narratives are explicitly telling us about masochism.

I have chosen to talk about two films that follow their central figures' struggles to come to terms with their condition as members of repressive societies and, at the same time, make the transition from youth to manhood—*if...* and *Lord Jim*. In both films, masculine subjectivity is overtly connected to, although not conflated with, masochism through central scenes in which the young man's subjection to variously eroticized violent abuses is represented as the catalyst for his sudden attainment of male identity and power. There are marked differences in the films' presentations of these moments in which the possibility of a masochistic response is offered. Plot details work with visual cues to contextualize this possibility as a temptation to be resisted or an opportunity to be grasped. Each film takes a position on masochism that is deeply colored by radical political concerns.

Of the two, Lindsay Anderson's 1969 film *if...* is the most blatantly political and the most uncompromisingly radical. *if...* reenvisions the sixties in microcosm as a clash between remarkably free-spirited boys and tight-lipped, repressive prefects in an English public school, and concludes with a fantasy of armed revolution in which "the system" is destroyed. Posters of revolutionary leaders dignify the activities of the rebellious boys through association. While the Kiplingesque standard of restrained masculinity alluded to in the film's title and epigram is savaged, the concept of a heroic masculinity is retained. The rebels are idealized according to their ability to escape restraints and resist internalizing repression.

In its vision of heroic masculinities the film is unusually generous. Homosexuality is not excluded; instead, scenes of idyllic homoeroticism are matched to scenes of glorious heterosexuality. For instance, in one scene shot as a silvery dream, the nude wife of the housemaster wanders through an empty dormitory, her pale body glowing, while in another scene equally lustrous and slow, a classically beautiful boy plays on a trampoline under the adoring gaze of a younger adolescent watching from a balcony. However, one effect of this narrative strategy is that the arousal that many audience members will feel watching the beautiful boys on the screen is mirrored within the frame, so all the contacts between the boys seem saturated with homoerotic possibility. Consequently, the set piece caning of the rebel leader is eroticized, not simply by the perverse eyes of the viewer, but within the fiction.

Here a Foucauldian recognition that power and resistance lie in each others' arms seems to lurk just beneath the surface of the action. But as the protagonist's self-satisfied bravado is broken by unexpected additional blows, the almost emergent image of dominance as seduction and rebellion as erotic play is effaced by the redramatization of the old Promethean/romantic opposition between hegemonic power and heroism. The protagonist becomes a hero—and a man— when he refuses to accept even a negative definition from those placed above him and sets out to obliterate them.

Rather than representing a space in which power could be seized and identity negotiated, masochism is simply coded and rejected as collusion with the enemy. Because the beating scene evokes a favorite situation in masochistic pornography, because it is placed at the end of a series of increasingly explicit scenes of sexualized activity, and because it occurs within an atmosphere of open homoeroticism, the viewer may well be tempted to consider the scene sadomasochistic. But the film urges resistance of that temptation. In fact, the story concerns itself with the political necessity that masochism be absent so that a difficult and risky resistance can be maintained.

We may argue with the film's position on masochism—although a more politically useful response might be to examine the ways in which it reflects leftist ideology of its times—but we cannot locate masochistic pleasure within the film's depiction of the beating except through projection. We must interject our own responses into the film to find within its frame anyone enjoying the reception of violence. And to do so is to ignore rather than to deconstruct the story that unwound before our eyes. Like Freud listening to Dora, we would have to translate the emphatic "no" we hear into a "yes" we wish to hear.

If we hear "yeses" that have never been voiced, how shall we hear the voiced affirmatives? Richard Brooks' 1965 film *Lord Jim* is generally understood to be about masochism, but that it is virtually unique in valorizing masochism as the preeminent road to both successful revolutionary activity and manhood seems seldom remarked. Masochism is suggested by Peter O'Toole's playing of the title role. Not only is the character of the protagonist inflected by the prior text of O'Toole's performance in *Lawrence of Arabia* (1962), which includes a graphic whipping scene, and by the association of the actor with T. E. Lawrence's masochism, but it is also informed by his large features and theatrical acting style, which exaggerate his expressions of emotion so that in numerous close-ups he appears grotesquely agonized. From the Conrad novel on which it is, often rather loosely, based, the film inherits the theme of guilt and expiation. But in contrast to the novel, the film detaches Jim's pleasure in pain from guilt and instead represents it as the ultimate satisfaction his world has to offer a decent white man.

Conrad's suggestion that Jim is flawed by pride, which forces him into situations that can only be redeemed through self-sacrifice, is stated by one of the characters, but without much conviction. What we are shown, repeatedly, is that because of Jim's birth into a specific race and class, his masochism has been predetermined as the only possible noble response to the needs of the colonized people who surround him. *Lord Jim* represents the masochist as the exemplary male subject but in accordance with a very different ideology than the one Silverman uncovers in *It's a Wonderful Life*. The film is the most faithful to Conrad in its abhorrence of imperialism, but least faithful in its insistence that imperialism must be resisted through masochism.

The masochism of *Lord Jim* fits Deleuze's descriptions better than Freud's. Deleuze writes, "Masochism is a story that relates how the superego was destroyed and by whom. . . . Sometimes the story is misunderstood and one is led to think that the superego triumphs at the very point when it is dying" (130). The words "the Father," "the patriarchy," or "imperialism" can be inserted interchangeably in place of "the superego" without altering the statement's applicability to *Lord Jim*. Jim first appears on the screen inscribed with his culture's signifiers of value and truth, which are read for us by a voice-over that is quickly identified as proceeding from the respectable captain of Jim's first ship, a man whom he will later call Father. The rest of the film is devoted to Jim's subversions of the inscriptions he bears, through his ardent pursuit of tortures that will mark him as inferior to the colonized Other.

On the *Patna*, Jim faces the false choice between taking the ship's wheel and captaining the "natives" as he has been commissioned to do or deserting them. As he will slowly learn, the choice is false because either action would be a betrayal. In his obsessive returns, rendered through flashbacks, to the decisive moment, he discovers new possibilities, all ways to destroy the power that his tall, blond, uniformed body represents. When his judge angrily confronts him, after the *Patna* trial, with the accusation that his confession and humiliation have hurt all his fellow white men, Jim suggests with an enigmatic smile that this was his intention. Within this context, the apparent ecstasy that twists Jim's face as he awaits the application of a burning knife to his flesh is much less suggestive of the gratification of moral masochism than of the wild pleasure of the boy who cuts himself to spite his father's race. Finally he becomes the imperialist father, *Lord* Jim, only to sacrifice himself along with all he represents.

Deleuze's view of masochism as an attack on the father through the person of the son seems apropos here (125–26). But far from suggesting, as both Deleuze and Silverman in her discussion of his theory do, that male masochism can merely disavow paternal power, *Lord Jim* dramatizes the moment of resistance in which the fathers are crushed to dust (Silverman, "Masochism" 56). When Jim falls, there are no more patriarchs or heirs on the screen. Even the native chief, already rendered virtually meaningless by his deference to Jim and the subsequent loss of his son and descent line, confirms his own impotence when he becomes the agent of the death Jim has chosen.

The culmination of Jim's story and of the film comes when his shrouded body is displayed on the funeral pyre of the tribal prince, indistinguishable from any native Patusanan's, recognizable only because of the attention of the camera and the beatific expression of fulfillment on the face of his mistress. Jim is dead, but the fathers are far from having triumphed. They have died in his person in the instant of his death, and in that same instant he has acceded to manhood, attaining the manly power both to define himself without reference to the father and to satisfy his woman. His power is realized in the assent he makes to punishment; it is exercised in his choice to share his humiliation with the oppressive group to which he has been assigned; and its pleasure is registered in his surprising smiles in painful situations.

Much more can be said about gender in these films. My intention has been to show that the most obvious plot elements in films must provide a basis for further discussion of their construction of masculinity. For how can we know what these two films made in the 1960s, each speaking from the depths of a fierce politics, have to say to each other if we see them both as depicting masochistic pleasure? How can we recognize the disruptions in their representations of exemplary manhood if we begin with the assumption that all scenes in which the protagonists receive punishment signify masochism? The films themselves envision masochism, as does Deleuze, not as an omnipresent response to abuse but as a contract negotiated by the punished with the punisher, a contract that can be negotiated because it can also be rejected. If the dismal truth of life really is that it makes masochists of us all, no matter what we believe we want or feel, then perhaps we should be all the more attentive to narratives that in their "disavowals" of such profound powerlessness at least allow us to dream of meaningful resistance.

Notes

1. I wish to distinguish here not between types of feminists but between types of feminist activity, and between the feminisms, theories formal and unarticulated, which guide them. While I believe that feminist literary and film criticism will eventually help bring about social change, I do not see these as political activities so direct as, for example, working in a shelter for battered women. Since many feminist critics participate in such direct political actions, my point is that we should bring our own feminisms into fuller and more harmonious communication with each other.

2. See Jennifer Nedelsky's "Law, Boundaries, and the Bounded Self" for a balanced discussion of the implications for women of the centrality in the U.S. Constitution of the concept of a bounded self that must be protected from invasion.

3. For one of Freud's most convoluted "explanations" of the seductiveness of paternal brutality, see "A Child Is Being Beaten," in which he claims that men's heterosexual fantasies of being dominated by women always mask the unconscious desire to be beaten by the father, which "also stands for being loved (in a genital sense)" (198).

Works Cited

Cooper, Arnold M. "Masochism as a Character Trait." Keynote Address. Masochism Symposium Sponsored by the Psychiatric Services of Children's Hospital of San Francisco. San Francisco, 25 Oct. 1986.

Deleuze, Gilles. *Masochism: Coldness and Cruelty.* Trans. Jean McNeil. New York: Zone, 1989.

Dirty Harry. Dir. Don Siegel. 1971.

Freud, Sigmund. *The Standard Edition of the Complete Psychological Works of Sigmund Freud.* 24 vols. Trans. James Strachey et al. Ed. Strachey. London: Hogarth, 1974.

———. "'A Child Is Being Beaten': A Contribution to the Study of the Origin of Sexual Perversions." 1919. *Standard Edition* 17: 179–204.

———. "Fragment of an Analysis of a Case of Hysteria" [Dora]. 1905. *Standard Edition* 7: 1–122.

Grossman, William I. "Notes on Masochism: A Discussion of the History and Development of a Psychoanalytic Concept." *Psychoanalytic Quarterly* 55 (1986): 379–413.

if... Dir. Lindsay Anderson. 1969.

It's a Wonderful Life. Dir. Frank Capra. 1946.

Lord Jim. Dir. Peter Brooks. 1965.

Modleski, Tania. *The Women Who Knew Too Much: Hitchcock and Feminist Theory.* New York: Methuen, 1988.

Nedelsky, Jennifer. "Law, Boundaries, and the Bounded Self." *Representations* 30 (1990): 162–89.

Reik, Theodor. *Masochism in Sex and Society.* Trans. Margaret H. Beigel and Gertrud M. Kurth. 1941. New York: Grove, 1962.

Scarry, Elaine. *The Body in Pain: The Making and Unmaking of the World.* New York: Oxford UP, 1985.

Silverman, Kaja. "Fassbinder and Lacan: A Reconsideration of Gaze, Look and Image." *Camera Obscura* 19 (1989): 54–85.

———. "Male Subjectivity and the Celestial Suture: *It's a Wonderful Life.*" *Framework* 12 (1981): 16–22.

———. "Masochism and Male Subjectivity." *Camera Obscura* 17 (1988): 31–68.

———. "White Skin, Brown Masks: The Double Mimesis, or With Lawrence in Arabia." *Differences* 1.3 (1989): 3–54.

Smith, Paul. "Action Movie Hysteria, or Eastwood Bound." *Differences* 1.3 (1989): 88–107.

Studlar, Gaylyn. *In the Realm of Pleasure: Von Sternberg, Dietrich, and the Masochistic Aesthetic.* Urbana: U of Illinois P, 1989.

Valverde, Mariana. "Beyond Gender Dangers and Private Pleasures: Theory and Ethics in the Sex Debates." *Feminist Studies* 15 (1989): 237–54.

Vertigo. Dir. Alfred Hitchcock, 1958.

Williams, Linda. "Submission and Reading: Feminine Masochism and Feminist Criticism." *New Formations* 7 (1989): 9–19.

Revisionary Interdisciplinarity:
A Selection of New Approaches

Razing the Framework:
Reader-Response Criticism after Fish

David R. Anderson

Although reader-response criticism has shifted critical attention from works to readers' dynamic structuring of texts over time, reader-response theorists have failed to answer difficult questions about interpretive limits, interpretive change, and the social exchange of meaning. This failure is due, in part, to cultural-framework models of communication, such as Stanley Fish's idea of interpretive communities. Cultural frameworks cannot model the dynamic processes of textual structuring because they are formalist models of reader response. Without acknowledging it, Fish is arguing that meaning is embedded in cultural frameworks, an idea no better than the idea that meaning is embedded in literary works. Fish's model ignores the reading process, allowing him to impose his own predilections upon the results of that process. Additionally, framework models mistakenly equate societal and physiological processes of organization, leading not only to reductive reasoning but to representational theories of communication. Ultimately I object, personally and politically, to theorists' use of cultural frameworks to homogenize diversity and thereby obliterate the tremendous agency that all readers (and minority readers in particular) exercise daily to construct viable selves and meaning in indifferent or hostile social environments.

By contrast, I argue that readers are self-organizing and self-stabilizing systems for whom structuring is an instrumental process based on probability and personal economy. My type of reader-response criticism would emphasize the agency of the reader. It would be qualitative rather than quantitative, following the shape and probability of response rather than predicting specific responses for specific readers at specific times. My approach is akin to mathematical catastrophe theory, which maps major changes in a system following minor changes in conditions. Accordingly, I discuss shifts in reading strategy to demonstrate how steady continuous input into a system can lead to sudden, catastrophic shifts in strategy. I contend that reader-response criticism informed by Jamesian pragmatics and nonlinear dynamics (such as catastrophe theory) can model both the temporal structuring of texts and the social negotiation of meaning, and thereby describe the complexities of reading better than framework relativism.[1]

1

Although reading is often done in solitude, it is also a social act, and criticism oriented to the process of reading has had tremendous difficulty explaining the simultaneous construction of texts and the negotiation of meanings based on those texts. Stanley Fish makes an important contribution to reader-response theory with the idea of "interpretive communities," whereby readers construct meaning based on social as well as personal interests. But Fish never incorporates readers' construction of these communities into the *dynamic* process of reading. Instead, he argues that a shared "point of view or way of organizing experience" engulfs and controls the process. Readers are "embedded" in a common social matrix, so that "community-constituted interpreters . . . in their turn, constitute, more or less in agreement, the same text, although the sameness would not be attributable to the self-identity of the text, but to the communal nature of the interpretive act" (*Doing* 141). By imposing interpretive communities upon the reading process rather than incorporating their construction into that process, Fish creates a formalist model of reader response.

For this reason, Fish's model is subject to the same charges of formalism that he leveled at stylisticians and literary critics over twenty years ago. In "Interpreting the *Variorum*," for instance, he attacked any literary analysis "gen-erated by the assumption that meaning is embedded in the artifact" because "evidence brought to bear in the course of formalist analyses . . . will always point in as many directions as there are interpreters; that is, not only will it prove something, it will prove anything" (*Is There a Text* 150). Instead, Fish argued, "It is the structure of the reader's experience rather than any structures available on the page that should be the object of description" (152). But in later work he claims that readers are themselves "embedded," and consequently meaning is embedded, in a social structure where categories and presuppositions are culturally determined and already in place. With this argument, Fish's idea of interpretive communities becomes a formalist model of reading. Marvin and Netta Kaplan point out, however, that "assumptions of integrative hierarchical control" such as Fish's interpretive communities have no connection to the processes described but are merely theorists' "imposition of rules of orderliness" on experiences long after the processes are over: "[Such] constructions that we make regarding the development of control or regulatory functions are . . . merely metaphors of control, regulation, and direction that reflect the theorist's framework of as-sumptions as well as the limitations imposed by observational methods" (164). Fish is not modeling the reading process itself but imposing metaphors of control on the results of that process. Instead of integrating control, regulation, and direction into the decision processes of readers, he imposes his own preferred rules of orderliness and social homogeneity upon reading and the social negotiation of meaning. He is free to construct interpretive communities any way he wishes, and to make whatever assertions he can about them. Fish's cultural frameworks, then, are subject to the same criticisms as other formalist models of reading. No matter what the circumstance, his model will always prove what he wants to prove—namely, that cultural frameworks produce meaning.

Accordingly, critics and theorists alike can create interpretive communities for any literary occasion. Since the theorist, rather than the reader, defines the cultural framework, the theorists can impose relationships onto the results of the reading process to generate self-validating descriptions. Communities become ad hoc generalizations about any social coordination or coincidence of activity. The characters in Robert Frost's "Mending Wall" can be said to constitute an "interpretive community" of wall builders. People who drive on the right side of the road can be said to belong to yet another "intepretive community." Many of us belong to an interpretive community of toilet-paper pullers, some of whom prefer to unravel the roll from over the spool, some from under. But although this interpretive community is "homogeneous with respect to some general sense of purpose and purview," that is, unraveling the toilet paper, the community is "heterogeneous with respect to the variety of practices it can accommodate," namely, unraveling over or under the spool (Fish, *Doing* 149). By failing to describe the way that readers dynamically construct the communities to which they belong, Fish relabels communal behavior without explaining it.

In truth, Fish must fall back on a formalist account of reading because, without frameworks, he cannot explain how or why we structure texts or the world. In formalist theories of process, "The stability and continuity of systems are assumed to be anchored to the properties of their physical structure" (Kaplan and Kaplan 164). Fish anchors readers' activities to the engulfing community, so he cannot otherwise explain interpretive change. For instance, he argues that readers make interpretive assumptions at line breaks of Milton's sonnets but modify or abandon those assumptions immediately after the line break (*Is There a Text* 149–57). He does not believe, however, that readers could change their interpretations if left to their own devices. In "How to Recognize a Poem When You See One," he describes how students could interpret a list of names on a blackboard as a seventeenth-century religious poem, concluding that "indeed definitions of poetry *are* recipes, for by directing readers as to what to look for in a poem, they instruct them in ways of looking that will produce what they expect to see" (*Is There a Text* 327). Potentially, readers could produce a virtually infinite number of texts from the blackboard list.[2] And if the mind can create almost at will, it can interact at will, so we are free to interact with the text as much or as little as we like. The question arises, why read or act when we can simply imagine Nirvana, withdraw from the world, and die in bliss? Fish assures us, however, that we do not withdraw from the world—he "doesn't mean that [the objects we experience] are not objects or that we don't have them or that they exert no pressure on us" (*Doing* 153). His community becomes like a parent making sure we eat our carrots and make friends at school, supposedly providing sufficient economic reason for our continual interaction with the world, and our varying interaction with literary works.

Clearly, we must have motives for structuring the world, and for structuring texts in particular ways, but instead of discussing the economic interests and evaluative abilities of readers, Fish personifies the entire interpretive community, granting it physiological processes and economic interests that only individuals could possess. When asked how people can change their minds within such a community, he answers that "the mind (and, by extension, the community) is an engine of change," as if both perform similar mental functions (*Doing* 146). Fish later describes cognitive *set*, the physiological preparation to perceive expected information, as a societal response. Set becomes "a general background of irrelevance . . . that informs the community, telling it what it must pay attention to and what it can afford to ignore" (148). Fish begs the question of how hundreds, perhaps thousands of people could coordinate their physiological responses—he simply assumes that they are already coordinated (*always already coordinated?*).

No model of communication can afford to dismiss the motives behind communication, but Fish is so concerned with social homogeneity that he ignores the varying responses within any social situation, as well as the complex motives behind those responses. In "Change," he cites an example from the sociologist D. L. Weider of a halfway house where ex-convicts abide by the convict code—"to show loyalty to the residents by displaying resistance to the staff" (*Doing* 150). When the director of the house asks a resident to organize a baseball team, the resident refuses on the basis of the code. Fish argues that the resident's decision proves the dynamic nature of interpretive communities. The resident extends the code to structure a new experience, but that extension changes the code and all future actions within it (151). By such logic, the code becomes "an entirely flexible instrument for organizing contingent experience" (151).[3]

But Fish is so worried about homogeneity that he neglects the experience of the resident. Did the resident refuse the director's request for moral reasons, for revenge, out of exhaustion, as a favor to another resident, or in fear of his or her life? For Fish, the resident's decision does not matter, because all decisions occur within the code. But the individual qualities of the resident's decision are clearly important. He or she must decide to apply the code, then weigh the advantages and disadvantages that the code makes possible. Consequently, the resident's conscious and unconscious evaluation of social repercussions is crucial to his or her decision. Only through evaluating does a code exist or continue to function. Fish suppresses evaluation within the reading process because he is concerned only about homogeneity, not an individual's construction and main-tenance of the code. Fish does precisely what he accuses formalist literary critics of doing in "Interpreting the *Variorum*"—flattening out or suppressing difficulties that readers experience over time, and thereby creating a self-validating model of reader response. Within his system, readers' motives for predicting social responses to their interpretive behavior vanish without a trace.

By suppressing evaluation, and by equating social and individual processes of organizing texts, Fish constructs yet another representational theory of mean-ing. Instead of mirroring the world, however, language mirrors the ideas of the community. By contending that language conveys meaning with considerable precision, Fish must create a totalizing cultural framework to explain such precise communication. He argues in "Change" that individuals modify a social code while using it, but because the social code simultaneously modifies the individual, personal response and social frameworks are equated. Social negotiation of meaning becomes identical to individual physiological processes of constructing meaning. Individual and society are so coordinated physiologically that language mirrors mental activity and social interaction simultaneously. Fish approvingly quotes Richard Rorty's assertion that "there is no way to think about either the world or our purposes except by using our language," nor "of breaking out of language to compare it with something else" (qtd. in *Doing* 143). Language mirrors the cognitive and cultural presuppositions we use to organize experience, because both sets of presuppositions are identical. The cognitive ability of individuals and the cognitive ability of communities are one and the same.

Fish's argument is reductive: communities control the organization of mean-ing, individuals organize meaning, therefore communities must control the or-ganization of meaning. By arguing that societies organize themselves in the same way that individuals do, Fish commits the fallacy of composition (the argument that what is true of the part must be true of the whole) that Jon Elster warns about in *Ulysses and the Sirens*: "In societies there is no general mechanism—corresponding to natural selection [or human cognition]—that could permit us to infer that the latent functions of a structure typically maintain the structure by feedback" (2). In other words, social groups cannot maintain themselves; people maintain social groups. Societies, unlike people, cannot physiologically anticipate environmental events or modify behavior to satisfy needs and inter-ests. Similarly, people are not homunculi who resemble their societies on a microscopic scale. Fish argues reductively to defend his assertions of social homogeneity, arguing that individual physiological processes of self-organization are also social processes of structural maintenance.

We need to go beyond explaining communication through some supposed homogeneity in linguistic usage. "Communication" is not the conveyance of ideas but, in its archaic sense, an act of working in common. We do not exchange ideas or experiences through language, but we construct corresponding (but not identical) versions of those ideas and experiences based on probability, past experience, current needs, and personal resources. For instance, when my friend Elise tells me, "My mother is dead," I cannot know Elise's precise experience through language, but I can construct my own version, drawing probable connections between the words she uses and my own personal experience, and guessing what aspects of the situation are important enough to figure out. Because my experiences of her mother differ from Elise's, I construct an adequate version of what I believe she was like based on memory, past description, and the purposes of our conversation. I understand the mother's death only through my own experiences with death. I empathize with Elise's mourning because of my own past losses, loves, and concern for Elise. In other words, my friend has not conveyed meaning to me, but I have created meaning *for myself with respect to her.* I have literally made sense of language, and remade that sense for the shifting purposes of the conversation. People do not convey information intact. Instead, they make it easier for others to construct meaning in such a way that they can work together, and they continually test and modify those constructions based on changing conditions and interests.

Just as two people coordinate very different interests while talking, so audience members of mass entertainment have different interests and construct different, if corresponding, versions of movies, texts, and so on. Karen Chandler points out in her research on women's reception of melodrama that "movies contributed to the illusion of homogeneity since persons of middle- and working-class status attended them" (32). Although melodramas with female protagonists were popular with women regardless of social status, "Nevertheless, black women's embrace of melodrama does not indicate their assimilation of middle-class white women's tastes. Women did not comprise the homogeneous audience that the film and publishing industries addressed" (32). Chandler refers to Alice Dunbar-Nelson's adverse reactions to early sound films such as *Hearts of Dixie,* which contained racial stereotypes, as well as Dunbar-Nelson's enthusiastic reviews of various melodramatic novels with female protagonists (33–34). "Although most works of popular culture do not acknowledge black women's conditions, these conditions do pointedly shape [those] readers' and filmgoers' acts of interpretation. They guide her rejection of negative stereotypes of blacks, her acceptance of positive ones, and her, at times, ambivalent identification with black or white protagonists and their trials" (35–36). In other words, when watching a film or reading a book, people continually reconstruct their social relationships to other members of the audience and to the filmmaker or author. Accordingly, readers constantly coordinate their own personal and social interests with respect to those which other audience members, or the filmmaker or author, are presumed to possess. At varying times, readers' interests correspond with, or are antagonistic to, those of other races, classes, and groups.

Stanley Fish could argue that all African-American readers make up one homogeneous interpretive community, or he could arbitrarily clump them together into various groups, but those procedures obscure diversity among African-Americans, as well as the agency behind their diversity. The more we know of Alice Dunbar-Nelson's taste, the less she can be clumped arbitrarily with others. If her intense dislike of *Hearts of Dixie* associates her with some readers, her interest in melodramatic novels with female protagonists whittles that interpretive community down, and each additional film or novel gradually reduces that community to a grand total of one—either that, or the shared assumptions would be so few and so general that they would hardly characterize what Fish would call an interpretive community. Dunbar-Nelson's tastes do not reflect the shared assumptions of a large community, but the continual construction and negotiation of meanings with others.

As an African-American scholar, I am frustrated with the widespread abuse of field or framework models in the literary profession, particularly because these models suppress, ignore, or fail to explain the tremendous agency minorities must exercise daily to construct viable selves and meaning in a hostile social environment that my colleagues continually assure me is "homogeneous." Field theories can provide useful ways of thinking about social groups, but once we think of groups as frozen structures rather than as continually shifting processes of social interaction, we are in trouble. And once we think that these structures can mysteriously maintain themselves like some creature out of a science-fiction film, it is time to abandon them. Besides, field theories in the social sciences are pseudoscientific and mechanistic. They are borrowed either from nineteenth-century physics (the same physics that influenced Eliot's theory of the canon) or from theories of biological function (for instance, the function of a cell within an organism), and neither biology nor physics uses intention among its modes of explanation (Elster, *Ulysses* ix). Not only minorities but all readers in contemporary theory are just so many electrons within a magnetic field, so much protoplasm within cell walls. Such theories are a luxury other theorists can afford, but I cannot, Frederick Douglass could not, other members of minorities cannot—and I believe most readers cannot.

Framework models of communication fail because they only explain the possibility of communication but never consider the *use* of communication for the purposes of adaptation. Language does not enforce or reflect homogeneity, it helps people coordinate, and perhaps fight for or defend, separate interests and processes of interpretation. Reader-response theorists must recognize that if people negotiate meanings for a sufficient period of time, they learn to coordinate their interests and construct corresponding meanings with increasing success. When I communicate with someone, I try to get our conceptual worlds to correspond *just enough* so that we can work together. From this, people can engage in collective action, that is, form social groups and ultimately cultures. Regardless of whether groups form because of coercion, economic necessity, or geography, these groups stay together partly because individuals must negotiate interests with others. Members of groups learn to negotiate with one another with considerable success, lending the appearance of homogeneity. But any person can construct *some* version of another's experiences and negotiate interests with that other person, if perhaps less successfully or with less complexity if they cannot find past experiences and present interests that enable them to coordinate the construction of meaning. For instance, the question whether African-Americans are always better interpreters of their own literature remains unanswered, because even though imagination cannot replace experience, and black literary theorists and critics have the advantage of a particular cultural knowledge, others can become increasingly skilled in negotiating meanings from those texts, and some exceptionally skilled.

Communication, including reading, is a process of adapting to changing social conditions to maintain and expand our interests. That process is based on past experience and subjective probability. In the rest of the paper, I will begin to develop such a model of reader response.

2

Jamesian pragmatism is a highly useful model for reader response because, as William James argued at the turn of the century, people continually predict, test, and reevaluate probabilities to adapt to changing conditions. Like James, I assume that "the world [is] constituted by the activity of mind or consciousness acting upon a confusion of unorganized data . . . to satisfy human needs and purposes" (Kuklick xii). To experience, then, is to structure and value. Leonard Meyer states: "Experienced naively—without any psychological predispositions or cultural preconceptions whatsoever—the world, as William James observed, is a buzzing, booming confusion of discrete, unrelated sense impressions. . . . It has neither process nor form, meaning nor value. . . . It merely exists" (3). To make sense of this barrage, we organize experience within a set of instrumental assumptions and predictions, hypothesizing about material reality to achieve our ends efficiently.[4] We establish boundaries of probability around our experience, separating usable from unusable stimuli. When these boundaries are small enough, we have a manageable number of impressions that we can combine according to probability and convention. These structures, in turn, become the bases for new hypotheses. Structuring is functioning, and a necessary part of goal-oriented activity. Hence, evaluation is implicitly part of experience. As Barbara Herrnstein Smith argues, a "subject's experience of an entity is always a function of his or her personal economy," namely, needs, interests, and resources ("Contingencies of Value" 16). By structuring sense impressions into individual "gestalts" (unified psychological configurations) and contextual frames that link gestalts together, people construct versions of their environment for personal use:

> Clearly there are in the mind no objects or events—no pigs, no coconut palms, and no mothers. The mind contains only transforms, percepts, images, etc., and rules for making these transforms, percepts, etc. . . .
> In any case, it is nonsense to say that a man was frightened by a lion, because a lion is not an idea. The man makes an *idea* of the lion. (Bateson 271)[5]

Knowledge is a probabilistic, instrumental construct readily adapted to changing circumstances.

Reading is like any other goal-oriented activity. Readers bring large numbers of preconceptions to texts, differentiating finally between literary and nonliterary discourse and between poetic and prosaic discourse. These differentiations in turn differ from reader to reader and time to time. Any theory of reader response must recognize that readers have different goals while reading, bring different experiences to a text, and adapt to changing conditions, constantly reevaluating progress toward goals, reevaluating those goals, reevaluating the hypotheses, and renegotiating meaning with others.

Furthermore, reading is probabilistic rather than representational because structuring must be economical. We lack the resources to structure every potential bit of information a work might contain. Additionally, most potential information is irrelevant to our needs and interests. Finally, objects continually change, and if my idea of an object were photographically precise, I would soon be unable to recognize it. Neither ideas nor language can be strictly representational— neither Bateson's idea-lion, nor the linguistic sign "L-I-O-N" which corresponds to the idea. Instead, both perception and linguistic use are adaptive processes that coordinate our complex interests with our physiological experience, and that coordination depends heavily upon probability.

Communication relies so heavily on probabilistic processing that encoding and decoding meaning are "equally imprecise and approximate and . . . therefore, there is no possibility of recovering complete meaning from a text." Rather than recovering sense from a text, we *make* sense of it. People use language as "a set of directions . . . indicat[ing] to the decoder where he must look in the conceptual world of his knowledge and experience for the encoder's meaning." Because reading depends upon probability and personal economy, "the amount of information contained in a text . . . is incalculable since it depends on how much knowledge the reader brings to the text and how much he wishes to extract from it" (Widdowson 174).

Our cognitive systems are "self-referential" rather than representational—

that is, we construct an environment from within our own assumptions and concerns about our surroundings, about who we are, and about our relationship to that environment. Human psychological functioning is what Marvin and Netta Kaplan describe as "a self-organizing system" that is far more concerned with organizing and sustaining adaptive mental processes than with mirroring the environment (161). Structuring and functioning, forming and informing, are the same act seen from different perspectives (see, e.g., 166).

Because our cognitive systems are self-organizing, they must also be self-stabilizing—that is, they must coordinate all mental processes to change together. Stability, then, is not permanence or persistence but active and successful change. This may seem illogical, but for the system to continue functioning, all processes must adapt together. In the simplest terms, if I am walking and I reach a point where I face oncoming traffic, I had better stop or change directions, or I will die. If I assume that Marianne Moore's "The Jerboa" is about a quest for the Holy Grail and my assumptions are never borne out, I had better change my assumptions if I want to get anything valuable from the text. In other words, the *system* remains stable by changing—adapting processes and structures to new conditions. All constructing is part of a larger unitary process that coordinates while it organizes.

No adaptive system can remain functionally stable without some means of correcting itself—that is, some means of reorganizing its behavior. Consequently, self-referential knowledge is not nihilistic relativism but an evolving process of engaging the world from within continually modified assumptions. "In all cases [for adaptive systems] . . . there must be a process of *trial and error* and a mechanism of *comparison*" (Bateson 274; see also Guilbaud 21; Koestler 42). We predict, define evidence, decide the requisite amount of evidence, compare the evidence to our predictions, and decide what to do from there. Our cognitive systems need negative feedback (a means of disconfirming our hypotheses) so that they can successfully reorganize themselves with respect to the environment. Positive feedback confirms our expectations, encouraging our systems to continue on their paths of functioning, much like a person walking into oncoming traffic. Negative feedback, however, alerts the system that its predictions are wrong, and that its functioning must adapt to unexpected conditions. Nevertheless, negative feedback does not proscribe particular responses, only that we should do something else. Just as error is self-determined, corrections are also self-determined. Since our minds do not try to mirror our surroundings, neural activity "does not have a direct correspondence with environmental conditions" (Kaplan and Kaplan 171). Changes are self-determined, since our systems reorganize behavior within a continually modified set of probabilities and predictions. Adapting is part of a large unitary process of self-organization that structures by means of subjective probability and modifies those probabilities by means of feedback loops.

Because our systems are self-stabilizing through feedback, we experience ourselves and our environments, and therefore textual structures, as relatively persistent. Visual attention during reading is a good example of self-stabilizing: "What is being distinguished as a 'fixed' object of attention [in our case, a text] does not exist as such but is being created along the lines of an ongoing organizational 'theme' that is being labeled as the identified object" (Kaplan and Kaplan 170). When we read a text, we often assume that our eyes move in a straight line from left to right (for English orthography), except for those times that we look back briefly to reread. In fact, our eyes move in a series of quick jerks (or saccades), fixating briefly on one part of the text or another (Smyth et al. 2).[6] Nearly 20 percent of all reading eye movements (for all ages) are backward and right to left (Crowder 8–9; Smyth et al. 2–3).[7] Sequential focusing brings out or explores new or special features in the text based on shifting needs and orientation. (Some saccades are also random means of organizing the visual field.) Each focus relates to the one before and the one after, so that attention evolves as part of the organizational process of the entire system (Kaplan and Kaplan 170).[8] Because my cognitive system continually adapts, I experience myself and the environment as "stable, enduring, and continuous," I form "discrete linear constructs such as objects, events, ideas, or memories," and I learn to label broader psychological functions such as "perception" and "emotion" (175). But objects and functions seem enduring and continuous only because of successful adjustments made by our cognitive systems. Seemingly fixed objects or ideas are really changing processes of organization, particularly shifts in attention (170).

Using language is a similarly dynamic, if more complex, cognitive process because we must coordinate simultaneous processes of defining referents and signifiers. When ideas change, language changes. We must coordinate the construction of visual marks or sound patterns with the construction of referents, and we must continually modify both sets of constructions and the relationships between them when interacting with the world and with other people. Just as my house keys never form the same geometric pattern twice, no two sound patterns or printed marks are identical, yet I am able to say with some confidence, "These are my house keys," or ask somebody "Can you hand me those house keys?" depending upon my shifting interests, what I believe is necessary to know about the environment, and what I believe are the corresponding interests of others. Neither marks nor ideas are ever the same twice, but organized and coordinated within the same unitary process of self-organization.[9]

Since readers are self-organizing and self-stabilizing systems, texts, experiential selves, intended meaning, and our roles as readers within interpretive communities are all constructions that change when we respond to new conditions. All these seemingly rigid structures are really coordinated processes of self-organization that are modified simultaneously during the course of reading. When our conception of intention changes, for instance, we must modify simultaneously our conception of the text and the interpretive communities to which we respond.

This "rearrangement" of ideas, as James once put it (78), can be demonstrated by various readings of William Carlos Williams's "The Yachts." The poem can read as stream of consciousness unless a reader makes certain assumptions about the author, and therefore about the text and communities reading the text.[10] When reading the first five lines, many readers will notice by the third or fourth line that the poem rhymes, and some will assume that the poem is written in *terza rima* (after seeing the *a b a b c* rhyme scheme of the first five lines).

contend in a sea which the land partly encloses
shielding them from the too-heavy blows
of an ungoverned ocean which when it chooses

tortures the biggest hulls, the best man knows
to pit against its beatings, and sinks them pitilessly.
(Williams 101)

With each new detail, their conception of the author changes (for instance, Williams's knowledge of other formal poetry, his purposeful choice of a *particular* form such as *terza rima*, his purposeful reference to Dante). When assumptions about intention change, the text is modified, too (the poem's organization seems carefully controlled, the organization of the poem mimics the organization of nature, the poem is a vision of hell), and the interpretive community is also modified (readers should catch references to abstract forms or to Dante, the yachts are a symbol of wealth, particularly for readers during the Great Depression, and so on). By lines six and seven, rhyme becomes irregular ("Mothlike in mists, scintillant in the minute / brilliance of cloudless days, with broad bellying sails"), and it disappears by the fourth stanza. Readers must then try to explain the sudden disappearance of rhyme and the increasingly convoluted syntax. Accordingly, they must modify or reinforce their constructions of the author, the text, and the interpretive community (the poem is not as organized as it first appeared because nature and society are not as organized as they first appear, the poem is still a vision of hell, and so on). If we read on, more assumptions would change or be reinforced.

For reading "The Yachts" (or other texts) to be a communal act, we must believe that somebody intends textual meaning to a given audience. Unless we assume linguistic intention, we cannot organize texts into linguistic structures. Intention is indispensable to reading, but when readers construct intention, they do not always assign it to a single author. Many times, they divide or disperse intention throughout a community, depending upon the expected roles and abilities of its members. Whether we attribute intention to an author, to several authors, to an editor, to a literary critic, to the reader, to other readers, or to various combinations thereof, the processes of constructing intention are similar across the board. Consequently, rumors of the death of the author are greatly exaggerated, because we must construct *some* intender or intenders in order to construct meaning.[11] The two are inseparable. When critics assert that the author is dead, they never abolish intention or some concept of an intender. They merely construct different notions of intention and an intender, and different notions of acceptable interpretation within constructed discursive communities. Even by asserting "the author is dead," these critics are necessarily constructing a traditional author, if only to contrast him or her with the new intender. Finally, their new ways of organizing the text imply a protoauthor, because their organization of the text is necessarily related to past performances of organizing texts, some of which may presume authorial intention.

In addition, there is no interpretive "free play" as an absolute, even though interpretation is adaptable and poems can have an infinite number of meanings. As a practical matter, interpretation is limited by self-organization and self-stabilization. Our minds are "wedged tightly," as James would write, not only because we must organize experience, but because we must coordinate all processes of organization (96). Reading takes place within a larger self-organizing process in which we constantly reorganize our experiential selves, our discursive communities, and the texts we are reading. Free play is a luxury only certain literary critics can afford. Our cognitive systems cannot tolerate free play. They are too concerned with adaptation and survival.

But when we coordinate the activities of reading, authorial intention need not be hierarchically privileged. Changes in the text or community may change our construction of intention. If I see that a poem is a sonnet, I may assume the author was alluding to other sonnets. I may wish to interpret Robert Frost's "Nothing Gold Can Stay" as an attack on the gold standard, but I am loath to do so because my interpretive community (other scholars) would demand evidence showing that Frost was actively concerned about economic matters. (In that case, I would be coordinating my conception of the author with what I believe to be others' conceptions of the author. I can still maintain that "Nothing Gold Can Stay" is about the gold standard, but I would realize that my interpretation has no currency.)

Constructing intention is more complicated than simply attributing ideas to an author. We bring assumptions about encoding and decoding meaning, as well as human ability, to the construction of texts. We construct intention based upon these assumptions. In psychoanalytic criticism, for instance, practitioners attribute some intentions to the author, but some must be attributed either to the author's unconscious or to the critic who reconstructs meaning from unconscious signs. Nevertheless, these critics construct unconscious meanings *as if an author had intended them,* even though they assume the author did not intend everything he or she wrote. In other words, the processes for organizing psychoanalytic readings of texts resemble those in which complete authorial intention is assumed. The case of the psychoanalytic critic is not unusual. Readers and literary critics frequently question or modify authorial intention because they know encoding and decoding meaning is imprecise ("You didn't mean to say *that,* did you?"), or because historical and cultural remove reminds us of human frailty ("Well, A. D. Hope was wrong—free verse didn't die out"). Concessions to human limitation, as well as theories of communication and meaning, influence our construction of intention.

Even when reading "found poetry," when intention, textual meaning, and interpretive roles are suddenly open to question, readers continue using probability to limit speculation and construct efficiently.[12] Under what conditions do we organize nonpoetic discourse with the processes we use to organize lyric poems? We can start by looking at Stanley Fish's blackboard assignment/religious lyric:

Jacobs-Rosenbaum

Levin

Thorne

Hayes

Ohman (?)

(*Is There a Text* 323)

Fish's 1971 summer class at SUNY-Buffalo interpreted these lines as a seventeenth-century religious lyric because, well, they were in a religious poetry class, and Fish told them to. Because of social context, the students' subjective probabilities were stacked in favor of organizing these lines as a poem, and classmates' corroborating interpretations helped confirm this assumption.

Outside of Fish's class, however, their subjective probabilities would shift drastically. Those five lines, if encountered on the street, would not resemble any poem the students had seen before. It would be so improbable that those lines were a poem that the students would not even consider constructing them into a poem (except, perhaps, as a joke). This is because of psychological set (a preparational state for perceiving phenomena). Floyd Allport points out: "Sets . . . stand in an *antagonistic* relation to one another and have a *negative* or *inhibitory* as well as a positive aspect. . . . Sets are . . . inhibitory only with respect to *other* acts and their corresponding sets" (214). Sets inhibit other sets within similar activities (so that hypotheses about texts compete with one another, and stronger hypotheses cancel out weaker hypotheses). The stronger the students' assumptions (that is, the more probable the phenomenon), the less evidence they need to confirm their hypotheses, and the more likely that their assumptions will be confirmed. Similarly, the weaker their assumptions, or the more evidence that contradicts their hypotheses, the more supporting evidence they need for confirmation (Allport 381–83).

In the case of Fish's students, the most likely hypothesis—a list of names—would be so strong that it would eliminate other possibilities of construction. The students would recognize the lines as a list of names, although they would probably not be able to decide what kind of list it might be. Even if the students did recognize the lines as a poem, they would not recognize it as any type of poem, but most likely as a lyric because of its short length, and there is no guarantee they would like the poem. Even though sense impressions can be understood in a multitude of ways, not every representation is feasible or possible at the *same* time. Our hypotheses bound interpretations by introducing unequal probabilities, making some representations more likely than others, and some virtually impossible. Predictions about text, self, and community all limit the range of my interpretations, and all limits must be coordinated as part of a large unitary process of self-organization. Under such extraordinarily demanding conditions of adaptation, "our mind is thus wedged tightly" (James 96).

Readers bring their experience with general linguistic usage to bear on works, and thereby bring a subjective knowledge of the frequency distributions of rhythmic, syntactic, typographical, and narrative structures to free verse. When hypotheses about textual information are not confirmed, readers eventually shift strategies abruptly, trying to develop a new strategy for structuring based on the poem in question.

Because of such strategic shifts, qualitative modeling (especially catastrophe theory) is useful for reader-response criticism. Catastrophe theory models "a major change in [a] system, consecutive to a minor change in the external variables" (Ekeland 90). "A catastrophe occurs when a stable equilibrium vanishes during a continuous modification of the external variables. . . . that is, we get a discontinuous response to a continuous change" (90, 91). Catastrophe theory is a qualitative model because it predicts particular types of catastrophes given a particular type of system. It does not predict *when* a catastrophe will occur, only that one will occur if certain conditions persist. Qualitative models, then, enable "us to understand the patterns which the system will follow in the long run, even if definite predictions cannot be made" (75). A qualitative model of reading helps us follow the shape of readers' responses without predicting specific responses at specific times.

To demonstrate catastrophic shifts in structuring, I will examine the process of reading the first section of Walt Whitman's "Out of the Cradle Endlessly Rocking," a poem one early reviewer, in the *Cincinnati Daily Commercial*, declared meaningless (Whitman 247). I, too, had immense trouble constructing a context for the first section of the poem. As George Dillon argues in *Language Processing and the Reading of Literature*, "Processing strategies are probabilistic in nature: they are based on expectations and likelihoods . . . they are indeed a quintessence or abstract of previous performances" (xxvi). When I read the first prepositional phrase ("Out of the cradle endlessly rocking"), I assumed that it modified a nearby noun phrase, which I expected to find in the next line. Instead, I found another prepositional phrase ("Out of the mocking-bird's throat, the musical shuttle"), but still assumed a noun phrase lurked in the next line to help me contextualize the first two lines. Although increasingly uncertain by the third phrase ("Out of the Ninth-month midnight"), I still believed the parade of prepositional phrases would end, partly because one more phrase was highly improbable, and partly because the third line contained two signs of closure—relatively fewer syllables, and three strong alliterative stresses. With the fourth line ("Over the sterile sands and the fields beyond . . . "), prepositional phrases became more likely than noun phrases, because my expectations had been consistently thwarted. I decided, therefore, that my original hypothesis was improbable and must be discarded. Consequently, I had to devise another strategy for reading the poem, and began to read the poem phrase by phrase rather than as a sentence. I no longer tried to find a noun phrase that the prepositional phrases were linking to the rest of the sentence, and abandoned the hope of quickly contextualizing the poem. By processing the poem line by line rather than within a larger frame, I consequently failed to find the subject, verb, and object of the sentence (I sing a reminiscence).

Because my previous reading strategy did not work for me, I had to modify my approach to the poem. From a processing strategy based on generalized past reading experience, I had to develop a processing strategy based on my experience of the free-verse poem before me. The sudden shift in strategy could have come after the second prepositional phrase, the fifth, or the tenth—it does not matter. What does matter is that I eventually had to adjust my strategy to the poem I was reading. By noting syntactic and rhythmic parallelism, I was able to construct a contextual frame, but more importantly, I began to understand the syntactic cataloging of experience to be an epistemological jumble that, in the last line, becomes a simulated gestalt (a sung reminiscence). By organizing this jumble, I emulated the process of constructing a poem and learned to become a poet like Whitman through the act of structuring. Needless to say, I was quite pleased with myself.

I can generalize about my own experience with "Out of the Cradle Endlessly Rocking" for several reasons. Readers bring their general linguistic experience and their subjective probabilities to literary discourse. Norms, and deviations from those norms, are based on the frequency distribution of structures within the language. Readers bring their experience with general linguistic usage to bear on literary works, and thereby bring a subjective knowledge of the frequency distributions of rhythmic, syntactic, typographical, and narrative structures to free-verse poems. Similar members of a linguistic community have roughly similar experiences with the frequency distribution of rhythmic, syntactic, typographical, and narrative structures in general usage. No two sets of subjective probabilities are alike, but they do not need to be identical to be meaningful. Subjective probabilities of syntactic structures within a community form a bell curve of possible response to Whitman's poem. At one end of the curve, readers will immediately surmise that the first section consists of a series of prepositional phrases. At the other end, readers will be lost from the very beginning of the poem (or will read it as a quest for the Holy Grail). But in between, there will be many readers who will have to switch strategies abruptly when the expected noun phrase consistently fails to appear. When that switch takes place will vary from reader to reader—some may need only two lines to switch strategies, some will need eight or ten lines. I can predict only that a switch will eventually occur if their hypotheses are not confirmed, and that the switch will be abrupt. What the new strategy will be, nobody can predict. But once again, it will follow a bell curve of response. The complexity of coordinating continual processing shifts makes every reader's response unique, but the closer readers' probabilities are to mine, the more easily I can generalize from my experience to theirs.

Such contexts and meanings that I generated from "Out of the Cradle Endlessly Rocking" are not permanent because new conditions lead to modified structures. For example, when I first read the opening three lines of Robert Frost's "The Oven Bird" ("There is a singer everyone has heard, / Loud, a mid-summer and a mid-wood bird, / Who makes the solid tree trunks sound again" [Frost 119]), I constructed a context in which "sound" was most likely a verb that meant, roughly, "to reverberate loudly." When I noted a theme of natural degeneration in the rest of the poem, my context gradually changed, and I brought that new context back to the beginning of the poem. To my surprise, "sound" had suddenly become ambiguous. It was not only a verb but an adjective as well, meaning, approximately, "healthy, rejuvenated."

Semantic structures such as "sound" must be modifiable because reading is a temporally linear and mistake-ridden process. Because I obtain information sequentially rather than all at once, I must anticipate new information by hypothesizing. Informed guesses, however, are always subject to error (nonconfirmation). Errors (or rather, improbable hypotheses that I abandon as unconfirmed) are potentially costly (I cannot go back in time and change the initial hypothesis). Reading, then, becomes a complex process of adaptation in which I try to satisfy needs, anticipate information efficiently to minimize the likelihood and severity of errors, evaluate progress, and correct errors.

As it turned out, I was able to use my interpretation of the ambiguity of "sound" in other acts of discourse. For instance, when I mentioned the ambiguity to one professor, she responded, "Yes, 'sound' can be a noun—the bird is turning the woods into sound, that is, a poem."[13] Now this is not what I had meant, but since I was already prepared to interpret "sound" as ambiguous, I could easily interpret it as a noun, as well as a verb and adjective. By doing so, I was able to exchange information and new ideas to further develop my own interpretation. Because of the possibility of new meaning, I reorganized my concept of authorial intention, as well as my relationship to another reader.

Of course, my professor and I had very different ideas about the poem, and very different ideas about the ambiguity of "sound" in that poem. This is because, as Widdowson states, encoding and decoding meaning are "equally imprecise and approximate and . . . therefore, there is no possibility of recovering complete meaning from a text." Encoding is not the transmission of messages, but "the devising of a set of directions . . . indicat[ing] to the decoder where he must look in the conceptual world of his knowledge and experience for the encoder's meaning." Interlocutors negotiate meanings through "reciprocal exchanges," and in place of such exchanges, readers may decode a text by "assum[ing] the dual role of addresser and addressee, and reconstitut[ing] the dialogue" (Widdowson 174, 177). But as the interpretive community grows, the standard deviation of possible responses widens. With increasing social interaction (in a classroom, for instance), we increase the likelihood of modifying our interpretations to correspond with, or repudiate, the interpretations of others. The precision of the informational exchange is lessened, but the possibility for new constructions of information increases. Consequently, the amount of information in a work is incalculable, depending not only upon the reader's past experience and personal economy when constructing a text but also upon the number of readers of a particular work, and therefore on the social interaction among particular readers.

The imprecision of exchange and the potential for information both grow with the size of the interpretive community, *but only to a point*. The text does not degenerate into meaninglessness or free play. We do not get complete information from a text, but the text does not become a chaotic jumble, either. If my professor and I had continued talking and had pushed one another on every possible meaning, we would have left the conversation bewildered. Fortunately, our conceptual worlds did not have to be identical, but only roughly in correspondence for us to interact (Widdowson 176). We assumed for the purpose of discussion that our conceptual worlds corresponded, continually tested that assumption, and negotiated agreement on such troubling concepts as the meanings of "sound" (177). Eventually, we walked away with new and potentially useful ideas. There is no need to specify ultimate motivations because, in a sense, there are no ultimate motivations—my decisions during reading were contingent upon a wide variety of intertwining factors, and later uses of that conversation will be similarly contingent.

My generalizations about readers' responses are possible because my theory of reader response, like catastophe theory, is loosely predictive. Catastrophe theory argues that, given certain types of events, steady continuous input will lead to sudden discontinuous output. The theory traces the shape of the behavior of a system but does not try to predict an outcome at a *specific* moment in time. Similarly, I am arguing that the longer textual hypotheses go unconfirmed, the more unable readers will be to modify and salvage those hypotheses, and the more likely to shift strategies abruptly. Nobody can predict when that shift will take place, or what the new strategy will be. Qualitative modeling is ideally suited to reader-response criticism because of the complex agency of readers, and because the construction of knowledge is a probabilistic process. As critics, we want to make sure that we do not confuse interpretive stability with structural rigidity. Interpretive stability is a process, the continual ability to construct and negotiate texts within a larger unitary process of self-organization. A theory that emphasizes change rather than persistence can best describe such interpretive stability.

I hope I have emphasized the problems with framework models of communication—not only their similarity to other formalist models but their crude insistence upon homogeneity and their inherent reductive reasoning of premising the absence of agency to prove the absence of agency. Without returning to a representational theory of meaning, I have tried to show that readers construct texts from within their own changing interests, and have tried to model the reading process by using probability in much the same way that readers themselves use probability to construct meaning.

Notes

1. For a far more detailed attack on framework relativism, see Paisley Livingston's *Literary Knowledge*.

2. I say "virtually" because, as Fish points out, we would always construct the text from some set of preconceptions that allow some constructions but constrain or curtail others. The number of potential preconceptions, however, would be infinite if interpretive communities did not regulate and constrain them.

3. Fish's idea of interpretive communities eerily resembles T.S. Eliot's conception of the literary canon. In "Tradition and the Individual Talent," Eliot compares the canon to an electromagnetic field in which a new work of art changes the field in which it is placed, while the field simultaneously changes the work of art (38–39). Fish is creating an Eliotic model of reader response

in which, as an observer from outside the field, he can preserve social meaning as carefully as Eliot preserved his hierarchy of texts.

4. Although our cognitive systems try to structure efficiently, efficiency is not an end in itself. In other words, adaptation is far more important than optimizing efficiency. For a fuller discussion of possible problems with maximizing or optimizing, see Slote's *Beyond Optimizing* and Elster's *Sour Grapes.*

5. A percept is simply a "phenomenological experience of an object," which is really an ongoing process of organizing physiological stimuli (Allport 23). A transform is a group of elements (all the physiological information about a perceived object) qualitatively changed into a gestalt (the lion).

6. "Saccades and fixations are not unique to reading; they happen whenever we inspect a static scene" (Smyth et al. 2).

7. The percentage of regressive, or backward, eye movements does not include dropping down to a new line of text.

8. Within this self-organizing system, there are "no discrete parts, no enduring subprocesses, and no fixed structural differentiation," only a continual organizational process (Kaplan and Kaplan 166). Such seemingly discrete functions as emotion and perception occur simultaneously and are inseparable from one another during psychological functioning. Because of selective attention, people sometimes notice them separately.

9. By arguing that language is a dynamic, instrumental process, I am implicitly repudiating Jacques Derrida's contention that language is a static, autonomous system that people unsuccessfully try to impose upon a dynamic world. I should point out that Derrida's model of communication depends upon the autonomy of signs, which severs them from human use. By contrast, I am arguing that communication depends upon the synonymy or similarity of signs (that is, the continually redefined equivalence or sameness of two or more signs). Since people constantly redefine equivalence or sameness of meaning, language can never be severed from human use, and writing can never be an autonomous machine.

10. Here, "stream of consciousness" refers only to Williams's literary style, which draws attention to readers' shifts in interpretive strategy. By contrast, William James's concept of the stream of consciousness emphasizes that because of cognitive adaptation we experience ourselves and our environments as relatively persistent. In this sense, James's work resembles that of Kaplan and Kaplan.

11. A constructed intender does not have to be an author, so my discussion of meaning and intention differs markedly from that of Steven Knapp and Walter Benn Michaels in "Against Theory." In addition, I would argue that our theories about human psychology and communication necessarily influence our construction of an intender, and therefore our construction of texts.

12. Literary criticism abounds in such examples. See, e.g., Terry

Eagleton's sign in the London underground (6–7), Fish's blackboard assignment (*Is There a Text* 323), Vanzetti's last courtroom speech in Barbara Herrnstein Smith's *Poetic Closure* (22), and a piece of French journalism in Jonathan Culler's *Structuralist Poetics* (161).

13. I am indebted to Elisa New for my discussion here.

Works Cited

Allport, Floyd. *Theories of Perception and the Concept of Structure.* New York: Wiley, 1955.

Bateson, Gregory. *Steps to an Ecology of Mind.* San Francisco: Chandler, 1972.

Chandler, Karen. "Melodrama and Its Audiences." Unpublished essay, 1991.

Crowder, Robert G. *The Psychology of Reading.* New York: Oxford UP, 1982.

Culler, Jonathan. *Structuralist Poetics: Structuralism, Linguistics, and the Study of Literature.* Ithaca: Cornell UP, 1975.

Dillon, George L. *Language Processing and the Reading of Literature: Toward a Model of Comprehension.* Bloomington: Indiana UP, 1978.

Eagleton, Terry. *Literary Theory: An Introduction.* Minneapolis: U of Minnesota P, 1983.

Ekeland, Ivar. *Mathematics and the Unexpected.* Chicago: U of Chicago P, 1988.

Eliot, T. S. "Tradition and the Individual Talent." *Selected Prose of T. S. Eliot.* Ed. Frank Kermode. New Haven: Farrar, 1975. 37–44.

Elster, Jon. *Sour Grapes: Studies in the Subversion of Rationality.* Cambridge: Cambridge UP; Paris: Editions de la Maison des Sciences de l'Homme, 1983.

―――. *Ulysses and the Sirens: Studies in Rationality and Irrationality.* Rev. ed. Cambridge: Cambridge UP; Paris: Editions de la Maison des Sciences de l'Homme, 1984.

Fish, Stanley. *Doing What Comes Naturally: Change, Rhetoric, and the Practice of Theory in Literary and Legal Studies.* Durham: Duke UP, 1989.

―――. *Is There a Text in This Class? The Authority of Interpretative Communities.* Cambridge: Harvard UP, 1980.

Frost, Robert. *The Poetry of Robert Frost.* Ed. Edward Connery Lathem. New York: Holt, 1969.

Guilbaud, G. T. *What Is Cybernetics?* Trans. Valerie MacKay. New York: Grove, 1959.

James, William. *Pragmatism.* Ed. Bruce Kuklick. Indianapolis: Hackett, 1981.

Kaplan, Marvin L., and Netta R. Kaplan. "The Self-Organization of Human Psychological Functioning." *Behavioural Science* 36 (1991): 161–78.

Knapp, Steven, and Walter Benn Michaels. "Against Theory." *Against Theory: Literary Studies and the New Pragmatism.* Ed. W. J. T. Mitchell. Chicago: U of Chicago P, 1985. 11–30.

Koestler, Arthur. *The Ghost in the Machine.* London: Arkana, 1967.

Kuklick, Bruce. Introduction. *Pragmatism.* By William James. Ed. Bruce Kuklick. Indianapolis: Hackett, 1981. ix–xv.

Livingston, Paisley. *Literary Knowledge: Humanistic Inquiry and the Philosophy of Science.* Ithaca: Cornell UP, 1988.

Meyer, Leonard B. *Explaining Music: Essays and Explorations.* Chicago: U of Chicago P, 1973.

Slote, Michael. *Beyond Optimizing: A Study of Rational Choice.* Cambridge: Harvard UP, 1989.

Smith, Barbara Herrnstein. "Contingencies of Value." *Canons.* Ed. Robert von Hallberg. Chicago: U of Chicago P, 1983. 5–39.

———. *Poetic Closure: A Study of How Poems End.* Chicago: U of Chicago P, 1968.

Smyth, Mary, et al., eds. *Cognition in Action.* London: LEA, 1987.

Whitman, Walt. *Leaves of Grass.* Ed. Sculley Bradley and Harold W. Blodgett. New York: Norton, 1973.

Widdowson, H. G. *Explorations in Applied Linguistics.* Oxford: Oxford UP, 1979.

Williams, William Carlos. *Selected Poems.* Ed. Charles Tomlinson. New York: New Directions, 1985.

Remodeling Truth, Power, and Society: Implications of Chaos Theory, Nonequilibrium Dynamics, and Systems Science for the Study of Politics and Literature

Barbara Riebling

The intellectual should constantly disturb, should bear witness to the misery of the world, should be provocative by being independent, should rebel against all hidden and open pressure and manipulations, should be the chief doubter of systems, of power and its incantations, should be a witness to their mendacity.
—Václav Havel, *Disturbing the Peace*

Usually provinces go most of the time, in the changes they make, from order to disorder and then pass again from disorder to order, for worldly things are not allowed by nature to stand still.
—Machiavelli, *Florentine Histories*

Questions of power are central to contemporary literary studies. In recent years, the most "unlikely" works have become vehicles for political analysis, since many scholars now assume that *all* texts reflect or enact power relations. To some this "politicization" of the critical discourse is deeply disturbing. However, as one who does historical work in Renaissance literature, I have found that the recognition of literature's political potential has opened more doors of critical inquiry than it has closed. I am, nevertheless, concerned about the direction contemporary work in politics and literature has taken—not because I feel the subject area is inappropriate but because I find the methodology unsound. Specifically, I believe that the models literary scholars use to describe power relations are fundamentally flawed. In what follows, I will attempt to delineate why contemporary modeling is theoretically inadequate and inaccurate, and I will offer alternatives based on recent breakthroughs in the hard and social sciences, briefly applying these theories to a select group of Renaissance works.

In recent years, the ideas of Michel Foucault have dominated theories of power in literary studies, particularly in the Renaissance, where his political models have been applied mainly by the "new historicists." Two central Foucauldian tenets are particularly relevant to the study of politics and literature: (1) the idea that in all societies power "constructs" truth, and (2) the notion that the social dynamics of control are a continuous equilibrium process of subversion and containment.[1]

To Foucault and his followers "truth" is simultaneously an effect of power and its mode of domination. It has no transcendent (essential) existence outside power relations, and it can never be an instrument of individual or collective agency. "Truth" reflects and sustains social systems in which all (including the nominally powerful) are subjugated. Foucault's assertions about truth harmonize with poststructuralist epistemological nihilism.[2] They are also attempts to define truth *functionally*—its power or lack of power, its role in history, and its representation in a variety of texts. Foucault is right to look at truth functionally, especially in the study of politics; he is also right that truth bears a strong relation to power. What his theory fails to explain, however, is the kind of truth that can bring down regimes and empower the powerless. Specifically, if we look at the history of "the politics of conscience," we can see that truth can *be* power; it does not simply reflect, enact, or perpetuate it. The simplest way to highlight the limitations of Foucault's totalitarian theory of truth is to look at an example from recent history. When a group of women whose children had "disappeared" at the hands of the Argentine junta dared to defy its official silence about their children's fate, they were empowered by their act of witness. Their vigil in the central square of the capital, where they stood with the photographs of their missing sons and daughters, was a daily indictment of the regime, its murders and its lies. Most significantly, by forcing Argentina to face the truth about the junta, the women's actions were a significant factor in its eventual collapse. This is just one instance from the history of political activism; there are many others, each serving to call into question the crippling cynicism of Foucault's theory of power and truth.

Building on Foucault's general political theory, new historicists have also adopted his model of a continuous subversion of power and containment of subversion, which they apply to both social systems and literary works. Like deconstruction's cardinal principle of self-cancellation in texts, this theory displays a compulsive symmetry leading to nihilism: for every +1 there will arise a −1, so that all human equations result in 0. Although it may appear dynamic, this model is essentially static and determinist. In the end, the system in question (whether society or text) always maintains perfect equilibrium; power "circulates," but nothing really changes. This is true whether the model is applied "pessimistically" (any attempt at subversion of the social order is automatically contained) or "optimistically" (any effort at control by the ruling power is automatically subverted).

Foucauldians maintain that their theories escape the reductive determinism of "vulgar Marxism" by no longer locating power in a single class or mode of control. Like Althusser, who "dethrones the God economy," Foucault spreads out the mechanisms of domination, diffusing them throughout the social structure until they seep into every aspect of life. Power is "everywhere and nowhere," so that even though "sites of resistance" continually arise, all resistance is in the final analysis futile, or at most cathartic. In other words, these theories have decentralized determinism, not dismantled it. Indeed their models of power, particularly their rejection of collective power bases and their belief that subjective consciousness is entirely controlled by internalized social mechanisms, make them "ultradeterminist."[3] Because it obviates individual and collective agency, Foucauldian theory fosters a politics of despair and enervation similar to what Václav Havel has called "degenerate realism"—the tendency to wallow in a sense of one's own helplessness (*Open Letters*, 98). Besides being demoralizing, the death of agency gives rise to serious theoretical problems; there is nothing in the subversion/containment model that can account for genuine conflict or change. These are grave flaws in what purports to be a comprehensive theory of political history, since politics and history are the social sciences that deal with conflict and change, respectively.[4]

For decades the theoretical grounding for the formal study of power politics among social scientists has been general systems theory. However, this theoretical base has not carried over into political analyses within the humanities. The neglect of systems theory is partly a result of the dauntingly technical nature of the material and partly a reaction to the reductive modeling done by early behaviorists working in social cybernetics (the study of control systems). Ironically, the theory of subversion and containment is itself a simplistic cybernetic model, which has been adopted by humanities scholars at the very moment when the sciences are opening up possibilities for nonreductive systems modeling. Grégoire Nicolis and Ilya Prigogine argue that unexpected discoveries about the behavior of matter at far-from-equilibrium states have given "hard" science a new relevance to the social world.

> According to the classical view, there was a sharp distinction between simple systems, such as studied by physics or chemistry, and complex systems such as studied in biology and the human sciences. Indeed, it would be hard to imagine a greater contrast than the one that exists between the simple models of classical dynamics . . . and the complex processes we discover in the evolution of life or in the history of the human societies.

It is precisely because this gap is narrowing that we now may consider applying new knowledge to situations for which the concepts of
classical physics were insufficient or inappropriate, or even essentially
meaningless. (3)

Whether they realize it or not, new historicists are practicing a kind of
cybernetic modeling based on the theoretical assumptions of classical physics,
assumptions that are rapidly becoming obsolete. Chaos theory, Prigogine's theory
of "dissipative systems," the study of turbulence, new theories in ecology, and
catastrophe theory, among others, have all adopted "lifelike" models that are
disequilibrial, symmetry breaking, and potentially stochastic. In other words,
these models reflect the fact that complex, living systems cannot exist in *perfect*
balance or symmetry, and that their behavior is inherently unpredictable. Perfect
equilibrium (the condition of opposing forces exactly balancing or equaling one
another) is characteristic of systems that are either artificial or dead. Foucauldian
notions of social systems dynamics, which are equilibrial, unchanging, and symmetrical—the dynamics of a perpetual motion machine operating in a vacuum—
could not be further from current scientific thinking. Not only do they violate
the second law of thermodynamics (which is now expanding its range of applications in the new physics),[5] but they also display a kind of mechanistic determinism most scientists no longer accept.
    Philosophies of mechanistic determinism originated in the Enlightenment
and continue to shape our views. Whether teleological or fatalistic, they assert
that human actions, regardless of any appearance of freedom, are determined
exclusively by external forces acting upon the will and that these forces are
themselves driven by a necessary and unbroken chain of causation. Given enough
information, human actions and the course of history are transparent and predictable, and individual acts are without significance, overwhelmed by the global
forces that shape their origins and obviate their effects. Philosophical determinism
is closely intertwined with the "classical determinism" of Enlightenment scientists
like Newton and Laplace. Laplace, for example, in his *Philosophical Essays on
Probabilities*, asserts that "an intellect which at any given moment knew all the
forces that animate Nature and the mutual positions of the beings that comprise
it, if this intellect were vast enough to submit its data to analysis, could condense
into a single formula the movements of the greatest bodies of the universe and
that of the lightest atom: for such a being nothing would be uncertain; and the
future just like the past would be present before its eyes" (qtd. in Stewart 11–
12). If Laplace's statement seems painfully naive, it might be well to remember
how many contemporary theorists within the hard sciences, the social sciences,
and the humanities are searching for universal algorithms, and how many disciplines still see history (whether human or cosmic) as "given" and the future as
equally "given," albeit unknown.

However compatible philosophical determinism may be with classical scientific determinism, it is at odds with chaos theory and the new sciences of
complexity. Indeed, "Laplace's demon" has become a synecdoche among chaos
theorists for all the reductive certainties that underlie mechanistic determinism.
The new paradigms of order and disorder proposed by chaos theory, catastrophe
theory, and Prigogine's "order through fluctuations" model call into question the
two fundamental assumptions of classical scientific and philosophical determinism: (1) that events are tied to one another in an unbroken chain of causation;
(2) that actions at the "local" level (the scale of the individual) are always
determined by larger "global" forces on which they can have no significant
impact. One can still speak of "determinism" in the new sciences, but its operation
is now seen as strictly limited. As Prigogine and Stengers state:

> Our universe has a pluralistic, complex character. Structures may disappear,
> but they also may appear. Some processes are, as far as we know, well
> described by deterministic equations, but others involve probabilistic pro-
> cesses. . . . The models considered by classical physics seem to us to occur
> only in limiting situations such as we can create artificially by putting
> matter into a box and then waiting until it reaches equilibrium.
>   The artificial may be deterministic and reversible. The natural contains
> essential elements of randomness and irreversibility. This leads to a new
> view of matter in which matter is no longer the passive substance described
> in the mechanistic world view but is associated with spontaneous activity.
> This change is so profound that, as we stated in our Preface, we can really
> speak about a new dialogue of man with nature. (9)

Prigogine and Stengers describe the history of complex systems as anything but
an unbroken chain of predictable causes and effects. Their "order through fluctuations" model describes complex systems as traveling an evolutionary path
characterized by a mixture of necessity and chance, "a succession of stable regions,
where deterministic laws dominate," punctuated by instabilities, "bifurcation
points" at which the system's behavior is governed by chance (169–70).
    Prigogine's description of the evolution of physical systems finds a parallel
in the historical sciences with Niles Eldredge and Stephen Jay Gould's theory
of evolutionary dynamics known as "punctuated equilibria." This theory has
supplanted Darwinian gradualism as the dominant model for evolutionary change
among paleontologists. For instance, on the largest scale, discoveries in the
geologic record indicate that, for whatever reason, the course of evolution on
this planet has been one of long periods of stability punctuated by catastrophic
mass extinctions (where as many as 90 percent of the species are randomly wiped
out); this is followed, in turn, by a proliferation of new classes of species or a
new order of dominance that initiates another long period of stability. On the

smaller scale of species evolution, the patterns of change are also nongradualist. Although neither Prigogine nor Gould acknowledge one another, Daniel Brooks and E. O. Wiley in *Evolution as Entropy* have attempted to find a basis for macroevolutionary dynamics in Prigogine's theories. In addition, life scientists like Stuart Kauffman use "dissipative systems" theory to build computer models of evolution that display a tendency to evolve stable states, which then become unstable and "crash" only to evolve new stabilities.[6]

In mathematics, recent work in chaos theory and catastrophe theory also undermines mechanistic determinism. Ivar Ekeland and Ian Stewart both describe "deterministic chaos," randomness flowing from lawful behavior. If there is one deterministic system, says Ekeland, it is the whole universe. However, predicting its operations would require infinite information, and its subsystems (about which a finite amount of information could be obtained) become unpredictable when they are studied in artificial isolation from the whole. Thus, "like the queen of England, determinism reigns but it does not govern. Its power nominally extends over vast territories, where local rulers are in fact independent, and even turn against it" (63). In addition to undermining mechanistic determinism, catastrophe theory also provides a new kind of modeling for systems dynamics. Its models are "qualitative" rather than "quantitative," that is, they describe the shape of a behavior rather than attempt to plot its occurrence as a prediction. The behaviors catastrophe theory was designed to describe are the kind of "nonlinear" events where steady continuous input produces sudden discontinuous output.[7]

Traditionally, systems theorists have relied upon simple "linear" models. A linear relationship can be expressed as a straight line on a graph, and a linear system has the virtue of being modular—it can be broken down into components, each of which can be understood and all of which "add up" to describe the system as a whole (Gleick 23). A linear system also has "homogeneity," that is, proportional input and output (Kramer and de Smit 88–89). Unfortunately for the model makers, the universe is fundamentally nonlinear, a fact that explains why mechanistic models so often fail to describe reality. Nonlinear dynamics resist orderly analysis, as Briggs and Peat make clear in their overview of choas theory:

> In a nonlinear equation a small change in one variable can have a dispro-
> portional, even catastrophic impact on other variables. Where correlations
> between the elements of an evolving system remain relatively constant for
> a large range of values, at some critical point they split up and the equation
> describing the system rockets into a new behavior. Values that were quite
> close together soar apart. In linear equations, the solution of one equation
> allows the solver to generalize to other solutions; this isn't the case with
> nonlinear equations. (24)

Gleick compares the difficulties encountered in trying to solve problems in fluid dynamics with the nonlinear Navier-Stokes equation to "walking through a maze whose walls rearrange themselves with every step you take" (24). The reason nonlinear systems remain so intractable to prediction and orderly analysis is that even small variations in a single variable or minor perturbations (disturbances) to any part of these systems can become magnified by their dynamics and result in wildly unpredictable behavior. This is particularly true of complex systems with a tendency to iterative positive feedback (systems that repeatedly feed back their output as input) and those in far-from-equilibrium states.

The study of nonlinear dynamics is revolutionizing systems theorists' conceptions about the relationship of the "local" and the "global." For years, systems theory tended to reinforce the classical determinist idea that minor individual actions would naturally be overwhelmed by the giant system containing them and could not be critical in determining the path a system would follow. Often for no better reason than analytic convenience, they imposed an orderly dynamics on the natural world, asserting that small disturbances or inaccuracies of measurement would be insignificant when predicting the behavior of large systems. Edward Lorenz's discovery of the "butterfly effect" in the early sixties exploded this assumption, thereby destroying myriad fantasies of creating models that could predict the behavior of complex systems—from long-term weather forecasting to stock market predictions (Gleick 9–31). Although it took a while for the rest of the scientific community to notice Lorenz's discovery, in retrospect the "butterfly effect" was the beginning of the end for mechanistic, linear systems analysis in all but the most limited applications. The story is by now familiar, but it illustrates one of the fundamental principles of chaos theory so well that it bears repeating.

In 1961 Lorenz, a meteorologist, was trying to create a computer model that could lead to long-term weather prediction. All of the relevant physics were well understood, and Lorenz designed his primary model to operate with a few simple equations. After one particularly long run of the computer simulation, Lorenz wanted a rerun of the final phase and took the shortcut of simply entering the data for that position as it was recorded on the printout, using these figures to delineate the initial conditions of the final phase. He walked away from the computer for a few hours, and when he returned found to his amazement that the weather in the second version of the final run had taken an entirely different course. What had happened was that the computer had used six decimal points to calculate but only printed three. Although the inadvertent "round-off error" represented only the tiniest deviation, its results had amplified exponentially through simulation. This was not a programming error but a consequence of the nonlinear character of any system as complex as the weather. The name "butterfly effect" alludes to the fact that over sufficient time the movement of a butterfly's wings in Hong Kong can mean a storm in New York. The more technical name for the effect that threw Lorenz's model weather system into chaos is "sensitive dependence on initial conditions." Lorenz's discovery did not mean that the equations used by meteorologists were faulty or even that *very* precise measurements would be needed in order to forecast the weather accurately; rather, it meant something far more profound: that prediction in complex dynamic systems is *theoretically* impossible because of the iterated nonlinear equations involved, equations that represent the interconnected dynamics of the system (Briggs and Peat 69).

The discovery of the butterfly effect has wide-ranging implications that spread across disciplinary boundaries. "On a philosophical level," say Briggs and Peat, "chaos theory may hold comfort for anyone who feels his or her place in the cosmos is inconsequential. Inconsequential things can have a huge effect in a nonlinear universe" (75). From a social science perspective, "sensitive dependence on initial conditions" necessitates a reevalution of the power relations between the global and the local, the governors and the governed, society and the individual. Political and social relations are by their very nature complex and dynamic; therefore social systems should display the same nonlinear potentialities as all other complex systems, especially in times of crisis. Individual words and actions take on *much* greater significance in light of the new systems theory than was allotted to them by determinist social philosophies. To some degree these "new" attitudes represent a return to proverbial wisdom. As Gleick points out, "sensitive dependence on initial conditions" is a part of historic folklore:

For want of a nail, the shoe was lost;
For want of a shoe, the horse was lost;
For want of a horse, the rider was lost;
For want of a rider, the battle was lost;
For want of a battle, the kingdom was lost! (23)

If the "butterfly effect" helps to free individual agency from global determinist systems, and it does, it is nevertheless vital that we not "totalize" from the description of this phenomenon and see powerful, unfettered agency everywhere. First of all, even complex systems are not all equally chaotic or chaotic on the same time scale. For example, while local weather systems are highly nonlinear and tend not to be predictable beyond three days, a current like the gulf stream, which is also part of a complex chaotic system, can remain roughly predictable for centuries (Wunsch). Second, even the same system can behave differently over time. In looking at the role individual action can play in the fate of a complex system, Prigogine and Stengers emphasize the relative position of that system on its evolutionary path—is it near equilibrium or far from it? Is it at a critical bifurcation point? Since individual actions have different effects depending on the equilibrium status of the system, the generalizations drawn about the relative power of the local and the global to determine events are complex and contingent. One must distinguish between "states of the system in which all individual initiative is doomed to insignificance on the one hand, and on the other, bifurcation regions in which an individual, an idea, or a new behavior can upset the global state. Even in those regions, amplification obviously does not occur with just any individual, idea, or behavior, but only with those that are 'dangerous'—that is, those that can exploit to their advantage the nonlinear relations guaranteeing the stability of the preceding regime" (206). Thus, Prigogine and Stengers conclude that "*the same* nonlinearities may produce an order out of the chaos of elementary processes and still, under different circumstances, be responsible for the destruction of this same order, eventually producing a new coherence beyond another bifurcation" (206).

The kinds of processes that Prigogine and Stengers are describing are exemplified by some common occurences in nature. Small disturbances and individual actions become more critical the further a system gets from a state of equilibrium—for example, on the threshold of a "phase change," when matter changes from one state to another. When water boils in a pot, the first bubbles will form around dust particles or at sites where there are small imperfections in the surface of the vessel. These bubbles become the formal nuclei for others that proliferate around them and then invade the rest of the system. The instigating role of such nuclei is especially dramatic when water is "superheated." Very pure water in a perfect vessel can be heated without boiling to a point above normal boiling temperature. Then if a few dust particles drop into the water, it will come to an instantaneous rapid boil (Briggs and Peat 132). Similar dynamics of "nucleation" are at work when a supersaturated vapor transforms into a liquid: "In a gas, . . . condensation droplets incessantly form and evaporate. That temperature and pressure reach a point where the liquid state becomes stable means that a critical droplet size can be defined (which is smaller the lower the temperature and the higher the pressure). If the size of the droplet exceeds this 'nucleation threshold,' the gas almost instantaneously transforms into a liquid" (Prigogine and Stengers 187).

The implications of these kinds of models of change for social systems theory are fairly obvious, and numerous historical examples bear them out. When a regime or system is in a highly unstable state at the threshold of change, it can be toppled by a single act or word—provided that the act or word can take advantage of the system's dynamics, and especially if it predicts the system's next stable state, as the water droplet in a supersaturated vapor "predicts" the liquid state (in social terms, if it can represent or prophesy a new stable state toward which the system is already potentially tending). Recent events in Eastern Europe provide particularly striking evidence of this phenomenon. The 1989 Romanian revolution started in Timisoara when a single voice in the crowd shouted "Down with Ceauşescu!" and the city spontaneously rose in revolt. That revolt was then brutally repressed, but five days later a voice in a Bucharest crowd shouted "Timisoara," all of Romania rebelled, and within four days Ceauşescu and his wife were dead. Václav Havel speaks of the "nuclear" power one single word of truth has in a totalitarian regime—a power, he adds, that it does *not* have in a regime where free speech is more or less the rule. Comparing the impact of individuals in totalitarian and Western democratic societies, Havel states that a "single, seemingly powerless person who dares to cry out the word of truth and dares to stand behind it with all his person and all his life, ready to pay a high price, has, surprisingly, greater power, though formally disenfranchised, than do thousands of anonymous voters" (*Open Letters* 270).

Havel's assertion, certainly supported by recent events, raises the question why, in systems terms, totalitarian states should be more vulnerable to perturbation. In two essays that in retrospect seem particularly prescient, Havel gives a possible answer to this question. In "Dear Dr. Husák" (April 1975), he predicts to Czechoslovakia's ruler a moment when a "tornado [will] whirl through the musty edifice of petrified power structures" (*Open Letters* 77–78). At this moment, "The machine that worked for years to apparent perfection, faultlessly, without a hitch, falls apart overnight. The system that seemed likely to reign unchanged, world without end, since nothing could call its power into question amid all those unanimous votes and elections, is shattered without warning. And, to our amazement, we find that nothing was the way we thought it was" (77). In "The Power of the Powerless" (October 1978), Havel explains the dynamics of just such a total collapse and the role that the individual truth teller can have in the system's demise:

> For the crust presented by the life of lies is made of strange stuff. As long as it seals off hermetically the entire society, it appears to be made of stone. But the moment someone breaks through in one place, when one person cries out, "The emperor is naked!"—when a single person breaks the rules of the game, thus exposing it as a game—everything suddenly appears in another light and the whole crust seems then to be made of tissue on the point of tearing and disintegrating uncontrollably. (*Open Letters* 150)

Clearly, Havel is saying that late totalitarian societies, which he calls "post-totalitarian," are fragile *because* power constructs truth. A monologic social system is delicate when the monologue is a lie, and for Havel and other dissident political philosophers, all state monologues are invariably lies. This means that Havel sees weakness where Foucault and Althusser see monumental strength.

Havel can look at states living the Foucauldian carceral nightmare—from the inside out—and declare them systems in extremis. Havel would agree with the poststructuralist theorists that modern states (including Western capitalist states) make truth and the individual subjects of power. However, he would add that when Soviet bloc societies succeeded so thoroughly in subjugating their citizens, they made themselves intensely vulnerable. Instead of gaining the complete control that was their aim, they inadvertently transferred power to individuals, making it possible for them to disconfirm the totalized system of manufactured truth by a single word. In these regimes acts of truth telling are neither the kind of subversion that simply perpetuates the status quo nor momentary blasts of saturnalian energy coming from below that merely release pent-up frustrations. In Havel's view, they can be catalysts for real change.

Havel's beliefs about the power of truth and the vulnerability of totalitarian systems doubtless grow out of his historical situation; however, there are theoretical grounds for asserting that his views are basically valid. Since its inception, systems science has explored the relationship between stability and the flow of information, especially within the field of cybernetics, the study of control systems. It has long been recognized that the more freely information flows in a system, the more readily it can withstand perturbations. In political terms, a constant flow of truth, "negative feedback," keeps states adaptable and therefore stable under stress—in systems terms, "robust." Rigid regimes, on the other hand, where communication has atrophied, are brittle and subject to catastrophic failure. In physical systems, the phenomenon of "nucleation" reflects this crucial relationship between stability and effective communication: "Theoretical studies and numerical simulations show how the critical nucleus size increases with the efficacy of the diffusion mechanisms that link the regions of systems. In other words, the faster communication takes place within a system, the greater the percentage of unsuccessful fluctuations and thus the more stable the system" (Prigogine and Stengers 187).

The connection between communication and stability is easily observed in the thermostatic control of a home heating system, which operates by "negative feedback." The furnace controls are tied to constant readings of inside temperature. The system is in effect always asking "is it hot enough?" "is it cool enough?" and when it gets a negative answer, it takes corrective action by turning the furnace on or off. Disable the thermostat, and the system will keep on the same course until it breaks—frozen pipes or a burst boiler. Although this particular example is mechanical, not all systems controlled by negative feedback loops are man-made. The delicate balances between predator and prey populations in ecosystems are examples of naturally evolved stabilities employing negative feedback. Conversely, populations of species like the gypsy moth which have no natural predators explode and crash in chaotic patterns. These patterns exemplify "positive feedback" (the system's output becomes its input), which is always associated with instability. It is the presence of iterated positive feedback and its power to amplify deviations that make a highly nonlinear system like the weather so unstable and produce phenomena like the butterfly effect.

Other theoretical models in nonequilibrium dynamics can help to refine our approach to questions of control and stability in social systems. One of the most influential (and controversial) theories of evolving dynamic systems is the "Gaia Hypothesis" developed by James Lovelock to explain the highly improbable persistence of life on earth.[8] Throughout life's history, the earth has maintained a relatively constant temperature during periods of vastly different energy output from the sun. Lovelock asserts that life makes its own persistence possible by self-regulating its environment; its nonequilibrium dynamics save the earth from the deadly alternative equilibrium fates of Venus and Mars, which are respectively too hot and too cold for life. Lovelock sees life and its environment as one vast evolving superorganism—a view that is gaining considerable ground in environmental sciences and paleoecology (the study of the evolution of ecosystems).[9]

If the butterfly effect calls attention to the fundamentally nonlinear properties of complex dynamic systems, the Gaia Hypothesis emphasizes their resiliency— a difference that may explain Lovelock's hostility to chaos theory. From a broad perspective, however, both theories can coexist in the new systems sciences, since nonlinearity is relative. Although chaos is certainly the fate of all complex systems eventually, for some systems the time frames involved are measured in minutes, for others in days, years, or centuries, and for Gaia in eons. Furthermore, although the Gaia Hypothesis asserts that life itself is persistent, it sees any given life form as highly perishable. Thus it is in harmony with the earth's turbulent history of mass extinctions. Stability is once more a matter of scale— high on the global scale, but punctuated by periods of chaos on the smaller scale of the species.

To explain the mechanism by which the earth maintained its own life-sustaining climate, Lovelock and Lynn Margulis created the elegant model "daisy world." This world has two kinds of daisies—black daisies that thrive in cool weather and white daisies that thrive in warm weather. If the planet's surface cools, it begins to be covered by black daisies, which because they are dark have the natural property of "low albedo" (they absorb heat from sunlight). Therefore, as they thrive, the surface of the planet begins to warm, creating conditions that favor white daisies. And since white daisies have "high albedo" (they reflect the sun's energy), the planet will begin to cool again. Eventually, a state of homeostatic stability evolves through negative feedback: populations of black and white daisies gently rise and fall, regulating the planet's temperature and ensuring their own survival. Lovelock's research into the earth's climatological history and especially its regulation of "greenhouse gases," which are produced and consumed by living organisms, has confirmed that systems more complex than those in "daisy world" but analogous to them have kept our planet's temperature fluctuating within the narrow range that sustains life despite serious climatic disturbances and uneven solar output.

Summarized in a few lines, Lovelock's contribution to the modeling of complex dynamic systems may seem simplistic; it is not. He developed "daisy world" to illustrate that even a very modest system can evolve homeostatic mechanisms without teleology (the grounds on which his early critics had dismissed Gaia), and his real-world climatological models are anything but reductive or mechanical. They encompass the astro- and geophysical forces that have shaped our planet's history as well as the roles played by some of the humblest species in the biota. Thus among Gaia's most important contributions to systems science is a holistic design that works across scales, integrating and enmeshing subsystems without collapsing their unique qualities into the whole. Other contributions are its demonstration that living systems must exist in persistent states of homeostatic *dis*equilibrium, and its description of the mechanisms through which living systems coevolve with their environments.

The systems insights that Gaia brings to environmental sciences provide an avenue of escape from reductionist views in the social sciences and literary studies. Specifically, if applied to political history, an emphasis on the coevolution of systems with their environment would require that no nation state be studied without reference to its larger context. On these grounds, new historical practice is open to serious critique.

In general, new historicist studies of Renaissance England have treated Britain as if it were more or less detached from Europe, immune from all the forces of hegemonic, religious, and ideological conflict that mark pan-European history in the sixteenth and seventeenth centuries. New historicists who focus on colonialism have made some effort to see England from a global perspective, but they have erred by ignoring European hegemonic conflicts played out both inside and outside its borders. They have tended either to erase Europe altogether or to collapse its states and England into one imperial superpower with a unified concept of the "other" and a single colonial strategy driven by identical economic constraints.[10]

New historicists have also ignored the massive civil and religious conflicts in which European powers were engaged—conflicts that had a significant impact on Engligh political life and literature despite the isolationist policies of Tudor and Stuart monarchs. England was deeply involved in the religious struggles that racked Europe, as we can see from its efforts to liberate the Spanish Netherlands, its outrage over the massacre of the French Huguenots and other Protestant minorities, and its consistent association of internal treason with external (Catholic) conspiracies. In addition, since Europe's royal families intermarried, intimate connections were forged among reigning monarchs. For example, in his collected works, James I can be seen writing directly to foreign "brother" princes and their populaces. Finally, throughout the sixteenth and seventeenth centuries, England felt the impact of ideas that originated in Europe—among them various forms of humanism, Reformation theology, Counter-Reformation theology, political resistance theory, Continental absolutism, Machiavellianism, republican philosophies, and neo-Stoicism. A systems theory approach could provide the theoretical framework within which literary scholars would be able to sort out such complex matters of historical context. Renaissance Europe's political and intellectual history is England's coevolving environment in the sixteenth and seventeenth centuries; nothing happens in one that does not affect the other, yet the two remain distinct. Although holistic, this kind of theoretical approach does not completely collapse the boundaries between a system and its environment. In other words, it need not repeat the "history of ideas" error of assuming a homogeneous Europe by drowning England in great tides of Renaissance thought, and it can recognize England's separateness without joining the new historicist erasure of the European context.

At this point it should be clear that no single algorithm can be drawn from chaos theory and the sciences of complexity and applied uniformly throughout social history. Large dynamic systems can be robust or display a "sensitive dependence on initial conditions." They can be relatively stable, even determinist, at some points in their evolutionary history, and at other points follow a course that leaves them prey to chance events or small disturbances. In other words, the relationship between a given system's complexity and its stability is itself complicated. This does not mean that complex systems cannot be analyzed; it means, however, that we must begin to think in terms of more than one simple model. A model in which systems experience long periods of stability interrupted by "bifurcation points" where chance and individual actions become critical (such as Prigogine's description of "order through fluctuations" and Gould and Eldredge's parallel theory of "punctuated equilibria") seems to provide the best overall description of political and social systems moving through time (indeed the cybernetic theorist Ervin Laszlo has adopted just such a model for societal histories).

In literary studies, the application of varied models derived from the new systems theory would mandate an increased sensitivity to the *contingent* nature of the interplay of text and context. Political texts participate actively in their world, and their stabilizing or destabilizing potential is a product of political qualities that are simultaneously textual and contextual. Shakespeare's *Richard II* could therefore be revolutionary, subversive, stabilizing, or neutral, not because it is all of these things at once, but because its political impact would be contingent on its context's stability.

In order to determine a social system's equilibrium status at a particular point in time and a text's relation to that status—in other words, in order to do theoretically valid work in the field of literature and politics—broad historical knowledge is necessary. When studying a given period, we need to understand power relations among specific groups—the source and extent of their power, the history of their conflicts, and the strength and variety of their ideological commitments. Bluntly, we need more than the idle assertion that power is "everywhere and nowhere," paired with a few great anecdotes. A systems approach also requires that we understand the larger historical contexts and trends surrounding specific societies, that we reach beyond the artificial barriers of period "epistemes" and national borders to gain some idea of the system's evolutionary path and external environment.

Ironically, in their attempt to assume a truly "theoretical" perspective, new historicists have for the most part closed themselves off from just these larger concerns by rejecting the work of traditional historians. Reflecting the influence of the *Annales* school, they have effectively substituted social for political history. Obviously, there is nothing wrong with emphasizing social history, but such an emphasis becomes problematic when the social completely subsumes the political. (The exclusive focus of earlier politically oriented historians on the struggles of the powerful, ignoring the daily life of the people, was equally problematic.) Social and political realms are two distinct but interacting subsystems. Like other enmeshed subsystems (e.g., weather patterns and ocean currents), they can be nonlinear on vastly different time scales. In seventeenth-century England the pace of political change was rapid (it was the "Age of Revolutions"), but social change was comparatively slow. Social and political systems should neither be collapsed into one another nor analyzed in isolation. Their synergistic relationships need to be studied with a sensitivity to each system's unique dynamics.

Another methodological problem is raised by new historicists' reliance on the concept of "thick context" derived from the work of the anthropologist Clifford Geertz, which translates in their critical practice to a disturbing dependence on anecdotal evidence and a nearly obsessive topicality. Such problems in methodology, like those of earlier "worldview" critics, spring from the assumption that the local simply mirrors global forces. The new systems science presents alternatives to this reductive view in its precise and complex models of local/global dynamics and subsystems interactions.

To illustrate systems theory applications to historical literary studies, I will focus briefly on a group of politically self-conscious texts from medieval and Renaissance Europe—counsel and statecraft literature. In this or any other period, the role political literature plays vis-à-vis its social context can be variously modeled. For the purposes of this analysis, I want to suggest that politically charged texts not only constitute a distinct subsystem but also function as "feedback." One reason counsel and statecraft literature fits well within this theoretical framework is that it saw itself playing just such a role. Since feedback is crucial to achieving stability, systems whose dynamics are characterized by "negative feedback"—the process of communicating from the governed to the governor that all is not well—tend to be relatively robust. Systems without negative feedback (and especially those with "positive feedback" that merely amplifies and reamplifies the system's "message") are highly unstable.

As Arthur B. Ferguson has illustrated in *The Articulate Citizen and the English Renaissance*, political authors in the late Middle Ages and the Renaissance prescribed "good counsel" as *the* master remedy for whatever ailed the state (17). Throughout this period, "good counsel" meant the frank delivery of unpleasant truths to the monarch, in other words, "negative feedback." Whether conceived of morally, as they generally were in medieval counsel literature, or prudentially, as they increasingly were in Renaissance statecraft literature, these critical truths were considered vital to the maintenance of social and political order. It was a dangerous and often futile task, but the duty of the sage counselor was to correct the course of government by courageous truth telling, leading the monarch away from a natural, almost entropic tendency to abuse or neglect his subjects.

Mum and the Sothsegger, an allegorical poem written shortly after the deposition of Richard II, provides an especially clear and detailed exposition of counsel ideology. The work has survived as two fragments. The first is a surprisingly frank postmortem of Richard's reign that blames the king for his own fall. By surrounding himself with young and foolish advisers who flattered him and encouraged his every extravagance, Richard became so alienated from his subjects that in his time of crisis they abandoned him to his enemies. The Prologue condemning Richard's council offers up the work as a "treatise" to any English king interested in preserving his reign (lines 40–55). The second fragment is a political allegory set in a disordered kingdom, where the poet witnesses the struggle between Mum (a character representing the path of least resistance in the councils of government) and Sothsegger (the Truthteller); unfortunately, he finds out that telling the truth is no way to rise at court. As the poet travels through the corrupt and disordered realm in search of answers, he learns that Mum's universal triumph is at the root of the world's ills. In a final dream vision, the poet is instructed by a beekeeper (bees were considered ideals of social harmony) to find the "sothsegger" that lives in each man's heart and seek every opportunity to advise his lord; he is instructed, that is, to rescue his world by writing counsel literature. *Mum and the Sothsegger* defies contemporary political categories of "conservative" or "subversive"; for although the poet who laments Richard's fall obviously values political stability, he sees it as the product of disorderly counsel (negative feedback). And although this poem is a little bolder than most, its stance is typical of advice literature in the late Middle Ages and the Renaissance.

At first glance, the dynamics of order and disorder in counsel ideology may seem to exemplify the new historicist notion of subversion and containment. Actually, they are far from it. Counsel literature is not the imprint of royal self-subversion, nor is it a pressure valve through which marginalized populations blow off a little steam. Unlike the new historicist model of an essentially static system with an artificial equilibrium dynamics, the state that counsel literature tries to maintain is stable through real change. Counsel literature actively inter-venes in the political scene, albeit within a monarchial framework, to seek redress for subjects' grievances and the amelioration of their suffering.

Telling truths that affect social change and ensure political continuity is the theme of one of the sixteenth century's most politically radical texts, the anonymous play *Woodstock*. Although written two hundred years after *Mum*, *Woodstock* also explores the devastation wrought by bad counsel in the reign of Richard II. The truth teller in this work is "Plain Thomas" of Woodstock, the Duke of Gloucester, Richard's uncle and Lord Protector of the realm. Woodstock and the rest of the Lords Appellate are idealized in this play as noble, sage counselors whom Richard rejects in favor of young upstart flatterers. The king, in other words, chooses positive over negative feedback with predictably dis-astrous consequences. Among England's nobles, Woodstock is especially con-scious of how much Richard's extravagant favorites have cost the poor, and he champions the Commons at court, bluntly communicating their grievances to his king while trying to separate him from his corrupt flatterers. When he fails and the desperate Commons rebel, he stays sympathetic with their cause but intervenes to stop the rebellion and protect his king. He is Richard's ally, but Richard cannot tolerate his verbal defiance and has him killed. His death leaves the way open for favorites like Tresilian to loot the realm and persecute even the mildest resistance. In one scene, for example, commoners are arrested for "whistling treason." Not surprisingly, this oppression leads to open rebellion and Richard's defeat. Thus the play emerges as an object lesson in the dangers the crown brings upon itself when it feeds on flattery and ignores popular discontent.

Although less radical, Shakespeare's *Richard II* resembles *Woodstock* in many ways, displaying ideological affinities that go beyond shared subject matter and source material. Specifically, Shakespeare's play opposes the blunt but healing counsel of Gaunt and York to the smooth and destructive flattery of Bushy, Bagot, and Green. These representations of Richard's reign had contemporary political significance, and the performance history of *Richard II* highlights the dual and contingent role critical feedback can play in the political realm. Negative feedback enhances stability as long as a system is near equilibrium; however, the same act of truth telling that would further stabilize a robust system could "nucleate" disorder in a system far from equilibrium. Furthermore, it is very difficult, except in hindsight, to distinguish between system states. Counsel literature demonstrates that the Elizabethans understood the stabilizing effect of political criticism; however, they also seem to have conceived of political literature as having potentially "nucleating" effects, as is evidenced by *Richard II*'s performance history. It is widely known that Elizabeth was identified in her own mind and in the minds of her critics with the hapless Richard (a fact of historical record, whether or not she commented, "I am Richard II, know ye not that"). This identification was so strong that the play's deposition scene was censored during her lifetime for fear that the mere sight of it might spark an uprising (the scene appears to have been cut theatrically early on and not restored to the text until the Quarto IV edition of 1608). It was exactly this conviction, that the play had an inherent revolutionary potential, that led Robert Devereux, the second Earl of Essex, to sponsor a performance of *Richard II* as the initial act in his 1601 rebellion. Obviously, both Elizabeth's fears and Essex's dreams that simply representing Richard's deposition on stage would "nucleate" an imitative insurrection were unfounded—not because small events cannot trigger massive change, but because Elizabeth's regime was far more stable than either of them realized. Interestingly, fears about the play's destabilizing potential were not limited to Elizabeth's reign. They surface again in the volatile 1670s when Nathan Tate's adaptation of *Richard II* was suppressed by royal authorities, who saw it as potentially threatening to Charles II. However, unlike Charles, Elizabeth did not have the play banned; instead she allowed it to run (probably with the deposition scene cut) and complained bitterly about its popularity. Apparently, although Elizabeth did not like to hear criticism about a monarch who did not like to hear criticism, her subjects did. She could tolerate it, however. Indeed, by the time of the Essex rebellion, the play needed a paid sponsor because it was already "old news." Without intending it, Elizabeth's relative tolerance had blunted any potentially nucleating effect the play might have had. *Richard II* demonstrates counsel literature's political activism, its stabilizing effect, and its meta-advisory function. Above all, these works are candid advice on how healthy it is for the monarch to receive candid advice. In systems terms, they are negative feedback on negative feedback.

If Elizabeth was barely tolerant of unsolicited counsel, her successor was openly hostile to it. In fact James I usurps to himself the counselor function in government: he tells Parliament that he wants none of their advice and widely promotes his own work of counsel literature, *Basilikon Doron*. In this piece of royal pedagogy, he tells his son Henry to rely on the book itself as his "faithfull Praeceptour and counsellour," praising it as an adviser that "will not come vn-called, neither speake vnspeered at" (4). In other words, James subverts traditional counsel ideology by setting up a state system where the only feedback is positive, the amplification and reamplification of the monarch's voice. Indeed, many of the failures of Stuart monarchy can be traced to its emphatic rejection of independent counsel. If this seems an exaggeration, one need only look to the *Nineteen Propositions* of 1642, Parliament's final attempt to dictate an acceptable style of rule to Charles I. Its first article is a demand that all the king's counselors be approved by both houses of Parliament (Kenyon 223). This power struggle over counsel should not be surprising. Royal advisers and counsel literature play a crucial role in sixteenth- and seventeenth-century politics, because in a monarchy counsel is the chief avenue of communication between the governed and the governor.

In a democracy or a republic there are more-direct channels for popular feedback, and the sixteenth and seventeenth centuries were a time when Europe began to explore republicanism, a political ideology that mandates the vox populi be heard without being mediated through a few high-placed individuals. In the early and mid-seventeenth century—the period leading to the English Revolution and through the interregnum—English statecraft theorists actively searched for models of participatory governance where popular "feedback" would be not the province of counselors but the product of communal action. The English republican experiment in the mid-seventeenth century drew heavily for its political theory on Italian civic humanism, and especially on the works of Niccolò Machiavelli.[11]

In Machiavelli's republican *Discourses on the First Ten Books of Titus Livy*, statecraft literature reaches new levels of theoretical sophistication, displaying surprising parallels to modern systems science. Along with many of his contemporaries, Machiavelli was inspired by Polybius's *Histories* and its notion of the *anakuklosis politeion*, the cycle of constitutions. Like the new systems sciences, Polybian theory sees entropy as the driving force behind history. Uniting Platonic and Aristotelian political theory, it portrays all governing systems as decaying and yielding to the next system, which in turn decays. Thus monarchy decays into tyranny, then yields to aristocracy; aristocracy decays into oligarchy, then yields to democracy; democracy decays into anarchy, then yields to monarchy, and the cycle begins anew. In new science terms, the phase space model most closely approximating the *anakuklosis politeion* would not be a simple circle, since identical governments do not recur, but a "quasi-periodic" torus attractor with "asymptotic predictability," where forms cycle within predictable limits without repeating (Briggs and Peat 41).[12] In Polybius's view, the only way to escape from these destructive cycles is to create "mixed" governments that combine the best elements of all three forms. Although these mixed-form republics achieve greater stability and persistence than their monomorphic ancestors, they too eventually atrophy and die, so strong are the forces of decay in the universe.

Machiavelli subscribes to Polybian views, and in the *Discourses* he searches history for models of stability and relative permanence that can offer solutions for his own troubled times. He finds them in a most unlikely period in Rome's history: the tumultuous era after the death of the Tarquins that led to the creation of the tribunes. In his chapter "That Discord between the Plebs and the Senate of Rome Made this Republic both Free and Powerful," Machiavelli presents the counterintuitive thesis that a disorderly populace creates a powerful state:

> To me those who condemn the quarrels between the nobles and the plebs, seem to be caviling at the very things that were the primary cause of Rome's retaining her freedom, and that they pay more attention to the noise and clamor resulting from such commotions than to what resulted from them, i.e. to the good effects which they produced. Nor do they realize that in every republic there are two different dispositions, that of the populace and that of the upper class and that all legislation favorable to liberty is brought about by the clash between them. (113)

Machiavelli admits that the behavior of the discontented Plebs—running around "helter-skelter" in the streets and trooping out of the city en masse—is terrifying to read about, yet he goes on to recommend that every city find similar means for its people to express discontent (114). His aim goes well beyond civil catharsis. In Machiavelli's view "tumulti" force the creation of laws that protect the people (113–15). Thus a certain amount of civil disorder ensures the state's internal stability and protects it from external threats. People who have forced their city to treat them with decency do not become so desperate that they revolt and destroy their community, nor do they refuse to defend it with their lives when it is attacked. Very much like good counsel in a monarchy, popular tumults in a republic are the negative feedback the state needs to survive.

As Annabel Patterson has argued, Shakespeare's *Coriolanus*, which is set in the same period that inspired Machiavelli, also privileges the popular voice with all its disorderly expressions of discontent. Furthermore, she connects Shakespeare's play and its refrain that the people are starving to contemporary upheavals in England—the Midlands Rising and its aftermath. Patterson also connects the play to Machiavellian republican theory, suggesting that *Coriolanus* is an act of political intervention that offers a republican solution for England's current crisis:

> If, as Machiavelli had argued, the patricians were forced by effective popular protest to "grant the populace a share in the government," such an adjustment in the power relations of the Jacobean state was not, however unlikely, inconceivable; and to dramatize its occurrence in antiquity made the process of conceiving it visible and accessible to others. In *Coriolanus*, for the first time, Shakespeare's audience is invited to contemplate an alternative political system; and, more significantly still, to experience an entire dramatic action devoted to these questions: who shall speak for the

commons; what power should the common people have in the system; to what extent is common power compatible with national safety? (127)

I agree with Patterson's assessment of Shakespeare's play and its role in contemporary politics and would only add that the sorts of questions *Coriolanus* raises increase in frequency and strength as England approaches revolution.

These examples of Renaissance texts that lend themselves to a systems theory approach are by no means exhaustive, but I hope they serve to illustrate the point that models based on the sciences of complexity can be fruitfully applied to literary studies. This does not mean, by the way, that I look forward to a time when myriad literary articles bristle with phrases like "the butterfly effect," "catastrophe cusps," and "negative feedback." The last thing this profession needs is one more layer of alien terminology laid on its theoretical discourse. What I would hope this essay indicates, however, is the need for the profession to "break set" and realize that writers like Foucault do not have a monopoly on theoretical approaches to power. There are alternatives. We can afford to abandon simplistic, reductive, and dated models and begin the search for ways of talking about power, truth, politics, and literature that are complex, contingent, and open.

Notes

1. For Foucault's views on the relationship between power and truth see *Power/Knowledge;* for his theories about social control and domination see esp. *Discipline and Punish.* For general overviews of the new historicism see Goldberg, Howard. Works by Greenblatt like *Renaissance Self-Fashioning,* and *Shakespearean Negotiations,* which includes a reprint of his influential essay, "Invisible Bullets: Renaissance Authority and Its Subversion," constitute some of the clearest examples of Foucault's models of political power put into practice in literary studies. For a collection that represents varied positions on new historicism see Veeser. For materialist critiques of new historicist ideology and practice see, among others, Lentricchia, Holstun.

2. For an especially effective challenge to poststructuralist epistemological theories see Paisley Livingston's *Literary Knowledge.*

3. Lentricchia has argued that "because he leaves no shaded zone, no free space for real alternatives to take form, Foucault's vision of power, despite its provisions for reversals of direction, courts a monolithic determinism" (70). Edward Said similarly finds that Foucault's "interest in domination was critical but not finally as contestatory, or as oppositional as on the surface it seems to be. This translates into the paradox that Foucault's imagination of power was by

his analysis of power to reveal its injustice and cruelty, but by its theorization to let it go on more or less unchecked" (152).

4. Interestingly, Hayles sees chaos theory as a means whereby to rescue Foucault from the nagging charge that his theories cannot account for change because, as she points out, complex self-similar structures are ripe for sudden and drastic alteration (218–21). I believe there is a problem, however, with Hayles's strategy, which lies in the equilibrial nature of Foucault's model. The "sensitive dependence on initial conditions" is a characteristic of nonequilibrium dynamics. It is the property of a system that is either persistently nonlinear, like the weather (in which case it would be *constantly* changing), or one that has moved to a far-from-equilibrium state, like a "dissipative system" or matter on the verge of a phase change (in which case its internal dynamics would alter substantially before a massive change). Foucault's social systems are not in a state of continual disruption, nor do their dynamics alter on the threshold of change.

5. Much of current theory regarding the behavior of complex systems over time emphasizes the vital role of entropy. This is especially true of the work of Ilya Prigogine, who sees in the second law a simultaneous force for disorder *and* order in the natural world. Briefly, in "closed systems" (ones that do not draw energy from their environments) entropy dictates increasing disorder and the gradual loss of useful energy. However, in "open systems" (those that draw energy from their environments) entropy operates to create new patterns of order. It pushes open systems to far-from-equilibrium states where they demonstrate remarkable capacities to "self-organize." Prigogine has found "autopoetic" phenomena in a variety of physical, chemical, and biological processes, from the formation of "Bénard cells," "chemical clocks," and the "BZ reaction" to the life cycle of slime molds (see *From Being to Becoming, Order Out of Chaos,* and Nicolis and Prigogine's *Exploring Complexity*). For further confirmation of autopoesis in a variety of physical phenomena see, e.g., Eigen's theory of hypercycles (described in Bahg) and Bak and Chen's theory of "self-organized criticality." These theoretical developments in the physical sciences have not gone unnoticed by social scientists. As early as 1980 Erich Jantsch wrote *The Self-Organizing Universe,* where he applies Prigogine's theories of "dissipative structures" and autopoiesis to the social sphere. In 1981 an International Symposium on Order and Disorder was held at Stanford, bringing together a distinguished group of scientists and humanists (see Livingston, *Order and Disorder*). Systems analysts like Ervin Laszlo have been deeply influenced by these new theoretical paradigms, and recently a number of articles have appeared in *Behavioral Science* that apply new systems theory models drawn from the physical sciences to social organizations, psychology, politics, and history (see esp. Loye and Eisler). There is also interest in exploring the implications of chaos theory for the study of

literature: see, e.g., Brady, and, most notably, Hayles's *Chaos Bound*, and Argyros's *Blessed Rage for Order*. Hayles and Argyros differ on the implications of chaos for contemporary literary theory: Hayles sees deconstruction and chaos as fundamentally compatible, whereas Argyros sees them at odds. I share Argyros's belief that poststructuralist theory is more likely to find its nemesis than its savior in the new paradigm sciences.

6. For a description of Kauffman's work see Waldrop.

7. E.g., a catastrophe "fold" is used to model a balloon being inflated until it bursts or a span being weighted until it collapses; a catastrophe "cusp" models events that could break in one of two directions, like the fight or flight response of an animal under stress. For descriptions of catastrophe models see esp. Ekeland, Briggs and Peat.

8. The best introduction to the Gaia Hypothesis is Lovelock's recent *The Ages of Gaia*, in which he further refines his model "daisy world" and answers his critics.

9. I am indebted to William DeMichael and Scott Wing of the Smithsonian Institution, who are currently writing a book on paleoecology, for allowing me to sit in on their seminar "The Evolution and Revolution of Terrestial Ecosystems" at the University of Pennsylvania, spring 1991.

10. Actually, Spanish, English, and Dutch economies differed greatly in this period, and their corresponding forms of colonial expansion were also very different, although obviously devastating to all of the populations they conquered. English and Dutch imperialism in the sixteenth and seventeenth centuries was a product of early bourgeois mercantilism. Spain, on the other hand, remained a feudal economy, and in fact its particular brand of colonial exploitation ensured that it never developed a viable domestic bourgeoisie (see North and Thomas).

11. For the influence of Machiavelli and Italian civic humanism on seventeenth-century England, see Pocock, Fink.

12. Phase space models are "maps" used to visualize the dynamics of *changing* physical systems; they are especially useful, therefore, in talking about a system's history or qualitatively modeling its future states.

Works Cited

Argyros, Alexander J. *A Blessed Rage for Order: Deconstruction, Evolution, and Chaos.* Ann Arbor: U of Michigan P, 1991.

Bahg, Chang-Gen. "Major Systems Theories throughout the World." *Behavioral Science* 35 (1990): 79–107.

Bak, Per, and Kan Chen. "Self-Organized Criticality." *Scientific American* Jan. 1991:46–53.

Brady, Patrick. "Chaos Theory, Control Theory, and Literary Theory or: A Story of Three Butterflies." *Modern Language Studies* 20:4 (Fall 1990): 65–79.

Briggs, John, and F. David Peat. *Turbulent Mirror: An Illustrated Guide to Chaos Theory and the Science of Wholeness.* New York: Harper, 1989.

Brooks, Daniel R., and E. O. Wiley. *Evolution as Entropy: Toward a Unified Theory of Biology.* 2nd ed. Chicago: U of Chicago P, 1988.

Ekeland, Ivar. *Mathematics and the Unexpected.* Chicago: U of Chicago P, 1988.

Eldredge, Niles. *Time Frames: The Evolution of Punctuated Equilibria.* Princeton: Princeton UP, 1985.

Ferguson, Arthur B. *The Articulate Citizen and the English Renaissance.* Durham: Duke UP, 1965.

Fink, Zera S. *The Classical Republicans: An Essay in the Recovery of a Pattern of Thought in Seventeenth-Century England.* Evanston: Northwestern UP, 1945.

Foucault, Michel. *Discipline and Punish: The Birth of the Prison.* Trans. Alan Sheriden. New York: Random, 1977.

———. *Power/Knowledge: Selected Interviews and Other Writings, 1972–1977.* New York: Pantheon, 1977.

Gleick, James. *Chaos: Making a New Science.* New York: Viking Penguin, 1987.

Goldberg, Jonathan. "The Politics of Renaissance Literature: A Review Essay." *ELH* 49 (1982): 514–42.

Gould, Stephen Jay. *Wonderful Life: The Burgess Shale and the Nature of History.* New York: Norton, 1989.

Greenblatt, Stephen. *Renaissance Self-Fashioning.* Chicago: U of Chicago P, 1980.

———. *Shakespearean Negotiations: The Circulation of Social Energy in Renaissance England.* Berkeley: U of California P, 1988.

Havel, Václav. *Disturbing the Peace.* New York: Vintage, 1990.

———. *Open Letters.* New York: Knopf, 1991.

Hayles, N. Katherine. *Chaos Bound: Orderly Disorder in Contemporary Literature and Science.* Ithaca: Cornell UP, 1990.

Holstun, James. "Ranting at the New Historicism." *English Literary Renaissance* 19 (1989): 189–225.

Howard, Jean E. "The New Historicism in Renaissance Studies." *English Literary Renaissance* 16 (1986): 13–43.

James I. *The Political Works of James I.* Ed. Charles Howard McIlwain. New York: Russell, 1965.

Jantsch, Erich. *The Self-Organizing Universe: Scientific and Human Implications of the Emerging Paradigm of Evolution.* Oxford: Pergamon, 1980.

Kenyon, J. P., ed. *The Stuart Constitution: 1603–1688: Documents and Commentary.* 2nd ed. Cambridge: Cambridge UP, 1986.

Kramer, Nic J. T. A., and Jacob de Smit. *Systems Thinking: Concepts and Notions.* Leiden: Nijhoff, 1977.

Laszlo, Ervin. "Cybernetics in an Evolving Social System." *Kybernetes* 13 (1984): 141–45.

Lentricchia, Frank. *Ariel and the Police: Michel Foucault, William James, Wallace Stevens.* Madison: U of Wisconsin P, 1988.

Livingston, Paisley, ed. *Disorder and Order.* Proc. of the Stanford International Symposium. 14–16 Sept. 1981. Saratoga, CA: Anma Libri, 1984.

———. *Literary Knowledge: Humanistic Inquiry and the Philosophy of Science.* Ithaca: Cornell UP, 1988.

Lovelock, James. *The Ages of Gaia: A Biography of Our Living Earth.* New York: Norton, 1988.

Loye, David, and Riane Eisler. "Chaos and Transformation: Implications of Non-equilibrium Theory for Social Science and Society." *Behavioral Science* 32 (1987): 53–65.

Machiavelli, Niccolò. *The Discourses.* Ed. Bernard Crick. Trans. Leslie J. Walker. Harmondsworth: Penguin, 1970.

Nicolis, Grégoire, and Ilya Prigogine. *Exploring Complexity: An Introduction.* New York: Freeman, 1989.

North, Douglas C., and Robert Paul Thomas. *The Rise of the Western World: A New Economic History.* London: Cambridge UP, 1973.

Patterson, Annabel. *Shakespeare and the Popular Voice.* Cambridge: Blackwell, 1990.

Pocock, J. G. A. *The Machiavellian Moment: Florentine Political Thought and the Atlantic Republican Tradition.* Princeton: Princeton UP, 1975.

Prigogine, Ilya. *From Being to Becoming: Time and Complexity in the Physical Sciences.* New York: Freeman, 1980.

———, and Isabelle Stengers. *Order Out of Chaos: Man's New Dialogue with Nature.* New York: Bantam, 1984.

Said, Edward. "Foucault and the Imagination of Power." *Foucault: A Critical Reader.* Ed. David Couzens Hoy. Oxford: Blackwell, 1986.

Stewart, Ian. *Does God Play Dice? The Mathematics of Chaos.* Cambridge, MA: Blackwell, 1989.

Veeser, H. Aram, ed. *The New Historicism.* New York: Routledge, 1989.

Waldrop, M. Mitchell. "Spontaneous Order, Evolution, and Life." *Science* 247 (30 Mar. 1990): 1543–45.

Wunsch, Carl. "Computation and Data Analysis in Physical Oceanography for Understanding the General Circulation of the Ocean." Ninth Annual Princeton-Conoco Symposium in Geoscience on Computation and Data Analysis in the Earth Sciences. Princeton, 20 Apr. 1990.

For the Time Being:
Sideshadowing, Criticism, and the
Russian Countertradition

Gary Saul Morson

1. A Voyage to Uchronia

The greatest political novel ever written, Dostoevsky's *The Possessed*, meditates on the nature of temporality and focuses on the intelligentsia's understanding of time. Each of its main characters fabricates a peculiar and insane chronicity. Thus, the novel offers a catalog of temporal fallacies to which members of the intelligentsia are subject: fallacies about the moment in which they live, about the anticipated era of social harmony, and about the critical moment in which time itself is to be changed once and for all.

The revolutionary ideologue Shigalev is first described as someone who "looked as though he were expecting the destruction of the world, and not at some indefinite time in accordance with prophecies, which might never be fulfilled, but quite definitely, as though it were to be the day after to-morrow at twenty-five minutes past ten" (*Possessed* 135). The shadow of the Apocalypse hovers over all the novel's radicals.

Most famously, Kirillov offers to bring on the millennium by an unmotivated and completely irrational act of suicide. By killing himself for no reason at all, he expects to become the "man-god" and provide the model for a completely new type of human, or rather superhuman, being. Then the promise of the serpent to Eve—"Ye shall be as gods!"—will be fulfilled, indeed "overfulfilled" because we will actually *be* gods. Time as we have experienced it *shall be no longer*, as the Book of Revelation promises; and so we will have achieved immortality not in the other world but in this one.

> "Then there will be a new life, a new man; everything will be new... then they will divide history into two parts: from the gorilla to the annihilation of God, and from the annihilation of God to..."
> "To the gorilla?"

"...To the transformation of the earth, and of man physically. Man will be God, and will be tranformed physically, and the world will be transformed and things will be transformed and thoughts and all feelings. . . . He who kills himself only to kill fear will become a god at once."

"He won't have time, perhaps," I observed.

"That's no matter," he answered softly, with calm pride, almost disdain. (*Possessed* 114–15; unspaced dots indicate ellipsis in original)

We recognize in Kirillov's speech the phraseology of the Apocalypse and in his impatient disdain the mentality of the radical intelligentsia. For postrevolutionary Russian readers, his doctrine of a "new man" seems to anticipate the official Soviet doctrine of the New Man made possible by triumphant socialism. As so often happens with this remarkable book, such readers experience the eerie discomfort of encountering a novelist who somehow seemed to anticipate future horrors with uncanny accuracy.

The characters pursue the millennium, but their faith in the transmutability of temporality is usually accompanied by the novelist's ticking clock, his reminder that time—the same prosaic and everlasting time—is passing. As in Chekhov's plays, characters discuss the utopian future while present opportunities are being lost and human potential is wantonly destroyed. They are not only utopians but also *uchronians.* But time persists. One might locate the central irony of *The Possessed* by describing it as a *narrative* about the end of time.

When Kirillov explains his new chronicity to the always bored Stavrogin, for whom all this talk of infinite innovation is yet another repetition of the same old story, Stavrogin cannot help glancing at his watch. "You've begun to believe in a future eternal life?" Stavrogin asks.

"No, not in a future eternal life, but in eternal life here. There are moments, you reach moments, and time suddenly stands still, and it will become eternal."

"You hope to reach such a moment?"

"Yes."

"That'll scarcely be possible in our time," Nikolay Vsevolodovich [Stavrogin] responded slowly and, as it were, dreamily; the two spoke without the slightest irony. "In the Apocalypse the angel swears that there will be no more time."

"I know. That's very true; distinct and exact. When all mankind attains happiness then there will be no more time, for there'll be no need of it, a very true thought."

"Where will they put it?"

"Nowhere. Time's not an object but an idea. It will be extinguished in the mind."

"The old commonplaces of philosophy, the same from the beginning of time," muttered Stavrogin with a kind of disdainful compassion. (*Possessed* 239–40)

Here and elsewhere, Stavrogin cannot help thinking that each attempt to overcome time takes place at a given moment, and that there is a long history of futile escapes from history. There shall be a lot more time; and whatever the revolutionists say, the new man will resemble the old. We live in freedom by necessity and in temporality forever.

2. The Return of *The Possessed*

Dostoevsky's novel satirizes the predominant tradition of the Russian intelligentsia. The story of that tradition, constantly retold throughout the nineteenth and twentieth centuries, has often been identified as *the* story of modern Russian culture. The intelligentsia established its calendar of secular saints, its codes of behavior, its rituals of celebrating great events in its past; and it identified its mission, its purpose, and its successes with the salvation of the Russian people and, ultimately, of the whole world.

Dostoevsky was by no means unusual in seeing the dangers inherent in such a mentality. He was also far from unique in describing the intelligentsia as fanatically devoted to ideologies of various sorts. Time and again, some foreign philosophy was borrowed and adapted to the enterprise of creating socialism by the intelligentsia's activity. Even apolitical Western schools, if they were borrowed at all, were automatically made into yet another "algebra for revolution." The intelligentsia revered science, but, as was often pointed out, one aspect of science they never borrowed was a skeptical weighing of evidence and a willingness to submit theories to falsifiable tests. Science was accepted religiously, and its purpose was to guarantee the socialist millennium. In an often quoted *mot*, the philosopher Vladimir Soloviev mocked these mental habits in his parodic version of "the intelligentsia's syllogism": "Man is descended from the apes; *therefore*, we should sacrifice ourselves for our fellow man."

Russian novels repeatedly describe messianic "sciences" with considerable irony. One might even say that the great Russian novels are primarily about the intelligentsia's insane and dangerous attempts to transform time. The devil who visits Ivan Karamazov taunts him for his earlier adherence to naive schemes for ending all human suffering. Ivan, it appears, has compared his proposed transformation to a "geological cataclysm" that reshapes the world. But the devil reminds the parricidal *intelligent* that messianism plays right into the devil's hands.

Nothing leads to greater suffering than schemes to end it once and for all. The intelligentsia, with its contempt for bourgeois virtues and for undramatic daily activity, is especially drawn to such schemes. In *The Possessed*, Shigalev presents an infallible theory capable of solving all social problems at a stroke: "I am perplexed by my own data and my conclusion is a direct contradiction of the original idea from which I start. Starting from unlimited freedom, I arrive at unlimited despotism. I will add, however, that there can be no solution of the social problem but mine" (*Possessed* 409). In the prerevolutionary period, Shigalev came to represent the distilled essence of the intelligentsia's mentality; since 1917 it is his formulations, perhaps more than anything else, that have sustained Dostoevsky's reputation as a prophet. Dostoevsky is described as the foreseer of the central story of the twentieth century: the rise and fall of totalitarian ideologies established to save the world forever.

To be sure, not every Russian intellectual was given to such dangerous ideologizing. But those who were not could not, almost by definition, be *intelligenty* (plural of *intelligent*, a member of the intelligentsia). Because this paper is concerned primarily with those intellectuals who were *not* taken to be members of the intelligentsia, the point is an important one for our present purposes.

In Russia, where the word *intelligentsia* was coined, not every intellectual was an *intelligent* and not every *intelligent* could be described as an intellectual. The intelligentsia was identified, and identified itself, by a complex of attitudes and values, including socialism, atheism, and a mystique of revolution.[1] Codes of daily behavior—for example, bad manners of a specific sort—were important. Someone barely literate who shared those values would be regarded as a member of the intelligentsia more readily than, let us say, Leo Tolstoy, who disdainfully rejected the intelligentsia's mentality and its prescribed codes.

It is not surprising, then, that Russia generated a *countertradition* of thinkers deeply suspicious of the intelligentsia and its habits of thought. That countertradition generated the overwhelming proportion of Russia's greatest literary works and a sizable minority of its most remarkable critics, including Semyon Frank, Mikhail Gershenzon, and, most notably, Mikhail Bakhtin. A good first take on the Russian intellectual tradition would be to see it as offering a choice between two mentalities, two attitudes toward culture, and two approaches to morality. There was the tradition of Chernyshevsky, Mikhailovsky, and Lenin, and there was the countertradition of Tolstoy (before his conversion), Chekhov, and Bakhtin. The intelligentsia's tradition revered as its classics *What Is to Be Done?* and the criticism of the "radical democrats"; countertraditional thinkers cited *The Possessed*, *Anna Karenina*, and that remarkable polemical anthology *Signposts: A Collection of Essays on the Russian Intelligentsia*, edited by Gershenzon.

Countertraditional thinkers expressed deep suspicion of the intelligentsia's claims to have discovered the One True Theory that explains all of history and guarantees utopia. On the contrary, they tended to deny that history has laws or that such all-embracing theories could be anything but spurious. We may recall, for instance, the essays that interrupt the narrative of *War and Peace*, denying the possibility of historical laws. For Tolstoy, history has no hidden story; the world is fundamentally messy, the product of chance and choice as much as of regularities. And the most important moments are the prosaic ones of daily life, not the apocalyptic nodes or critical turning points that supposedly determine everything. For the countertradition, time is an everyday affair. God must have loved the ordinary events because he made so many of them.

Thus, *intelligenty* typically saw the key moments of life and history as dramatic and as splitting the past in two; their opponents tended to appreciate most highly the undramatic events of daily life. The famous opening sentence of *Anna Karenina*—"All happy families resemble each other; each unhappy family is unhappy in its own way"—alludes to a French proverb Tolstoy admired: "Happy people have no history." A life made of great events, a life like Anna Karenina's, is a life lived badly. The good life, like Dolly Oblonskaya's, is one we barely notice. We do not remark upon life's most important events because they are so commonplace. Cloaked in their ordinariness, they are difficult to discern.

The countertradition's fundamental values were prosaic. Its greatest writers —Chekhov, Tolstoy—therefore exploited the prosaic possibilities of prose. The countless small events leading nowhere that shape *War and Peace* and the trivialities that ruin lives in Chekhov's largely plotless plays derive from an impulse to take the "prosification" of prose and the "novelization" of literature as far as possible. Of course, the great theorist of such "novelization," the inventor of literary theory as "prosaics" rather than poetics, was Mikhail Bakhtin.

Bakhtin's attachment to prose, and above all to the novel, derives in large measure from what he called its "prosaic wisdom" and "prosaic intelligence." Novels, as he described them and as the great Russian authors wrote them, remain skeptical of grand events, ideological explanations, and socialistic "sciences." Instead, they locate wisdom in an appreciation of the ordinary.

As a rule, countertraditional thinkers saw morality as pertaining to specific people rather than to humanity in the abstract. Consequently, they insisted that morality cannot be deferred. What is most important is how we treat our contemporaries, the actual people we encounter. Countertraditional thinkers preferred the individual eggs to the socialist omelette. They viewed *intelligenty* as people who could not see the trees for the forest.

In *Signposts*, Frank remarks with dismay on the intelligentsia's active contempt for "simple, individual person-to-person aid," which it regards as either "a waste of time" or even "a betrayal of all mankind and its eternal salvation for the sake of a few individuals close at hand" (142). "Holding as it does the simple and true key to the universal salvation of mankind, socialist populism cannot help but scorn and condemn prosaic, unending activity of the kind that is guided by direct altruistic sentiment," Frank observes (143). In theory, of course, socialists are also guided by altruistic ideals. "But the abstract ideal of absolute happiness in the remote future destroys the concrete moral relationship of one individual to another and the vital sensation of love for one's neighbor, one's contemporaries and their current needs" (143).

Frank here echoes Alexander Herzen, who straddled both traditions and was appreciated by both. For the countertradition, Herzen's greatest work was probably *From the Other Shore,* in which he reflects on the damage done by neglecting the people of today in the name of a better future: "Do you truly wish to condemn all human beings alive today to the sad role . . . of wretched galley slaves, up to their knees in mud, dragging a barge filled with some mysterious treasure and with the humble words 'progress in the future' inscribed on its bows? . . . This alone should serve as a warning to people: an end that is infinitely remote is not an end, but, if you like, a trap; an end must be nearer— it ought to be, at the very least, the laborer's wage, or pleasure in the work done" (36–37). Bakhtin's early treatise on ethics also insists that morality obligates us to specific people today, not to people in general or some abstract humanity in the utopian future: "There is no person in general, there is me, there is a definite concrete other: my close friend, my contemporary (social humanity), the past and future of real people (of real historical humanity)" ("K filosofii" 117). Written shortly after the revolution, Bakhtin's observations have distinct countertraditional political implications.

In short, the countertradition traced a number of the most dangerous beliefs of the intelligentsia to its mistaken understanding of temporality. For the counter-tradition, time is open and what we do, and have done, makes a difference. No historical laws or teleological purposes give us an alibi for prosaic responsibility. The future allows for multiple possibilities, the traditions of the past enable as well as constrain, and morality is first and foremost a matter of present duties. Bakhtin's numerous writings on time—especially his essays "Epic and Novel," "The Bildungsroman," and "Forms of Time and of the Chronotope"—are perhaps best understood in this context.

Let me put my cards on the table: My interest in these Russian meditations on ethics, time, and the intelligentsia is threefold. I am concerned to understand the same set of issues and I am fascinated with the history of Russian thought. But I also see important implications for current American criticism and theory. It seems to me that today's prevailing critical trends repeat many of the Russian intelligentsia's characteristic mistakes, mistakes analyzed so brilliantly by their countertraditional opponents. Elsewhere I have focused on ethical, political, and epistemological problems, but in the current paper I wish to concentrate on some errors that reflect a mistaken sense of temporality. I begin with some observations about the present moment.

3. Being There

I sense myself writing this paper in the present moment, but I know that when you read it, it will have been completed. I have an idea of where my argument leads, but I do not know what thoughts may occur to me in the course of writing that will make my conclusion different from my anticipations. From experience, I know that some such changes will occur—in fact, they provide the special thrill of composition—but I cannot foresee their nature. I will then revise the essay to eliminate its loose ends, to give it the finished quality of a carefully expressed thought and a clearly unfolding intention. I will create the fiction of an intention concentrated in a single instant. Bakhtin would say, I will cover the scaffolding.

In short, for me, this essay is being created, but for you it is already created. For you it is past; for me it is still taking place in what Bakhtin called "the real present of the creative process." I keenly sense that it still has—in this moment of writing—what Bakhtin called "event-potential."

The present moment is in many respects truly special, but its distinctiveness leads us to draw some erroneous conclusions. People have an understandable tendency to treat the present as wholly different from other times. The future, after all, does not exist and never did exist, and the past is over forever. My eighteen-month-old daughter loves a song whose chorus repeats, "Dinosaur, dinosaur, gone forevermore!" The past is extinct. We can make a difference in the present, in fact it is *only* in the present that our decisions are made. The past is of importance only insofar as its effects are inscribed in the present situation, and the future depends entirely on what we do now.

In making these statements, I am not saying what I myself believe but on the contrary describing a feeling so natural, and so fraught with fallacies, that one has to think one's way out of it. From colloquial expressions such as "What's happening?" to "It's *now*, it's *in*" to the title of the old TV show *You Are There*, our language and our culture record the specialness of the present moment. Somehow one is truly alive only if one is up-to-date. Conversely, as Turgenev illustrated when he described the aristocrat whose "time has passed," Pavel Petrovich Kirsanov, to fall behind the times is to live posthumously. Nobody wants to be told that he is "living in the past," even though that phrase, when examined, turns out to be self-contradictory: after all, living in the past is something one can do only when that past is over, which is to say, it is just another way of occupying the present. There must always be an ever-changing way to do it. But for some reason we intuitively accept the judgment that it is not as good a way to live as being truly *contemporary* with "the times."

Publishers know: there appears to be something about the latest issue of a periodical that makes it especially desirable. That is why magazines go off sale an old magazine. That is so even when the articles deal with topics that are essentially timeless. After all, why should it matter whether one is reading this year's or last year's *National Geographic?* Or gazing at the Playmate of this month or last? But—they tell me—it does, it does. As theater operators know, there is something different about watching a movie that has just come out from waiting until it is in the video store or on HBO. *Back to the Future* is more exciting when it is "first run." The whole fashion industry depends on *being there.* Kant notwithstanding, existence—real, present existence—*is* a predicate, or at least is felt to be one. The question is "to be or not to be" rather than "to have been or not to have been."

The throb of presentness is in part a consequence of what Bakhtin called *unfinalizability,* the possibility of a choice that will render untrue any definitive statement. The present possesses what Bakhtin called "loopholes." We sense the present, which is to say, *our* present, as open. We sense the past as closed, because its outcome—our own situation—is already known and determined.

There is a perceptual fallacy here, which Tolstoy described very well in the epilogue to *War and Peace.* An event in the past seems inevitable, and the more distant in time the event is, the harder it becomes to imagine that something else might have happened. "It is this consideration that makes the fall of the first man, resulting in the birth of the human race, appear patently less free than a man's entry into wedlock today. It is the reason why the life and activity of men who lived centuries ago and are connected with me in time, cannot seem to me as free as the life of a contemporary, the consequences of which are still unknown to me" (1444). If an event happened yesterday, we can imagine something different. In fact, if we regret what we did, we often replay the scene and then have to remind ourselves that however recent the action and however strong our desire to have behaved more wisely, yesterday is as unchangeable as the Trojan War or the conquest of Peru.

But if an event happened two centuries ago, we are less tempted to grant plausibility, or even possibility, to an imagined alternative. The question "What if Caesar had not crossed the Rubicon?" has much less force (if it does not seem like a mere parlor game) than "What if Iraq had not invaded Kuwait?"; and this second question will doubtless have less force for you by the time you read this article than it does for me while writing it. "A contemporary event appears to us to be indubitably the work of all the known participants," writes Tolstoy, "but in the case of a more remote event we see only its inevitable consequences, which prevent our considering anything else possible" (*War and Peace* 1445).

If the American Revolution had not happened, would we exist? Would I be writing, and you reading, an essay on time—*this* essay, with its present argument? The suggestion that we, the observers of history, might not have been here at all is quite unsettling. And the possibility that we *would* be here but would see things quite differently is doubtless less unsettling psychologically but much more so epistemologically. In short, the past seems as if it had to happen the way it did, which is perhaps one reason why myths of historical inevitability are so popular even among politically committed people who urge us to action, a position one might otherwise deem a contradiction. "The intelligentsia asserts that the personality is *wholly* a product of the environment, and at the same time suggests to it that it improve its surroundings, like Baron Münchausen pulling himself out of the swamp by his own hair" (Bulgakov 36, my italics).[2] Logically, this is a contradiction, but psychologically, it often does not feel like one because it is the *past* that is proclaimed inevitable. The present *will* turn out to have been inevitable, too, of course, and whatever happens our political theorist will show why nothing else could have; but in the meantime things depend on us. The inevitability of the present—that's for later. Now there is work to be done!

4. Sports Time

There was a running gag on the old TV show *Magnum, P.I.* Magnum lives in Hawaii and so he can never watch his favorite team, the Detroit Tigers, play live. When the Tigers are in the World Series, he sets his VCR to record the game and then locks himself away so he can watch it before anyone can tell him the final score. He wants to re-create the sense of being a fan at the ongoing game, where cheering makes sense, where the winner is uncertain, where "it ain't over till it's over." Sports events lose an awful lot—not quite everything, but an awful lot—when they are recorded, because exertion in the present, the moment on which everything depends, and the sense of *being there now* are so important to what sports are all about.

In that respect, sports events resemble adventure stories, where crucial incidents, such as rescues and escapes, take place in "the nick of time." Sports time is etched all over with nicks. But it is, in a real sense, even more adventurous than adventure time because it exhibits an additional quality that the most suspenseful story lacks. In sports time the outcome *really* is uncertain, whereas when we read adventure novels or detective tales, we know, first of all, that the genre usually prescribes a certain sort of ending from the outset. Perry Mason gets the criminal to confess on the stand, and the district attorney, defeated yet again, comes back just as confident the next time. Still more important, when reading adventure stories we also know that the outcome has in a sense already happened because the author has already written it down. We cannot help knowing that. Adventure stories are not just told in the past tense, they have also been completed. Their suspense is ultimately—not immediately but ultimately—illusory.

We could flip to the end of an adventure story, or we might count how many pages are left and so guess at how many new complications are possible.

Or we could do what we all learn not to do: we could actually read the "foreword"—usually written by some professor or critic who has evidently forgotten what a first reading is supposed to feel like—before reading the story it introduces. There are lots of ways to circumvent the suspense of a published story.

Herodotus tells us, count no man happy until he is dead. The most important way in which novels are unlike our own lives is that novels are *over*. Serialized novels may seem less over, which may partially account for their popularity in the nineteenth century. Serialized dramas, like *Hill Street Blues*, strive for the same effect, which is one reason they also tend to incorporate recent real political or social events from episode to episode. Those events lend the episode the mark of presentness. Forgers do the exact opposite, of course, and stamp their work with signs of pastness. Both are spurious; and both are risky, though not for the same reason.

As in life, and for reasons Herodotus would have understood, "current events" incorporated into a serialized drama may create unintended ironies and unwanted meanings. For they may have unforeseen continuations in life that shed an unwelcome light on the story. That is why, by the time of broadcast, a disclaimer at the bottom of the screen—or actual cancellation of the episode—is sometimes necessary. These are especially noticeable reminders of the risks inherent in the "present-effect."

There is also a cost: nothing fades so fast as up-to-dateness, and so to the extent that shows depend on it, they date especially rapidly. They lose a lot more in reruns than, let us say, *The Cosby Show* or other dramas where each incident is a self-contained unit, where the episodes take place at no specific time, and where they can be watched more or less in any order. *M*A*S*H**, which cultivates a fake pastness, somehow even gains in reruns. *Hill Street Blues*, but not *The Cosby Show* and *M*A*S*H**, strives against its status as already recorded, already over. But sports events, unless they are fixed, do not have to strive in this way because they really are not over.

The joke on *Magnum*, of course, is that somehow, in spite of all his precautions to seal off the outside world, news gets through, Magnum learns the final score, and the game is spoiled. And yet one may conjecture that even if he were able to watch the recording without knowing the outcome, the edge of presentness would be dulled. There would still be suspense, of course, as there is suspense in a novel or detective story. But that's the whole point: that's a different kind of suspense, without the special *momentousness* of live sports. The suspense of a novel or of a recorded sports event comes from *not knowing* the outcome, rather than from the outcome being *still undetermined*, as in an ongoing sports event. Even instant replay—a recording broadcast a second later—can add to but never quite take the place of seeing the play actually being made. Wouldn't Magnum feel a little foolish cheering for an outcome, urging his favorite players on, wishing for a hit in a game that is already over and done with and recorded? You might as well cheer for the Athenians to win the Peloponnesian War.

5. Aperture and the Lie of Foreshadowing

Presentness leads us astray when we consider the past. Intuitively, if not deliberately, we think of the past as qualitatively different from the ongoing present. But it isn't—or rather, it wasn't. *Now* it is different, but then it was just another present. It *was* open. It was a "now," it was happening. And ethical decisions made then—made in that earlier now—had real weight because there *were* real alternatives.

What happened to have happened later was not somehow already present in what was happening then. That is one reason why the author of *War and Peace* disdained foreshadowing, which he deemed a fundamental violation of a true historical sense. When foreshadowing is used, alternative courses of action, which from a later perspective are difficult to see, are presented as if they were impossible from the outset. Foreshadowing operates by importing into events a future that (Tolstoy believed) need not have followed.

Only if time is closed and outcomes are inevitable is foreshadowing not a distortion. In *Oedipus the King*, where the hero's choices can only fulfill the oracle's predictions, the device is perfectly appropriate. But novelists who believe in a quite different temporality use it at the peril of unnoticed temporal incoherence. And people who read novels or histories that rely on foreshadowing may unwittingly come to shape their lives in a dangerously mistaken way. They may tacitly surrender their freedom to one or another version of fatalism and thereby fail to consider the choices and obligations they really have.

Anna Karenina believes in a world of omens. When the trainman is run over in part 1, she calls the incident an "evil omen," and when she has nightmares she persists in taking them as prophetic even after one of them—indicating she will die in childbirth—proves mistaken. Thus, when in part 7 she finds herself at the train station in a state of despair, her memory of her dreams and of the "evil omen" convince her that she "knows" what she "must" do. What is really ominous through this sequence is her belief in omens. Her relations with both Karenin and Vronsky are shaped by her tendency to project already determined outcomes onto situations in which choices are, though limited, nevertheless real and significant.

For Anna, the shadow of disaster lends her life heroism and tragic import. As her friends remark at the beginning of the book, she lives her life as if she were a heroine from a romantic novel. That is why she so often behaves as if she were Greta Garbo playing Anna Karenina. She tries to experience her actions as if they were already described. That tendency is her version of Bovaryism.

Or we might say: she lives (or imagines she lives) a foreshadowed life. In effect, omens are examples of foreshadowing that are visible to a character, signs of the already written future detectable from within experience. They create an oracular temporality in which choice can only be an illusion. Readers often misunderstand Tolstoy's point by assuming that it is he, not Anna, who treats time as already closed and real moral choice as precluded. But the novel's foreshadowing belongs to its characters rather than to its author, and is as much the object of parody as the chivalrous misperceptions of Don Quixote. In Tolstoy's world, Anna is wrong about time, and novels that rely on foreshadowing make essentially the same error.

In an essay he published while *War and Peace* was being written and serialized, Tolstoy claimed to have taken extreme measures to avoid even unintended foreshadowing. As he describes his creative process, he made sure that he wrote each section not knowing what was going to happen next to his fictional characters or how long he would continue writing. Rather, he created psychologically rich characters, placed them in richly detailed situations, and let them react. He claimed to have only the vaguest of "plans" in mind—to guide his characters "through the historical events of 1805, 1807, 1812, 1825, and 1856"— and he emphasized, "I do not foresee the outcome of these characters' relationships in even a single one of these epochs" (Drafts 55). To foresee outcomes would mean to incorporate some form of foreshadowing, to predetermine choices, and to impose closure on time: it would mean, in short, to falsify the past. It is worth noting that Bakhtin's theory of "polyphony" is also based on the author's deliberate ignorance—or as Bakhtin puts it, his renunciation of any "essential surplus" of knowledge inaccessible to the characters—in "the real present of the creative process."

Tolstoy also realized that wherever he ended his work, readers would take the ending not only as inevitable but as providing real closure. It would become the privileged point for judging all earlier incidents, because it would be, like a little Apocalypse within the text, the final revelation of authorial purpose and novelistic structure. Tolstoy disdained closure of this sort, which is false to the openness of time and the eternal tentativeness of judgment. Retrospectively, closure necessarily imposes some measure of foreshadowing, because readers treat everything as preplanned to lead to the ending.

Tolstoy was keenly aware that if readers, upon completing his work, imposed closure upon it, they would be committing the same errors for which he criticizes "the historians" in the book's essays. As historians privilege the moment from which they view the past and tend to treat everything as leading up to it, so readers would confer the same (if not greater) privilege on the novel's ending.

But life has no such moments, and Tolstoy, as a supreme realist, was concerned to offer a faithful representation of temporality. The amazing sense shared by so many critics from his time until now that Tolstoy's works are a piece of life rather than a piece of art—that they somehow seem to lack all artifice—derives in large measure from his incomparable understanding of the temporal flow of existence. Far from avoiding "literary devices," Tolstoy used them copiously and invented them frequently in order to convey the sense of existence as it is lived and not as it is read about.

Instead of closure, Tolstoy tried to create what I like to call *aperture.* A work that employs aperture avoids relying on any moment that does not invite continuation. It renounces the privilege of an ending. I am not speaking here of the device of parodic anticlosure so common in metaliterary works from Lucian to Lem, for anticlosure does emphatically place great weight on the ending. Its essential move is to make a violation of closural conventions an effective form of closure. It therefore confirms closural conventions with all the paradoxical power of an epigram. Anticlosure may reveal temporal artifice, but it does not avoid it, as aperture strives to do.

Aperture invites us to form a relative closure at several points, each of which could be a sort of ending, or at least as much of an ending as we are ever going to get. There will be no "final" ending, only a potentially infinite series of visions and revisions. In *War and Peace,* Tolstoy not only includes essays discussing temporal fallacies (such as "the fallacy of retrospection" and "the fallacy of reciprocity") but also warns his readers against reading this book as "a novel" with an ending. There will be no such ending, he tells them, just a series of installments. "I am convinced that interest in my story will not cease when [the section about] a given epoch is completed, and I am striving for this effect" (Drafts 56). The end of the work will simply be the last installment he has the energy to write, but he will always be able to add another one. In fact, he was later to do just that when some readers took Anna's suicide at the end of part 7 of *Anna Karenina* to be that novel's ending; Tolstoy later added part 8. And why not parts 9 and 10? Aperture encourages us to read with such expectations, so that we become practiced in assessing events forever free of foreshadowing, closure, and final signification. (It is interesting to note that readers have generally not drawn this conclusion: disdaining the naïveté of their predecessors who believed part 7 was the end, critics have usually affirmed how obvious it is that part 8 was required to provide a satisfying resolution to all themes.)

"I strove only so that each part of the work would have an independent interest," Tolstoy maintained; and then he wrote and struck out the following words: "which would consist not in the development of events, but in development [itself]" (Drafts 55). *Development itself* requires unpredetermined futurity, which means an escape from all those ways in which an end can be already given. One might put it this way: Tolstoy's war on foreshadowing and closure was ultimately an attempt to present a written artifact as if it were an artifact still being written, and therefore closer to lived experience. That is why serialization was not the way in which he just happened to publish *War and Peace* and *Anna Karenina* but was essential to its purpose. That purpose defines a key difference between Tolstoy's serialized novels and (let us say) Dickens's. Of course, this kind of temporal immediacy is something that could be fully operable only for the work's first readers. Today, it has to be re-created.

Above all, Tolstoy wanted to change our habit of viewing our own lives as if they were like novels. Earlier metaliterary writers who chose this theme were usually making fun of the distance between a given genre's view of reality and reality itself. Where the hero sees the helmet of Mambrino, we see a wash basin. Tolstoy uses this sort of satire, but his fundamental questions apply not to any specific genre of narrative but to narrative itself. The problem is not which genre we choose but whether we see our present moment as part of a prescripted story.

In the historical sections of *War and Peace*, the Tsar and Napoleon, both of whom have read too many histories, appear ridiculous as they try to behave according to anticipated narratives. Tolstoy's portraits might remind today's readers of a child playing a ball game as he narrates the sportscaster's account. Like the attempt to fulfill omens, this way of living while accompanied by an imagined foreshadow is a lie. Tolstoy's principled refusal of foreshadowing is one thing that differentiates *War and Peace* from Shakespeare's historical dramas, which rely heavily on our knowledge of the future as a way of creating narrative irony. And I think that on this question, at least, Tolstoy was right.

6. The Novelistic Past

Bakhtin makes a quite similar point about representing the past. He argues, rather paradoxically, that genres with too deep a reverence for the past, such as epic, are unable to represent it accurately. Such reverence, no less than the dismissive contempt characteristic of the radical intelligentsia, deceives. Epic as Bakhtin describes it relies on what Goethe and Schiller called "an absolute past," which is completely unlike the present. It tells of a time of "firsts" and "bests," a lost temporality that is the source of all values: "This [epic] past is distanced, finished, and closed like a circle." The values of the epic past are not subject to revision, as all merely historical values would be. This past is not "tied to the present by uninterrupted temporal transitions" because the difference between the absolute past and the present, or between the absolute past and the more recent historical past, is qualitative ("Epic" 19). Not only has time elapsed, it has changed.

But in the realist novel, beginning with the Wilhelm Meister narratives, time is understood quite differently. As modern geology was made possible by uniformitarianism—the principle that the forces governing the physical world have not changed qualitatively—so the novel reflects the discovery that time has always been a sequence of present moments.[3] The past as imagined by the novel consists of other presents and only of other presents; accurate description therefore requires an understanding of presentness. Bakhtin's paradox, then, is that it was the genre that focused on contemporaneity, and whose whole impulse was "to contemporize" everything, that made possible a superior disclosure of epochs gone by.

In his great writings of the late 1930s and early 1940s, Bakhtin developed the idea that different genres conceive of time quite differently and that the history of literature consists in part of a series of discoveries about temporality. "The field available for representing the world changes from genre to genre and from era to era as literature develops. It is organized in different ways and limited in space and time by different means. But this field is always specific" ("Epic" 27). The specificity of the novelistic field—its chronotope—includes a palpable sense of time as open, as "unfinalizable."

This sense in turn carries with it a whole series of remarkable implications: There are real alternatives. Therefore choice is not an illusion. Freedom is something more than "the consciousness of necessity." We consequently have real responsibility because what we do matters. Moreover, alternatives are *always* present, because the openness of time is not something that occurs occasionally (as in various forms of catastrophism) but is immanent in each prosaic moment. Time in the novel, unlike time in some other genres, is not "knotted." Thus ethical responsibility is not only real but unavoidable; or as Bakhtin puts it, *there is no alibi* for it. "That which can be accomplished by me cannot be accomplished by anyone else, ever" ("K filosofii" 112).

Real choice also establishes the genuineness of creativity, which cannot be reduced to mere discovery of outcomes already given but simply unknown. Life and human effort are capable of more than what Dostoevsky's underground man calls "the extraction of square roots." Depending on our choices, we can truly innovate. In this way, too, what we do matters. In short, life exhibits what Bakhtin called *eventness.*

People who live in such temporality truly "become." By "becoming" in this special sense Bakhtin means something more complex than mere change. He means, among other things, change that cannot be reduced to rules or laws, as it can be in dynamic structuralism or many forms of Marxism. Change of this sort contains a measure of "surprisingness." People do not "become" the way a seed grows into a plant. They do not just manifest qualities given from the outset, as in Plutarch's *Lives,* and their fundamental development is not over at an early age, as in Freudianism. For Bakhtin and in the novel, people are temporal to the core, and time is ever forging the new. Life is always eventful, and people are always becoming different, learning, creating.

So is the social world. As the novel understands it, history also undergoes genuine becoming, which is to say, the past shapes the present without exhaustively determining it. The past itself is the accumulation of present choices gone by; as such, it both constrains and offers potentialities for later present choices, which will have the same effect on futures to come. In the novel, that is true for both individuals and society.

As Bakhtin understands it, the novel, unlike genres with less profound chronotopes, not only comprehends both individual and social becoming but also sees the two as impinging upon each other. Their development is constantly interactive. Thus, people do not simply instantiate their socioeconomic epoch, nor is society just the passive background for individual action. This whole complex sense of unfinalizabilities in dialogue is part of what Bakhtin intends by his key phrase "the fullness of time."

Each of these qualities of time has always been present. We and our societies are and have ever been "becoming"; we have always had choices to make, responsibilities to assume, and works to create. It follows that the novelistic understanding of time leads to an appreciation of the unfinalizability of the past. A "task" of the genre is to allow the reader to sense palpably the contemporaneity of each past moment, the way it was experienced as present by those who lived through it. They lived it as open and inconclusive, as containing loopholes and as subject to experiment and probing. The novel represents the past, as it represents the present, in what Bakhtin calls "the zone of familiar contact."

This awareness of how past epochs resemble the present also creates the richest potential for sensing how they differ from it. The novelistic view of time makes it imperative that the true *otherness* of the past be understood. If people are always developing in interaction with specific situations at specific historical moments, and if those specificities shape personalities and social possibilities, then an understanding of any time and place requires a detailed picture of prosaic particularities in motion. The novel's "prosaic intelligence" tries to grasp all the infinitesimally small factors shaping the ethos of the time and the feel of the cultural milieu. Thus, the author of a historical novel must truly appreciate *anachronism*, the way in which actions and values characteristic of one time are uncharacteristic of, or impossible in, another. The same is true of novels set in other cultures of our own time: the novelist must appreciate what might be called *anatopism*.[4]

To understand people of any time and place is to comprehend the particular *field of possibilities* among which they continually choose and in reaction to which they develop. Having recognized that this is true of the present, and having understood that all times are present times, the novel evolved the best way to represent the otherness of others. That is why the novel, unlike the romance, eschews all forms of temporal flattening and all types of social abstractness. And it is also another reason why Freudian analyses usually seem to miss the very novelness of novels: in effect, such analyses turn novels into other forms—such as myth or allegory—with quite different chronotopes. The Freudian world is peopled by characters who resemble desiccated doubles of Konstantin Levin or Dorothea Brooke, in part because particularities are read as mere signs of an underlying pattern and in part because that world is governed by a simplistic and non-novelistic temporality.

For Bakhtin, the novel's appeal derives in great measure from its ability to let us experience how other people in quite different circumstances live and think. Its attention to detail is not mere "empiricism" but a way to convey a culture's "field of possibilities" at a given moment. The novel, to use Bakhtin's term, is adapted to "heterochrony," the comprehension of other times and other values.[5] Temporalities enter into dialogue. It follows that forms of reading that impose our own values, that judge people and situations according to the standards of the critic's own time, necessarily "de-novelize" novels, which by their very generic nature implicitly treat current standards as tested, contested, and contestable. But critics of this sort recognize only one temporality, their own. From their "homochronous" perspective, they engage in an impoverishing form of interpretation that Bakhtin calls "modernization and distortion."

As Bakhtin describes them, historical novels resist such interpretation:

> The depiction of a past in the novel in no sense presumes the modernization of this past. . . . On the contrary, only in the novel have we the possibility of an authentically objective portrayal of the past as the past. Contemporary reality with its new experiences is retained as a way of seeing, it has the depth, sharpness, breadth and vividness peculiar to that way of seeing, but should not in any way penetrate into the already portrayed content of the past, as a force modernizing and distorting the uniqueness of that past. After all, every great and serious contemporaneity requires an authentic profile of the past, an authentic other language from another time. ("Epic" 29–30)

We might modify Bakhtin's point about historical novels in this way: The historical novel as a genre brings into interaction two conflicting temporal perspectives. On the one hand, I think, the reader never forgets that the events described are not only over but have led (even if they were not fated to lead) to us. In this way, foreshadowing penetrates the narrative, because it is given in the very perspective that the novelist, himself the product of the events described, offers the readers. That is why the author of *War and Peace* had to struggle so mightily against foreshadowing. On the other hand, the past is described *novelistically*, that is, as open, as unfinalizable, and as having had many possible outcomes. The peculiar piquancy of the genre, its special appeal, derives from the interweaving of these perspectives, from the light they shed on each other, and from the ironies they make possible in both directions. Various historical novelists exploit the potentials of this temporal tension differently.

7. Sideshadowing and the Plurality of Truths

Bakhtin and Tolstoy understood profoundly that we and our opinions were not inevitable. "A hundred million chances" and choices could have led to quite different outcomes. Had people in past times chosen differently, we might very well hold different beliefs. The implications of this insight for the nature of conviction and for our attitudes toward our most cherished ideas are not trivial. Wisdom—the "prosaic wisdom" of the novel as Bakhtin described it—includes the sort of tentativeness about our own convictions that arises from the awareness of other possibilities in the past, present, and future: "Reality as we have it in the novel is only one of many possible realities; it is not inevitable, not arbitrary, it bears within itself other possibilities" ("Epic" 37). Heterochrony leads to a "decentering" of the "ideological world."[6]

To understand a moment is to understand what *else* might have resulted from it. It is to see time not under the foreshadow but accompanied by what might be called *sideshadows*. The initial critics of *War and Peace* objected that readers see why Prince Andrei *could* have developed the way he did but do not see why he had to develop that way; they sensed the possibility of other outcomes. Although these critics thought they had detected flaws of which Tolstoy was unaware, they were responding as Tolstoy meant them to respond. They described his sense of temporality accurately, even if they did not understand his central purpose and point: *to represent time accurately, one needs to sense its sideshadow.*

People of the past could have made other choices. Or if they could not have, then neither can we. To deny presentness to past moments when they happened is to deny presentness to the *present* present moment as it is now happening. In that case, the present becomes already over and turns into something resembling the part of a recorded program that happens to be playing. *All* hopes and efforts then become as senseless as rooting for the defeat of Sparta. Much as the strategies described by Thucydides have all already either failed or succeeded, so have ours if time is closed. Like readers of an already written novel, we simply do not yet know the unchangeable outcome of our own actions. In this view, our lives cease to be truly *our* lives but are instead lives we just happen to experience, the way an actor is assigned a part. Under the shadow of the future-already-present—under the foreshadow—all moments, including our own, turn out to be prescripted, prerecorded, already over before they have happened. That is what Tolstoy meant when he wrote, in the epilogue to *War and Peace*: "If we concede that human life can be governed [entirely] by reason, the possibility of life is destroyed" (1354).

If we really take seriously the openness of presents gone by, and therefore the possibility that the beliefs of our day might have been quite different, we become a lot less certain of those beliefs. For the thinkers of the Russian countertradition, the openness of time demanded epistemic modesty and suggested the folly of political systems closed to revision. It therefore made a lot of them into some sort of liberals.

From this perspective, the intelligentsia's characteristic sense of its own superiority, of the special insight afforded by the latest theories it has developed, ought to wane. To the extent that it does not, the intelligentsia's "truth" runs counter to the truth of novels, which is always aware of the prosaic messiness and diverse "surprisingness" of life. Bakhtin puts it this way: "Prophecy is characteristic for the epic, [but] prediction for the novel. . . . the novel has a new and quite specific problematicalness: characteristic for it is an eternal re-thinking and re-evaluating" ("Epic" 31).

Discounting other possibilities, those who believe they at last have the theory of theories forget that history did not lead inevitably to them. To parody this unearned theoretical confidence, the novelist has only to describe an earlier period when the intelligentsia professed with equal certainty theories that now appear palpably ridiculous. The novelist might also describe the intelligentsia's unbearable condescension to those who offered convincing but unfashionable objections to the latest theories and who were dismissed as unenlightened or reactionary. Scenes of this sort occur repeatedly in the great Russian philosophical novels. They develop the countertraditional sense that the intelligentsia yields with the utmost readiness to a faith—Tolstoy called it a superstition—in its own special insight.

That skeptical sense is central to the whole ironic structure of Turgenev's *Fathers and Children*, in which the sequence of generations becomes a series of claims to have at last achieved the eternally true beliefs. Each generation refutes its predecessor but will be refuted with equal, and equally unjustified, contempt by its successor. And as later countertraditional thinkers pointed out, Turgenev's prediction proved correct when the "children" were succeeded by the "grandchildren." *The Possessed* gives us both a version of Turgenev's generational argument and a conflict of simultaneous ideologists, each claiming that "there can be no solution to the social problem but mine."

In short, temporal wisdom lends the novel epistemic modesty and distinguishes it from the intelligentsia's ideological commitments. One way to tell the story of Russian thought is to describe the war between ideology and literature, especially the novel. The radical intelligentsia typically either rejected art altogether ("boots are more important than Pushkin") or tolerated only crudely didactic forms. For the countertradition, this attitude constituted not just an aesthetic but also a moral and a political offense. As Gershenzon observed in *Signposts*, "in Russia an almost infallible gauge of an artist's genius is the extent of his hatred for the intelligentsia" (60). Bakhtin's celebration of novelistic wisdom participates in the Russian countertradition's critique of intelligentsial ideology. Because Bolshevism was an obvious and longstanding target of such critiques, it is understandable why Bakhtin wrote for the drawer and why these essays remained unpublished for some thirty-five or forty years.

The struggle of the novel with ideology was to end in the victory of the latter. Understanding that they were dealing with a real enemy, the ideologists replaced the novel with socialist realism. The sideshadow was eclipsed when an essentially utopian understanding of time replaced the appreciation of "many possible realities."

Even before the doctrine of socialist realism was formulated, Soviet Marxism proffered the belief that the Party was the destined end of history and the realization of its hidden truth. The supreme answer to everything was to be found in *partiinost'* (Party-mindedness).

The teleological certainty of those who have successfully seized power is hard to oppose, especially when it means opposing the secret police. But for a while, the novel offered alternative truths. That is why, in Eugene Zamyatin's anti-utopian novel *We* (which until *glasnost'* could only be published abroad), the hero learns that the notion of a final truth, not subject to revision, is as ludicrous as the idea of a last number. It is not surprising that as he makes this discovery, Zamyatin's hero finds that his diary, originally intended as a poem to the State, has switched genres and turned into what he calls "an ancient, strange novel" (167). His friend I-330 suggests correctly that both the self and the novel rely on a sense of temporal openness: "Man is like a novel," she tells him. "Up to the last page one does not know what the end will be. It would not be worth reading otherwise" (151).

8. Theoretism vs. Literature

Appreciating the novel as a special and especially valuable form of thinking, countertraditional thinkers rejected the pretensions of criticism or theory to "account" for it. This issue—whether literature has a wisdom of its own inaccessible to the intelligentsia's theories—was constantly debated in Russian thought and was central to the battle between tradition and countertradition.

"If criticism, the authority of which you cite, knows what you and I don't, why has it kept mum until now?" asked Chekhov.

> Why doesn't it disclose to us the truth and immutable laws? If it had known, believe me, it would long ago have shown us the way and we

would know what to do. . . . But criticism keeps pompously quiet or gets off cheap with idle, worthless chatter. If it presents itself to you as influential, it is only because it is immodest, insolent, and loud, because it is an empty barrel that one involuntarily hears. Let's spit on all this. . . . (132–33)

Bakhtin's writings develop the countertraditional side of this debate with special force. Throughout his long career, Bakhtin insisted that theories that proceed from the assumption of their own superiority to great literature inevitably impoverish it. In his own time, he saw the two great rivals of the 1920s—formalism and Marxism—as equally vulnerable to this criticism.

Bakhtin's pejorative neologism for all such approaches was Theoretism. As the term is used in his early essay "Toward a Philosophy of the Act," *theoretism* names an approach to people and culture in terms of pregiven laws or rules. It assumes that existence is, at least in principle, exhaustively comprehensible in such terms. Real events are seen as the instantiation of rules (for example, in Saussurian linguistics and its heirs) or as the inevitable result of causal chains governed by abstract laws. Whatever residue is left over will either be accounted for later or is too unimportant to matter. Or as Bakhtin sometimes paraphrases the position, human action is seen as entirely "transcribable" by a set of abstractions, which the given Theory has provided. Bakhtin rejected this view in its entirety.

For Bakhtin, it is precisely what is *left over* after all transcription has taken place that allows for meaningful ethical choice and real creativity. Life depends upon what transcriptions leave out, that is, on what Bakhtin called "the surplus." The surplus is what allows for "eventness"—for unfinalizability and the openness of time. Great literature, and especially great novels, help us to understand the surplus, but theoretism reduces the surplus to zero.

It was obvious to Bakhtin that unless the specific person at a specific moment has real choice, creativity turns into mere discovery: theoretism can never think about creativity without thinking it away. In fact, both Russian Marxism and Russian formalism had boldly announced what we would today call "the death of the author" and the illusoriness of the individual creative act. To take just one celebrated example, the formalist Osip Brik contended that it is not authors engaged in the surprising process of creation but the abstract laws of literary history that produce works. Formalism "presumes that there are no poets and writers, there are only poetry and literature," Brik announced. "If there were no Pushkin, *Eugene Onegin* would have been written all the same. America would have been discovered even without Columbus" (213). With greater or lesser sophistication, various forms of Marxism and Freudianism arrived at basically the same conclusion.

The central problem of each of these schools lies not in what distinguishes them from each other but in the basic assumptions they all share. Consistently applied, theoretism always leads to reductionism and the closing down of time. To be sure, some theoretist thinkers back away from this conclusion, but they have none but purely ad hoc ways of avoiding it. If there was one reason why Bakhtin respected formalism more than its main rivals, it was that the formalists eschewed such avoidance mechanisms; arguing consistently from their theoretist premises, they allowed the real issues at stake to be clearly seen.

Formalism and Marxism both reflected the Russian intelligentsia's fundamental belief in Theories capable of explaining everything. They were semiotically totalitarian. Bakhtin evidently saw his own approach as deriving from the Russian countertradition's belief in the importance of particulars, the tyranny of "principles," and the multiplicity of temporalities. The Russian novel was not just his favorite topic but also his most important inspiration.

In Bakhtin's view, novels manifest a much truer ethical sensibility than any other form of thinking. That is because they focus on the particularities of each specific situation, all those momentous specificities on which informed ethical choice depends. In the root sense of the term, Bakhtin's approach to ethics was casuistical in that he believed there to be no substitute for an educated sensitivity to particular cases.[7] The generalities and impoverished (compared to novels) examples so familiar in theoretist ethical treatises "transcribe away" both real agency and the unrepeatable facts the agent needs to contemplate.

According to Bakhtin, the fundamental principle of theoretist ethics is "in no sense the principle of the [concrete] act, but the principle of possible generalizations from already completed acts in their theoretical transcription" ("K filosofii" 102). The concrete act "cannot be transcribed in such a way that it will not lose the very sense of its eventness, that precise thing that it knows responsibly and toward which it is oriented" (104). Those who would make moral decisions based on some prefabricated system of rules, whether already developed or only anticipated, tend to produce monstrous results, as the great Russian philosophical novels repeatedly demonstrate. Bakhtin's stress on "eventness" indicates the close connection he saw between ethics and a proper understanding of time.

With chronotopes unsurpassed in their sensitivity to specific cases, novels offer our richest portraits of real situations and constitute our greatest repository of ethical wisdom. For Bakhtin, then, the moral profundity of the great Russian novels could not be reduced to some set of philosophical or religious principles they exemplify. To think so would be to equate *Anna Karenina* or *Crime and Punishment* with a work like *What Is to Be Done?* No, what Bakhtin valued most in these masterpieces was two other sources of wisdom: first, the richness of each work's description of the prosaic circumstances shaping ethical choice, and second, the wisdom of the genre itself, which could be more or less appreciated through its greatest members. Bakhtin's real hero was the novelistic view of the world, and he apparently regarded his own writings as so many attempts to point in the direction of this wisdom, which was ultimately beyond all critical transcription.

In effect, theoretist critics place themselves in the position of the ideologues satirized *within* the great novels. Reading them, we may have the weird sensation that Bazarov or the heroes of *The Possessed* had chosen to analyze the novels of Turgenev or Dostoevsky. Bakhtin would doubtless have viewed the ideological criticism current in America today as he viewed its nineteenth- and twentieth-century Russian counterparts.

Familiar with Russian literary history, American Slavists often experience a strange sense of critical *déjà vu* in reigning American theoretical schools, particularly those that reduce works entirely to politics. Should we call this movement American socialist realism? For most Slavists, this *politicism*—the reduction of all things to politics—is as simplistic as psychologism, sociologism, historicism, or any other form of reductionism. Politicism is theoretism plus *partiinost'*. Its disastrous consequences for both writers and critics constitute the most obvious object lesson of Soviet cultural policy.

There is no doubt that Bakhtin saw greater wisdom in Dostoevsky than in any critic. Beginning with his earliest work, Bakhtin rejected all forms of reductionism, explicitly including politicism. Perhaps his importance today lies in his ability to express the values of the Russian countertradition to an audience that is much closer to its opponent, the predominant tradition of the politicized intelligentsia. This is why I prefer to say: not Bakhtin *and* current American theory but Bakhtin *versus* current American theory.

9. Stern Tribunals

Think, for instance, of the current critical practice of judging the great writers of the past according to the political orthodoxies of the present: Shakespeare was on the side of women, minorities, and people of color; or, conversely, he is culpable because he was not on their side; or he was on their side without knowing it; or perhaps he did not mention them at all, which is itself proof that he participated in (or undermined?) hegemony. There is a character in one of Solzhenitsyn's novels who wonders why she has to read Turgenev and Pushkin when they make ideological errors that today any fifth grader could detect.

In the epilogue to *War and Peace*, Tolstoy describes, with withering irony, how historians of his own day judge thinkers and political leaders of the past "progressive" or "reactionary" according to the historians' own values. "All the famous people of that period, from Alexander and Napoleon to Madame de Staël, Photius, Schelling, Fichte, Chateaubriand, and the rest, pass before their

stern tribunal and are acquitted or condemned according to whether they promoted *progress* or *reaction"* (1351–52). Tolstoy is careful to point out that the
tribunals are manned not only by historians but by *intelligenty* generally: "There
is no one in present-day Russian literature, from schoolboy essayist to learned
historian, who does not cast his little stone at Alexander for the things he did
wrong at this period of his reign" (1352).

With the supreme confidence so characteristic of the intelligentsia, these
critics say of Alexander: "He ought to have acted in such and such a way. In
this instance he did well, in that instance badly. . . . It would take a dozen pages
to enumerate all the reproaches leveled at him by historians, based on their
knowledge of what is good for humanity" (1352). But why should we assume
that the historians have the correct standards? And even if we did assume that
history as a discipline gives one the special knowledge needed to pass such
confident judgments, why should we believe the historians of today rather than
those of yesterday or, presumably, tomorrow? All that the historians' reproaches
mean, according to Tolstoy, is that Alexander "did not have the same conception
of the welfare of humanity fifty years ago as a present-day professor who from
his youth has been occupied with learning, that is, with reading books, listening
to lectures, and making notes" (1353).

Tolstoy's satirical defamiliarization of what professors actually do continues
an argument he advanced frequently. *Intelligenty* pass judgments with such confidence because they believe in the superior wisdom conferred by their special
way of living. The intelligentsia's way of life is implicitly or explicitly credited
with great epistemological power. The views of others are presumably distorted
by class interests, atypical experiences, or other forms of socially conditioned
false consciousness from which the intelligentsia is somehow exempt. And in
fact, the Russian intelligentsia was particularly energetic in enforcing on its
members codes of behavior and attitudes about the most diverse spheres of daily
and social life. One might even say that a group of professionals or intellectuals
constitutes an intelligentsia in the original Russian sense to the extent that they
share a self-conscious sense of corporate identity based on such codes and beliefs
rather than on other social or class connections. To that extent, countertraditional criticisms apply to other intelligentsias.

The Russian word *intelligentsia* suggests, among other things, that the group
it names is socially distinct and that this distinction is based on special insight
(intelligence). But from Tolstoy's perspective, the conditions of life among the
intelligentsia shape and distort its views no less than alternative conditions shape
the views of others. Tolstoy remarks: if we do not have histories that attribute
to shoemakers a decisive role in saving the people, as we have histories that
attribute such a role to the intelligentsia, that is only because it is intellectuals
rather than shoemakers who write histories.

Chekhov and the contributors to *Signposts* took this argument one step further. They contended that the Russian intelligentsia, defining itself in terms of a set of attitudes and a code of behavior, rapidly came to enforce a conformity of belief that was even more distorting than that of other groups. Dialogue is possible and often encouraged among other educated people, but political orthodoxies make it all but impossible among the intelligentsia. Asked to join a typical intelligentsia "circle," Chekhov replied with contempt for the conformism those groups promote. Shocking the *anti*bourgeois, Chekhov recommended prosaic virtues, for which "you've got to be . . . just a plain human being. Let us be ordinary people, let us adopt the same attitude *toward all*, then an artificially overwrought solidarity will not be needed" (letter of 3 May 1888, qtd. in Simmons 165).[8]

Allow *intelligenty* actually to attain the power they seek, Chekhov observed elsewhere, and they will be the worst oppressors of all: "Under the banner of science, art, and oppressed free-thinking among us in Russia, such toads and crocodiles will rule in ways not known even at the time of the Inquisition in Spain" (letter of 27 Aug. 1888, qtd. in Simmons 165). The editor of *Signposts* argues that the mentality of the intelligentsia was uncannily like that of the secret police and bureaucracy whom it opposed, and cited yet another (at that time, recently published) letter of Chekhov in support: "I do not believe in our intelligentsia, which is hypocritical, false, hysterical, ill-bred, and lazy. I do not believe in it even when it suffers and complains, for its oppressors come from the same womb" (letter of 22 Feb. 1899, qtd. in Gershenzon, *Signposts* 58). Of course, essentially the same insight informs Joseph Conrad's *Under Western Eyes.*

The very impulse of *Signposts* and related countertraditional writings to engage in a *sociology* of the intelligentsia's beliefs provoked deep hostility. Sociology was properly applied to the beliefs of others; its application to the intelligentsia was another affront committed by the great Russian novelists. If there was one major Russian work despised by the intelligentsia and published as rarely as possible by the Soviet regime, it was—understandably enough—*The Possessed.*

10. The Alternative to Us

The supreme confidence that underwrites the practice of judging great thinkers and writers of the past according to the intelligentsia's reigning political values derives from at least three interrelated sets of attitudes. It involves, as we have seen, an unwarranted faith in the power of current theories, which in turn underwrites the intelligentsia's claim to specially privileged insight. Russian countertraditional thinkers pointed out that such a mentality also involves a mistaken attitude toward time and specifically toward the present moment. A few more observations on intelligentsial temporality are in order.

Specifically, the Russian intelligentsia and their counterparts in American departments of literature often see the present moment as essentially *apocalyptic.* Such critics, like the historians Tolstoy describes, implicitly seem to presume the sort of knowledge that could be available only at the end of history, when all earlier views are revealed as partial and when no future experience could outdate present values. And so we hear the tone of certainty that only a final Revelation could warrant. Shakespeare and Alexander saw as through a glass darkly, but we see face-to-face.

It is not that such critics deny there will be a future, of course. Rather, one suspects that they do not imagine how naive or shortsighted their own views may soon look. They consequently lack the wisdom to adopt a more tentative tone. Usually missing are an acknowledgment of their own fallibility and a willingness to profit from diverse views. Instead, their first impulse is usually to attribute disagreement to benightedness or repulsive motives. The views of today's intelligentsia are the privileged vantage point for judging all others. They convey great confidence that values shared before a decade ago were morally offensive, but they seem to speak as if the process of change had at last essentially stopped. Have they leaped out of the river into which you cannot step twice into the heaven of Platonic forms?

Such critics seem to speak as if the future would undergo change, but only of a specified sort. It will change only by realizing and extending the values and insights of the present. One is tempted to call this sense of time *"preshadowing."* The future is to be like the present, only much more so: it will be, to use Lewis Carroll's phrase, "as large as life and twice as natural." And twice as present.

Preshadowing induces a mentality opposite to that inspired by side-shadowing: *"Reality as we have it in the novel is only one of many possible realities"* (Bakhtin, "Epic" 37, my italics). Accompanied by a sense of those unrealized possibilities, and aware of numerous sideshadows across our path, we come to appreciate that our views not only *will* be other but could easily have been other. Disagreement in our own time often reflects a diversity of experience from which we can learn.[9]

Had another present with different values arisen instead of ours, perhaps academics would have felt as confident in passing quite different judgments on the past. On quite different grounds, Shakespeare and Dostoevsky, Aristotle and Goethe, might have been summoned before the proud tribunal of associate professors. In vain would those writers have protested that in their time, too, it was tempting to see the present moment as a culmination rather than as a part of a process and one of several possible presents. Without effect would have been their warnings that in another decade or two the values of today will look as foolish and immoral as those of the 1950s appear to us.

Modern criticism condemns ethnocentrism but it is characteristically guilty of *chronocentrism*. Bakhtin expressed the import of Dostoevsky's novels with a credo of his own: "*Nothing conclusive has yet taken place in the world, the ultimate word of the world and about the world has not yet been spoken, the world is open and free, everything is still in the future and will always be in the future*" (*Problems* 166). By contrast, the chronotope of modern criticism implies: everything conclusive has happened in the world, we are in a position to speak the final word of the world and about the world, and the future will always be a vindication of the present present.

Notes

1. Among the countless studies, both Russian and foreign, on the Russian intelligentsia, I would single out the following as especially interesting from the present perspective: Berlin, J. Frank, Kelly, Nahirny, Paperno, Pipes, Schapiro, and the volume edited by Gershenzon, *Signposts*.
2. Bulgakov details a number of similar contradictions in his *Signposts* article.
3. Although Bakhtin was fond of scientific analogies, this comparison is my own. I have in mind the key idea that the laws of nature have remained constant, and not (as the term is sometimes taken to mean) that these laws do not allow for sudden changes.
4. The term is my own, not Bakhtin's.
5. I prefer this translation to the rendition in the English version of "The *Bildungsroman*" essay, "multitemporality." The Russian coinage Bakhtin uses, *raznovremennost'*, indicates variety, not just multiplicity; and it is an obvious analogue to *raznorechie*, "heteroglossia."
6. In this respect, heterochrony works much like heteroglossia. See "Discourse in the Novel" 365, from which the terms in my sentence are drawn. Bakhtin also notes that in the novel "a dialogue of languages is . . . also a dialogue of different times, epochs, and days, a dialogue that is forever dying, living, being born: co-existence and becoming are here fused into an indissoluble concrete unity that is contradictory, multi-speeched and heterogeneous" (365). There are several passages in "Forms of Time" and "Discourse" that link them to each other. For more on these connections, see Morson and Emerson.
7. For a discussion of casuistry quite in consonance with the spirit of the Russian countertradition, see Jonsen and Toulmin.
8. The theme of the conformity of the intelligentsia is treated in most studies on the intelligentsia; but see esp. Kelly.
9. The concept of sideshadowing is drawn from my study of the relation of morality, temporality, and narrative: *Narrative and Freedom: The Shadows of Time*. Michael André Bernstein is also completing a study of this and related concepts.

Works Cited

Bakhtin, Mikhail M. "The *Bildungsroman* and Its Significance in the History of Realism (Toward a Historical Typology of the Novel)." *Speech Genres and Other Late Essays*. By Bakhtin. Ed. Caryl Emerson and Michael Holquist. Trans. Vern McGee. Austin: U of Texas P, 1986. 10–59.

———. *The Dialogic Imagination: Four Essays*. Trans. Caryl Emerson and Michael Holquist. Austin: U of Texas P, 1981.

———. "Discourse in the Novel." Bakhtin, *Dialogic Imagination* 259–422.

———. "Epic and Novel." Bakhtin, *Dialogic Imagination* 3–40.

———. "Forms of Time and of the Chronotope in the Novel: Notes toward a Historical Poetics." Bakhtin, *Dialogic Imagination* 84–258.

———. "K filosofii postupka" [Toward a Philosophy of the Act]. *Filosofiia i sotsiologiia nauki i tekhniki*. Moscow: Nauka, 1986. 80–160.

———. *Problems of Dostoevsky's Poetics*. Ed. and trans. Caryl Emerson. Minneapolis: U of Minnesota P, 1984.

Berlin, Isaiah. *Russian Thinkers*. Ed. Henry Hardy and Aileen Kelly. Harmondsworth: Penguin, 1978.

Brik, Osip. "T.n. 'Formal'nyi metod" [The So-called Formal Method]. *LEF* 1 (1923).

Bulgakov, Sergei. "Heroism and Asceticism (Reflections on the Religious Nature of the Russian Intelligentsia)." Gershenzon, *Signposts* 17–49.

Chekhov, Anton. *Letters of Anton Chekhov*. Ed. Avrahm Yarmolinsky. New York: Viking, 1973.

Dostoevsky, Fyodor. *The Possessed*. Trans. Constance Garnett. New York: Modern Library, 1936.

Frank, Joseph. *Through the Russian Prism: Essays on Literature and Culture*. Princeton: Princeton UP, 1990.

Frank, Semen. "The Ethic of Nihilism (A Characterization of the Russian Intelligentsia's Moral Outlook)." Gershenzon, *Signposts* 131–55.

Gershenzon, Mikhail. "Creative Self-Consciousness." Gershenzon, *Signposts*, 51–69.

———. ed. *Signposts: A Collection of Articles on the Russian Intelligentsia*. Ed. and trans. Marshall S. Shatz and Judith E. Zimmerman. Irvine: Schlacks 1986.

Herzen, Alexander. *"From the Other Shore" and "The Russian People and Socialism."* Trans. Moura Budberg and Richard Wollheim. Oxford: Oxford UP, 1979.

Jonsen, Albert R., and Stephen Toulmin. *The Abuse of Casuistry: A History of Moral Reasoning*. Berkeley: U of California P, 1988.

Kelly, Aileen. "Self-Censorship and the Russian Intelligentsia." *Slavic Review* 46.2 (Summer 1987): 193–213.

Morson, Gary Saul. *Narrative and Freedom: The Shadows of Time*. New Haven: Yale UP, forthcoming.

Morson, Gary Saul, and Caryl Emerson. *Mikhail Bakhtin: Creation of a Prosaics.* Stanford: Stanford UP, 1990.

Nahirny, Vladimir C. *The Russian Intelligentsia: From Torment to Silence.* New Brunswick, N.J.: Transaction, 1983.

Paperno, Irina. *Chernyshevsky and the Age of Realism: A Study in the Semiotics of Behavior.* Stanford: Stanford UP, 1988.

Pipes, Richard, ed. *The Russian Intelligentsia.* New York: Columbia UP, 1961.

Schapiro, Leonard. *Russian Studies.* Ed. Ellen Dahrendorf. New York: Viking-Penguin, 1987.

Simmons, Ernest J. *Chekhov: A Biography.* Boston: Little, 1962.

Tolstoy, Leo. *War and Peace.* Trans. Ann Dunnigan. New York: Signet, 1968.

———. Drafts for an introduction to *War and Peace.* Vol. 13. Jubilee edition of his complete works. 90 vols. 13:53–57.

Zamyatin, Eugene. *We.* Trans. Gregory Zilboorg. New York: Dutton, 1952.

Notes on Contributors

David R. Anderson, a Consortium for a Strong Minority Presence at Liberal Arts Colleges Scholar-in-Residence at Bowdoin College for 1992–93, is completing his doctoral thesis at the University of Pennsylvania. His dissertation, entitled "The Evolving Art: Poetry as Process among Modernist and Negro Renaissance Poets," combines his model of evolving reader response with a study of poets whose poetics were similarly influenced by theories of evolution.

David F. Bell, Associate Professor of French at Duke University, has published *Models of Power: Politics and Economics in Zola's "Rougon-Macquart." Circumstances: Chance in the Literary Text*, a study of the notion of chance in Balzac and Stendhal, is forthcoming. He is currently studying the impact of the idea of statistical thinking on the novel.

William E. Cain is Professor of English at Wellesley College. His publications include *The Crisis in Criticism* (1984) and *F. O. Matthiessen and the Politics of Criticism* (1988).

Frederick Crews is Chair of the English Department at the University of California, Berkeley, where he has taught since 1958. He is the author of ten books, including *The Pooh Perplex* and, most recently, *Skeptical Engagements* and *The Critics Bear It Away: American Fiction and the Academy*.

Nancy Easterlin, Assistant Professor of English at the University of New Orleans, is a writer and critic. She has published essays on Michel Tournier and Byron, and is currently completing a book-length study of Wordsworth's poetry from the perspective of the psychology of religion.

Richard Levin, Professor of English at the State University of New York at Stony Brook, is the author of *The Multiple Plot in English Renaissance Drama* and *New Readings vs. Old Plays: Recent Trends in the Reinterpretation of English Renaissance Drama*.

Paisley Livingston is Professor of English at McGill University, and is the author of *Ingmar Bergman and the Rituals of Art; Literary Knowledge: Humanistic Inquiry and the Philosophy of Science; Literature and Rationality: Ideas of Agency in Theory and Fiction;* and *René Girard and the Psychology of Mimesis*.

Gary Saul Morson, Frances Hooper Professor of the Arts and Humanities at Northwestern University, is the author of *The Boundaries of Genre* (on Dostoevsky) and *Hidden in Plain View* (on Tolstoy). He is co-author with Caryl Emerson of *Mikhail Bakhtin: Creation of a Prosaics*.

Barbara Riebling, a Ph.D. candidate in English at the University of Pennsylvania, is currently completing a dissertation in Renaissance literature on stage representations of royal counselors and favorites. She has recently published "Virtue's Sacrifice: a Machiavellian Reading of *Macbeth*" in SEL (Spring 1991).

Carol Siegel is Assistant Professor at Washington State University, Vancouver. She is the author of *Lawrence among the Women: Wavering Boundaries in Women's Literary Traditions* and has published articles on the representation of male masochism in literature and film in *Twentieth Century Literature, Novel,* and *Genders.* She has just completed a book tracing the textual history of the concept of male masochism.

Robert Storey is Professor of English at Temple University. He has published *Pierrot: A Critical History of a Mask* (1978) and *Pierrots on the Stage of Desire* (1985) and is currently working on a book entitled *Mimesis and the Human Animal: On the Biogenetic Foundations of Literary Representation.*